WITHDRAWN FROM
TSC LIBRARY

TALLAHASSEE
LIBRARY
COMMUNITY COLLEGE

Learn, Teach...
Succeed...

With **REA's FTCE Exceptional Student Education K–12**
test prep, you'll be in a class all your own.

D1546770

WE'D LIKE TO HEAR FROM YOU!
Visit **www.rea.com** to send us your comments

FTCE

EXCEPTIONAL STUDENT EDUCATION K–12 (061)

FLORIDA TEACHER CERTIFICATION EXAMINATIONS

Nancy A. Tattner, Ed.D.
Associate Professor
Daytona State College
Daytona Beach, Florida

Ken Springer, Ph.D.
Professor of Education
Southern Methodist University
Dallas, Texas

**Updated and revised by
Maryann Gromoll, Ed.D.**
Associate Professor
Daytona State College
Daytona Beach, Florida

Research & Education Association

Research & Education Association
258 Prospect Plains Road
Cranbury, New Jersey 08512
Email: info@rea.com

Florida FTCE Exceptional Student Education K–12 (061), 2nd Edition with Online Practice Exams

Published 2020

Copyright © 2018 by Research & Education Association, Inc.
Prior edition copyright © 2014 by Research & Education Association, Inc.
All rights reserved. No part of this book may be reproduced in any form without permission of the publisher.

Printed in the United States of America

Library of Congress Control Number 2017954017

ISBN-13: 978-0-7386-1238-6
ISBN-10: 0-7386-1238-3

The competencies presented in this book were created and implemented by the Florida Department of Education and Pearson Education, Inc. For further information visit the FTCE website at *www.fl.nesinc.com*.

LIMIT OF LIABILITY/DISCLAIMER OF WARRANTY: Publication of this work is for the purpose of test preparation and related use and subjects as set forth herein. While every effort has been made to achieve a work of high quality, neither Research & Education Association, Inc., nor the authors and other contributors of this work guarantee the accuracy or completeness of or assume any liability in connection with the information and opinions contained herein and in REA's software and/or online materials. REA and the authors and other contributors shall in no event be liable for any personal injury, property or other damages of any nature whatsoever, whether special, indirect, consequential or compensatory, directly or indirectly resulting from the publication, use or reliance upon this work. Links to external sites in this publication or companion online materials are provided as a convenience to readers and for informational purposes only. Though every reasonable effort has been made to publish current links, URLs may change over time. No endorsement of any external link is made or implied, and neither the publisher nor the author(s) are responsible for the accuracy, legality, or content of any external site or for that of subsequent links.

All trademarks cited in this publication are the property of their respective owners.

Cover image ©iStockphoto.com/michaeljung

REA® is a registered trademark of
Research & Education Association, Inc.

Contents

Chapter 4:
Competency 4: Knowledge of the Positive Behavioral Support Process   97

Chapter 5:
Competency 5: Knowledge of Multiple Literacies and Communication Skills   117

About Our Authors

DR. MARYANN GROMOLL, who fully updated and revised this second edition for REA, has nearly four decades of experience in the field of exceptional education. Her insights draw upon her background as a schoolteacher in Pennsylvania, New Jersey, and Florida. Dr. Gromoll is an Associate Professor at the Daytona State College Educator Preparation Institute, where she prepares majors in exceptional student education as well as elementary and secondary education to become teachers. Dr. Gromoll has presented at the Florida Council of Exceptional Children Conference, the DSC Academic Excellence Symposium, and the Florida Association of Teacher Education Conference. She earned her Ed.D. in Curriculum and Instruction from the University of Central Florida. She also has an M.Ed. in Special Education from Temple University and a B.S. in Special Education from Bloomsburg State University.

DR. KEN SPRINGER, a developmental psychologist, is an Associate Professor and Chair of the school's Department of Learning and Teaching at the Simmons School of Education at Southern Methodist University. He teaches graduate classes in research methods, statistics, and program evaluation. His research focuses on academic achievement of students from economically disadvantaged environments. He is the author or co-author of a number of test preparation books. Dr. Springer works with several nonprofit organizations dedicated to serving families and children, and, through pro bono grant writing, has raised more than $1 million on their behalf. He earned his Ph.D. from Cornell University.

DR. NANCY TATTNER, a Florida educator for over 30 years, is an Associate Professor at Daytona State College where she supervises teacher candidates' field experience. She has taught kindergarten, and fourth and fifth grade, as well as serving as an interim principal for a private K-8 school named a Blue Ribbon School during her tenure. A recipient of the Junior Achievement of Central Florida Golden Service Learning Partner award, her mission at Daytona State is to arm teacher candidates with the knowledge and skills to be effective, passionate classroom leaders. Dr. Tattner earned her B.A. at Loyola College (now Concordia University) in Montreal. She earned her Diploma in Education from McGill University and a Master's degree in Educational Leadership from Nova Southeastern University. She received her Ed.D. from the University of Central Florida.

About REA

Founded in 1959, Research & Education Association (REA) is dedicated to publishing the finest and most effective educational materials—including study guides and test preps—for students of all ages.

Today, REA's wide-ranging catalog is a leading resource for students, teachers, and other professionals. Visit *www.rea.com* to see a complete listing of all our titles.

Acknowledgments

In addition to our authors, we would like to thank Pam Weston, Publisher, for setting the quality standards for production integrity and managing the publication to completion; Larry B. Kling, Editorial Director, for supervising development; John Paul Cording, Technology Director, for coordinating the design and development of the online REA Study Center; Alice Leonard, Senior Editor, for project management; Ellen Gong for proofreading; Terry Casey for indexing; and Kathy Caratozzolo for typesetting this edition.

Getting Started

Congratulations! By taking the FTCE Exceptional Student Education K–12 (061) exam, you're on your way to a rewarding career working with exceptional students. Our book and the online tools that come with it give you everything you need to succeed on this important exam, bringing you one step closer to being certified to teach in Florida. Our test prep package includes:

- a complete overview of the FTCE Exceptional Student Education K–12 exam
- a comprehensive review of every competency
- end-of-chapter quizzes
- two full-length practice tests, offered in the book as well as online, where you get the added benefit of timed testing conditions and diagnostic score reporting

How to Use This Book + Online Prep

About the Review

The review chapters in this book are designed to help you sharpen the skills needed to pass the FTCE ESE test. Each of the skills required for all six competencies is discussed at length to optimize your understanding.

Keep in mind that your schooling has taught you most of what you need to know to answer the questions on the test. Some of the education classes you took should have provided you with the know-how to understand and make important decisions about professional situations involving exceptional students.

Our review is designed to help you relate the information you have acquired to specific competencies. Studying your class notes and textbooks together with our review will give you an excellent foundation for passing the exam.

About the REA Study Center

The best way to personalize your study plan is to get feedback on what you know and what you don't know. At the online REA Study Center (*http://www.rea.com/studycenter*), we give you two full-length practice tests with detailed score reports that pinpoint your strengths and weaknesses.

Before you review with the book, go to the REA Study Center to take Practice Test 1 as a diagnostic. Your score report will identify the areas you should concentrate on. Studying the parts of the book where you're weakest will efficiently focus your study on the areas where you need the most review.

After reviewing with the book, take Practice Test 2 online at the REA Study Center to ensure that you have mastered the material and are ready for test day. Use your score reports to identify any other areas where you need extra study, and read those sections of the review chapters again.

If you are studying and don't have internet access, you can take the printed versions of the tests. These are the same practice tests offered at the REA Study Center, but without the added benefits of timed testing conditions, automatic scoring, and diagnostic score reports. Because the FTCE is a computer-based exam, we strongly recommend taking the practice tests online to replicate exam-day conditions.

An Overview of the Test

What is Tested on the FTCE Exceptional Student Education K–12 Exam?

The FTCE Exceptional Student Education K–12 exam assesses six broad competencies along with the skills aligned to each competency. Below are the competencies used as the basis for the exam, as well as the approximate percentage of the total exam that each competency covers.

These competencies represent the knowledge that teams of teachers, administrators, subject area specialists, and others have determined to be important for beginning teachers who work with exceptional students. Each review chapter discusses a competency in depth and is organized by the skills/categories used by the Florida Department of Education.

Competency	Approximate % of Exam
1. Knowledge of foundations of exceptional student education	24%
2. Knowledge of assessment and evaluation	13%
3. Knowledge of instructional practices in exceptional student education	21%
4. Knowledge of the positive behavior support process	12%
5. Knowledge of multiple literacies and communication skills	22%
6. Knowledge of the transition process	8%

What is the Format of the Test?

The FTCE Exceptional Student Education K–12 exam includes 120 scorable multiple-choice questions. All questions are designed to assess your knowledge of the competencies and the related skills reviewed in this book. In general, the multiple-choice questions are intended to make you think logically. You are expected in most cases to demonstrate more than an ability to recall factual information; you may be asked to think critically about the information, analyze it, consider it carefully, compare it with knowledge you have, or make a judgment about it.

Answering the multiple-choice questions is straightforward. Each question will have four choices labeled A, B, C, and D. Mark your answer choice directly below each test item on the computer screen.

You are given two and a half hours to complete the test, but be aware of the amount of time you are spending on each question so you allow yourself time to complete the whole test. Maintain a steady pace when answering questions and use your time efficiently.

When Should the FTCE Exam Be Taken?

Florida law requires that teachers demonstrate mastery of basic skills, professional knowledge, and the content areas in which they are specializing. A Professional Florida Educator's Certificate requires, among other things, that you pass all three parts of the FTCE battery: Professional Education, General Knowledge, and the Subject Area Exam. Temporary certificates are available to qualified individuals for three years, during which time you may teach while preparing to take the certification tests, including the one corresponding to your area of specialization.

This book helps you prepare for the area of specialization called Exceptional Student Education K–12. (Separate tests are required for certification in the areas of Hearing Impaired K–12, Speech-

Language Impaired K–12, and Visually Impaired K–12.) Whether you are a student, a graduate of a Florida state-approved teacher preparation program, or an educator who has received certification in another state, you should carefully read the requirements for working with exceptional students provided in the Educator Certification pages of the Florida Department of Education website at: *http://www.fldoe.org/teaching/certification/*.

Where Can I Test?

FTCE tests are available year-round by appointment, Monday through Saturday (except holidays), at more than 30 sites throughout Florida and over 250 sites across the United States (including Puerto Rico and other U.S. territories). To find the test center nearest you, visit *http://www.fl.nesinc.com*.

How Do I Register for the Test and Is There a Registration Fee?

You may register on the internet at any time. There are no registration deadlines for the exam, but it is wise to register early for the session you desire, as test sites tend to fill up fast. You must pay a registration fee at the time you register for the exam. Information about FTCE test registration and fees is online at: *http://www.fl.nesinc.com*.

Fee waivers may be available for military personnel, veterans, and their spouses or surviving spouses. Visit *http://www.fldoe.org/teaching/certification/military* for more information.

Are Special Arrangements Available for Candidates with Disabilities?

Yes. If you have a disability, you must file the correct paperwork during the registration process; special testing arrangements, such as extra time, may be provided. Accommodations are also available for nursing mothers. For more information, visit *http://www.fl.nesinc.com/FL_AltArrangements.asp*.

Scoring the Test

Each of the 120 multiple-choice questions on this test is worth one raw point, and your total raw score is determined by the number of questions answered correctly. No points are deducted for wrong answers.

To pass the FTCE ESE test, you need to earn a scaled score of at least 200; however, your passing status will be reported simply as "Pass" on your score report. Because there is no exact passing percentage across all test forms, the percentage needed to pass the FTCE ESE test is best expressed as the *maximum* percentage of correct answers needed to achieve a passing grade. As of spring 2020, that percentage is 70%, or 84 items. We recommend giving yourself a cushion of 75%, which equates with 90 items; achieving that level of performance on your REA practice tests will buoy your confidence on test day.

Our online practice tests are scored automatically for you. If you do not get a passing score on the practice tests, review your online score report and study the detailed explanations for the questions you answered incorrectly. Note which types of questions you answered incorrectly, and re-examine the corresponding portion of the review.

When Will I Receive My Score Report?

On the score report release date you will receive an email notifying you that your score report is available in your account. Be sure to provide your email address when you register.

Test scores are typically released on Tuesdays after 10 p.m. within four weeks of the test date. Your score will be sent directly to the school district, college, or university you indicated when you registered. Your score will also be automatically sent electronically to the Florida Bureau of Educator Certification.

If I Don't Pass, Can I Request that My Score Be Verified?

Yes, but only if you come within 10 scale score points of the passing scale score (200). If you qualify for a score verification session, you will have a chance to identify scoring errors.

Can I Retake the Test?

If you don't do well on the FTCE, don't panic! You can take it again, and in fact many candidates do. However, for any test, subtest, or section you do not pass, you must wait 31 calendar days to retake it. You will have to reregister for the test and pay a fee. There is no limit to the number of times you may retest.

Studying for the Test

When Should I Start Studying?

It is never too early to start studying for the FTCE. The earlier you begin, the more time you will have to sharpen your skills. Do not procrastinate. Cramming is not an effective way to study, since it does not allow you the time needed to learn the test material. It is very important for you to choose the time and place for studying that works best for you. Be consistent and use your time wisely. Work out a study routine and stick to it.

When you take the practice tests, simulate the conditions of the actual test as closely as possible. Turn off your electronic devices, and sit down at a quiet table free from distraction.

As you complete each practice test, review your score reports, study the diagnostic feedback, and thoroughly review the explanations to the questions you answered incorrectly. However, do not review too much in any one sitting. Concentrate on one problem area at a time by reviewing the question and explanation, and by studying our review until you are confident that you have mastered the material.

FTCE Study Schedule

Although our study plan is designed to be used in the six weeks before the exam, it can be condensed or expanded to suit your schedule. Be sure to set aside enough time (at least two hours each day) to study. The more time you spend studying, the more prepared and confident you will be on the day of the test.

Week	Activity
1	Take Practice Test 1 at the REA Study Center as a diagnostic. Your detailed score report will identify topics where you need the most review. Your target score should be 75% correct, or 90 items. Review the explanations for questions you answered incorrectly.
2–3	Study the review chapters. Use your score report from Practice Test 1 to focus your study. Useful study techniques include highlighting key terms and information and taking notes as you read the review, noting new terms and facts.
4	Reread all your notes and refresh your understanding of the exam's competencies and skills so that you can focus on your weak areas. You might also want to review your college textbooks, class notes, and any other supplementary materials that your advisor or the test administrator suggests. Visit *http://www.fl.nesinc.com* for more information.
5	Take Practice Test 2. Review topics based on your errors. Be sure to read through answer explanations for items you missed.
6	Retake Practice Test 1, either in the book or online to see how much your score has improved. If you still got a few questions wrong, go back to the review and study any topics you missed. Retake Practice Test 2 if you have time.

Test-Taking Tips

Taking an important standardized test like the FTCE might make you nervous. These test tips are designed to help alleviate your test-taking anxieties and increase your comfort level with the exam.

Tip 1. Become comfortable with the format of the test. When you are practicing, stay calm and pace yourself. After simulating the test even once, you will boost your chances of doing well, and you will be able to sit down for the actual FTCE exam with much more confidence.

Tip 2. Familiarize yourself with the directions on the test. This will not only save time but will also help you avoid anxiety (and the mistakes anxiety causes).

Tip 3. Read all of the possible answers. Just because you think you have found the correct response, do not automatically assume that it is the best answer. Read through each choice to be sure that you are not making a mistake by jumping to conclusions.

Tip 4. Use the process of elimination. Go through each answer choice and eliminate as many as possible. If you can eliminate two answer choices, you will give yourself a better chance of getting the item correct since there will only be two choices left from which to make your guess. Do not leave an answer blank; it is better to guess than to not answer a question on the FTCE exams as you won't lose points for wrong answers.

Tip 5. Work at a steady pace and avoid focusing on any one question too long. Taking the timed practice tests online at the REA Study Center will help you learn to budget your time, and it's a great way to prepare for the computer-based test.

Tip 6. Since you are taking a computer-based exam, be sure your answer registers before you go to the next item.

Tip 7. Watch for the limiters in a multiple-choice question stem, such as *initial*, *best*, *most*, *not*, *least*, *except*, *required*, or *necessary*. Especially watch for negative words (such as *not true*). Double-check yourself by asking how the response you like fits the limitations established by the stem.

Tip 8. Don't let anxiety stifle you. Take a moment to breathe. This won't merely make you feel good. The brain uses roughly three times as much oxygen as your muscles do. Give it what it needs.

The Day of the Test

Before the Test

Check your FTCE registration information to find out what time to arrive at the testing center. Make sure you arrive early. This will allow you to collect your thoughts and relax before the test, and will also spare you the anguish that comes with being late. (If you arrive late, you might not be admitted to the test center.)

Go online to check your admission ticket 24 hours before the test in case there is a change. If there is a change, you will have to print out a new ticket.

Before you leave for the test center, make sure that you have your admission ticket and two forms of identification, one of which must contain a recent and recognizable photograph, your name, and signature (e.g., driver's license). All documents must be originals (no copies). You will not be admitted to the test center and you will forfeit your test fees if you do not have proper identification. (More information about proper forms of ID is listed in the official registration booklet.)

Dress comfortably, so you are not distracted by being too hot or too cold while taking the test.

Test Center Procedures

The following are prohibited at the test site: smoking of any products, visitors, and weapons of any kind. In addition, you may not bring into the testing room any cell phones, smartphones, other electronic, listening, recording, or photographic devices including anything with an on/off switch, and eyeglasses with communication and recording devices. Food and drink, dictionaries, textbooks, notebooks, calculators, briefcases, or packages are also not permitted. If you bring any prohibited devices into the testing room, you will be dismissed from the test, your fee will be forfeited, and your test scores will be canceled.

Procedures will be followed to maintain test security. Once you enter the test center you will be signed in by a test administrator, who will collect your palm vein image digitally and take your photograph for the purpose of identity verification. Follow all of the rules and instructions given by the test supervisor. If you do not, you risk being dismissed from the test and having your scores canceled.

You will be supplied secure storage at the test site for your personal items. Only materials provided at the test site will be allowed during testing.

Be sure to check the official site in case anything changes (*fl.nesinc.com/FL_DayOfTest.asp*).

After the Test

When you finish, hand in your test materials and you will be dismissed. Then, go home and relax — you deserve it!

Good luck on the FTCE Exceptional Student Education K-12 (061) Exam!

CHAPTER 1

Competency 1:
Knowledge of Foundations
of Exceptional Student
Education

This chapter introduces some of the legal, professional, and scientific foundations of the education of exceptional students.

Skill 1

Identify state and federal legislation that govern the education of students with exceptionalities.

In this section you will find information about some of the federal and state laws that impact the education of students with disabilities.

IDEA

The **Individuals with Disabilities Education Improvement Act (IDEIA)** is the federal law that governs the education of children with disabilities. This law was first introduced in 1975 as the Education for All Handicapped Children Act, and was revised, renamed, and reauthorized in 1997 and 2004.

IDEIA is often simply referred to as the **Individuals with Disabilities Education Act (IDEA),** which was the name of the law immediately prior to its reauthorization in 2004. You will also see reference to the law as IDEA 2004. All material in this chapter pertains to the current version of the law.

An Overview of IDEA

Through IDEA, the federal government provides states with funding for exceptional student education. The states must in turn comply with numerous requirements that pertain to children ranging from birth to age twenty-one. These requirements can be briefly summarized as follows:

- States must conduct **Child Find** activities to identify and evaluate children who may have disabilities. Students who may have a disability must be evaluated, at no cost to parents, for their eligibility for exceptional student education services. Parents must be involved in the evaluation process. (Throughout this chapter, the term "parents" will be used as shorthand for "parent(s) or guardian(s).") Either parents or a school professional such as a teacher may request an evaluation, but parental consent is required before evaluation of an individual student can take place.

- Students with disabilities are entitled to the same kinds of educational experiences as their peers without disabilities. Schools must provide each child with a disability an educational experience that is appropriate to his or her age and abilities, at no cost to the parents. This requirement of IDEA is referred to as a **free appropriate public education (FAPE).**

- Students with disabilities are to be educated in the **least restrictive environment (LRE),** meaning that their educational experiences must be as similar as possible to those of children who do not have disabilities. The goal of the LRE requirement is for students with disabilities to remain in the general education classroom to the greatest extent possible, with the fewest possible changes to day-to-day routines, and to be removed from regular classes and/or provided with exceptional student education (ESE) services only when the severity of their disability requires doing so in order for them to be educated appropriately.

- Between the ages of three and twenty-one, each student with a disability must have an **individualized education plan (IEP)** that describes the child's present level of progress and learning capacity, the short- and long-term educational goals for the child, and the accommodations and services that will be provided in order to achieve those goals. (Prior to age three, each child who shows signs of developmental delay must have an **Individualized Family Service Plan**

(IFSP), a written document similar to the IEP that focuses on the family and the child's natural environment.) The IEP is a written document created by a team typically consisting of the child's parents, an exceptional student education professional, a general education teacher, a representative of the school, and others, as appropriate. The educational objectives described in the IEP must be aligned with state curriculum standards for general education. By age sixteen, the IEPs must include a description of the student's goals following graduation as well as the transition services needed to achieve those goals.

- The rights and interests of parents and their children with disabilities must be protected through confidentiality with respect to children's educational records, nondiscriminatory practices in the assessments used to determine disability status, the provision of information about parents' and children's rights to the parents in the form of procedural safeguards, and the opportunity for parents to express dissatisfaction with their children's educational experience through due process hearings and other means.

More detail about these and other requirements will be provided throughout this chapter. Further information about IDEA is available on the Internet at the U.S. Department of Education website. In addition, the Florida Department of Education website contains information about IDEA as well as state laws pertaining to the education of exceptional students.

Other Legislation

Along with IDEA, other federal legislation affects the education of students with disabilities. For example:

- The **Vocational Rehabilitation Act** and the **Americans with Disabilities Act (ADA)** forbid discrimination against individuals with disabilities.

- The **Family Educational Rights and Privacy Act (FERPA)** helps ensure the privacy of educational records such as IEPs.

- The **No Child Left Behind Act (NCLB)** increased the accountability of schools with respect to the academic progress of students with disabilities.

Every Student Success Act (ESSA) requires data on student achievement and graduation rates to be reported as well as action in response to that data. However, unlike NCLB, states, districts, and schools will determine what support and interventions are implemented. Exceptional student education in Florida is also regulated by state-level legislation. Within the Florida Department of

Education, the Bureau of Exceptional Education and Student Services publishes a summary of Florida laws and State Board of Education rules that concern exceptional students. These laws and rules are consistent with and extend the provisions of IDEA and other federal legislation.

Skill 2

Classify the characteristics of students with exceptionalities using the eligibility criteria of categories included in current state and federal laws and regulations governing K–12 education programs.

In this section you will find information about the classification of disabilities given in IDEA, as well as the general criteria for eligibility.

IDEA identifies numerous categories of disability as well as providing definitions and examples of each category:

Infants and Toddlers with Disabilities

IDEA defines "infants and toddlers with disabilities" as children between birth and age three who are experiencing developmental delays in one or more of the following areas:

- cognitive development
- physical development
- social or emotional development
- communication development
- adaptive development

Infants and toddlers with disabilities also includes children between birth and age three who have been diagnosed with a condition that is highly likely to produce one or more types of developmental delay. Finally, states and local education agencies have the option of using the term "developmental delay" for a child between the ages of three and nine, if the child exhibits delays in one of the aforementioned areas, and as a result of the delay the child needs special education and related services.

Children with Disabilities

For the age range three to twenty-one years, IDEA lists thirteen categories of disability:

- autism
- deaf-blindness
- deafness
- emotional disturbance
- hearing impairment
- intellectual disability
- multiple disabilities
- orthopedic impairment
- other health impairment
- specific learning disability
- speech or language impairment
- traumatic brain injury
- visual impairment

Eligibility

As discussed later in this chapter, eligibility for exceptional student education (ESE) services is based on the results of an evaluation conducted by a group known as the assessment team. Children who are considered eligible for exceptional student education (ESE) services must be reevaluated every three years, if not more frequently. The parents may at any time request a hearing to challenge the eligibility determination.

In general, a child is considered eligible for exceptional student education (ESE) services if the evaluation team concludes that the child has one of the thirteen types of disability listed above, and the child's educational performance is adversely affected by the disability. Both conditions must be met in order for the child to be eligible for special education services. The child need not be failing in school in order to be deemed eligible. Again, each particular state may choose to also consider developmental delay, along with the resulting need for special education and related services, as sufficient criteria for eligibility.

Skill 3

Compare typical and atypical development of physical, cognitive, linguistic, social, and emotional stages of students in the K–12 educational system.

This section consists of descriptions of the 13 categories of disability listed in the previous section.

- **Autism** refers to a developmental disability, generally detectable before age three, that affects communication, social interaction, and learning. The child with autism may show language delays, unusual speech patterns, aversion to eye contact and touch, repetitive behaviors, and resistance to change in daily routines.

- **Deaf-blindness** refers to simultaneous hearing and visual impairments that are so severe the student cannot benefit sufficiently from programs and services that are designed for exclusively deaf or exclusively blind children. Deaf-blindness is usually **congenital** (i.e., present at birth) but may be **adventitious** (i.e., acquired through illness or injury).

- **Deafness** refers to an extreme hearing impairment that adversely affects the student's educational performance. Deafness may be congenital or adventitious.

- **Emotional disturbance** refers to a condition that reflects at least one of the following characteristics over an extended period of time: (i) an inability to learn that cannot be attributed to other factors, such as intellectual or sensory deficits, or health problems; (ii) an inability to build or sustain satisfactory personal relationships with others; (iii) feelings or behaviors that are ordinarily inappropriate; (iv) pervasive unhappiness or depression; and (v) a tendency to develop physical symptoms or fears related to personal problems or problems at school. Schizophrenia, anxiety disorders, and depression are among the many examples.

- **Hearing impairment** refers to an impairment in hearing that undermines the student's educational performance but is not severe enough to be classified as deafness. Hearing impairments may be congenital or adventitious. Children with hearing difficulties are classified as hearing impaired only if the difficulties persist even after corrections (e.g., surgery and/or use of hearing aids).

- **Intellectual disability** refers to general intellectual ability that is significantly below average, combined with limitations in adaptive behavior, that adversely affects the student's educational performance. The primary example would be an intellectual disability, which is often congenital but may be adventitious. The phrase "adaptive behavior" in the definition indicates that intellectual disabilities involve not only much lower than average intelligence, but also impairments in the extent of the child's social competence and independence.

- **Multiple disabilities** refers to a combination of disabilities that is so severe the student cannot benefit sufficiently from programs and services that are designed for any one of those disabilities.

- **Orthopedic impairment** refers to musculoskeletal problems, congenital or adventitious, that adversely influence the student's educational performance. Examples include cerebral palsy, polio, amputations, and so on.

- **Other health impairment** refers to health problems affecting strength, energy, or alertness to a degree that adversely affects the student's educational performance. Among the many examples would be leukemia, epilepsy, diabetes, asthma, lupus, and sickle cell anemia.

- **Specific learning disability** refers to problems with the ability to comprehend or produce information when performing academic tasks. Dyslexia, dyscalculia, and minimal brain dysfunction are among the many examples. Such learning disabilities are usually congenital but may be adventitious. The term "specific" indicates that this disability is restricted to particular school subjects or tasks. A student with a specific learning disability may perform well in some subjects or tasks but poorly on others. These students are not impaired in general learning ability, in other words, but rather in some specific skill or skills.

- **Speech or language impairment** refers to communication disorders that adversely affect the student's educational performance. Examples include articulation disorders, stuttering, and mutism. Such learning disabilities are usually congenital but may be adventitious.

- **Traumatic brain injury** refers to any acquired injury to the brain that undermines the student's educational performance. Such injuries may result from accidents involving motor vehicles, sports, and other causes. Children with traumatic brain injury may have impairments in physical, behavioral, cognitive, social, and/or emotional functioning, depending on the nature and severity of the injury.

- **Visual impairment** refers to visual problems that adversely influence the student's educational performance. Visual impairments are usually congenital but may be adventitious. Children with visual difficulties are only classified as visually impaired if the difficulties persist even after corrections (e.g., surgery and/or use of corrective lenses).

Skill 4

Interpret principles and practices in the provision of education for students with exceptionalities based on legal and ethical standards.

In this section you will find additional information about these and other requirements discussed in the IDEA legislation.

Inclusion

Inclusion refers to the practice of educating students with disabilities in the general education classroom, so that they may participate in day-to-day routines alongside students without disabilities to the greatest extent possible. Inclusion is a general principle that is closely related to the legal concept of least restrictive environment (LRE) discussed earlier. IDEA does not guarantee inclusive education to students with disabilities, but through the LRE requirement it ensures that inclusion is a sort of default, or normative scenario, for which there may be exceptions. In other words, IDEA requires that students with disabilities be included in the general education classroom and only removed and/or provided with exceptional student services if the classroom environment cannot be modified to adequately support students' educational progress.

Inclusion can be contrasted with the older practice of **mainstreaming,** in which students with disabilities were included in the general education classroom only when their achievement would be near grade level without substantial support. The main difference between inclusion and mainstreaming is that inclusion treats the general education classroom as the student's primary placement, along with the general education teacher as the student's primary instructor. Educational practices that require the student with disabilities to spend time outside the general classroom, or to be instructed by other experts, are considered supplementary.

Transition Planning

The free appropriate public education (FAPE) requirement of IDEA was extended in the 2004 reauthorization to include not just current educational experiences but also preparation for additional education or training, employment opportunities, and independent living. This new emphasis on **transition** is intended to help prepare students with disabilities for life after their K–12 education. The IEP team is required to take responsibility for planning transition services. These services may include help with identifying and applying to college or vocational school, seeking employment, finding a place to live in the community, and so on. By age sixteen, the student's IEP must contain a postsecondary plan that indicates the goals for life beyond school and describes the transition services necessary to achieve those goals.

Confidentiality

Together with the Family Educational Rights and Privacy Act (FERPA), IDEA provides for the confidentiality of education records that are created and maintained for children with disabilities. Confidentiality must be maintained with respect to information that might unnecessarily identify a student as having a disability. Parents must be informed of this requirement and must give consent in order for personally identifiable information to be shared outside the school district. Parents must also have access to all such information maintained by the school.

The IEP is an education record created specifically for children with disabilities. The contents of the IEP must be kept confidential, except when school staff have a legitimate need to be aware of the contents. The amount of information a teacher, for example, may have about a particular child's IEP will vary from student to student. Parents may request that the teacher(s) have access to information in the IEP.

Procedural Safeguards

The **procedural safeguards** consist of a set of rules and procedures designed to protect the rights and interests of parents and their children with disabilities. IDEA requires that parents of children with disabilities be given an explanation of the procedural safeguards, also known as parents' rights, when their children are evaluated, when the parents are invited to early intervention or IEP meetings, when the parents file a complaint, and when they request the procedural safeguards. Following are some key examples of information conveyed in the procedural safeguards:

- Parents must receive notice in advance of any evaluations, services, or other activities involving the child. Parents can choose the language or mode of communication for such notices.

- Parental consent is required prior to any actions pertaining to the child, and prior to the sharing of any information about the child outside the school district. Parents can give consent to none, some, or all of the services recommended.

- Parents are entitled to see their children's educational records.

- Mediation will be provided to parents who have complaints, or who cannot agree with the IEP team on planning or services for their children. If mediation is unsuccessful, a due process hearing will allow parents' complaints to be addressed by an impartial, outside expert.

Due Process

In general, the phrase "due process" refers to principles that attempt to guarantee the rights of citizens. The rights and responsibilities that IDEA accords to parents, children, and schools are complex, and so there are many potential sources of conflict. Parents may disagree with the decision of the assessment team as to whether their child has a disability, or with the team's view of the nature of that disability. Parents may disagree with the school's placement of the child in or out of the general education classroom. They may disagree with other elements of the school's approach to educating the child, or they may feel that the quality of the educational experience is inconsistent or lacking. Owing to these and other conflicts that arise, **due process hearings** allow the parents to bring their complaints before an impartial, experienced individual from outside the school district. IDEA requires states to create a mechanism for due process hearings while allowing the states some latitude in procedural details. The hearings are conducted at no cost to parents, although parents are ordinarily responsible for their attorney's fees. Due process hearings can also be requested by schools, as happens sometimes, for example, when parents refuse to allow a child to be evaluated for the presence of a disability.

Skill 5

Apply knowledge of the requirements for developing individualized educational plans (IEPs), educational plans (EPs), and transition IEPs.

In this section you will find information about the requirements for IEPs and IFSPs that are specified by IDEA.

Within 30 days of determining that a child is eligible for special education services under IDEA, an **IEP team** must meet in order to create an IEP for the child.

Composition of IEP Team

The IEP team includes the following individuals:

- Parents
- An exceptional student education professional from the LEA or school district who works with students with the same type of disability
- At least one of the child's general education teachers, if the child participates, or may participate, in activities with general education students

- A representative of the LEA who is knowledgeable about available resources and the provision of exceptional student education

- A professional who is qualified to interpret and explain the results of testing and other aspects of the evaluation (if such an individual is not already part of the team)

Parents may invite anyone whose presence they consider helpful, including outside experts, family members, or anyone else with pertinent knowledge about the child. The school may invite anyone who is providing disability-related services to the child, as well as guidance counselors and/ or other experts. The child may be invited, as appropriate, and must be invited if one of the purposes of the meeting is transition services.

IEP Meeting

IDEA requires that school staff take responsibility for convening the first meeting to create a student's IEP, as well as for convening subsequent meetings. School staff must choose a meeting time and place that are convenient to the parents. They must inform the parents as to who will attend the meeting. They must also explain that the parents have the right to invite anyone else who has specific knowledge about the child.

Parents must be given a copy of the IEP. If parents disagree with the content of the IEP, they should attempt to negotiate an agreement with the IEP team. If an agreement cannot be reached, parents can request **mediation.** Briefly, mediation is a meeting between parents and school representatives conducted by a qualified, impartial mediator whose goal is to find a resolution that satisfies all parties. Mediation must be carried out at no cost to parents. Parents may also file a complaint with the state education agency and request a due process hearing concerning the IEP's contents.

The school is responsible for ensuring that the IEP is implemented. The IEP team must review the IEP at least once per year, as well as whenever the school and/or parents request a review.

IEP Content

IDEA requires that each IEP contain the following content:

- A summary of the child's current levels of functioning and educational performance. This summary is typically based on classroom performance (e.g., scores on tests and assignments), tests administered for the purpose of identifying a disability, and observations made by parents and school staff.

- A statement of annual goals. These are measurable goals that the child can reasonably accomplish in one school year, and they may pertain to the child's physical, behavioral, social, and/or academic functioning.

- A statement of short-term objectives. These are measurable goals that constitute steps toward achieving the annual goals.

- A list of services. This list consists of all services that the child needs in order to achieve the annual goals—both services directly provided to the child as well as support provided to school staff who work with the child.

- A description of timing for exceptional student education and related services. This description must indicate when the services will begin, as well as the frequency and duration of services. Location of services must also be indicated.

- An explanation concerning the extent of participation with nondisabled children. This explanation must account for situations in which the child is not present in the general education classroom and/or is not included in educational activities for children without disabilities.

- A statement concerning the child's participation in standardized testing. This statement indicates whether modifications are needed before administering any state- or district-wide achievement tests to the child. Also indicated is whether any of these achievement tests are not appropriate for the child to take (and whether alternative forms of testing will be provided).

- A description of how progress will be measured. This description indicates how the child's progress toward the annual goals will be measured, and how parents will be kept informed of the child's progress.

IFSPs

The Individualized Family Service Plan (IFSP) is similar to an IEP, in the sense that it is a written document that includes detailed information on the child's current level of functioning, a statement of goals, a summary of how those goals will be met, and so on. Both the IEP and the IFSP are based on a careful assessment of the child's needs. However, the IFSP only pertains to the age range birth to three years. Once the child turns three, the creation of an IEP must be discussed.

Another difference between the IFSP and the IEP is that the IFSP targets the family and those natural environments accessible to the young child, such as the home, child care programs, parks, and so on. The IFSP often describes services that will be provided by representatives of one or more agencies to families in the home. In contrast, the IEP is typically restricted to the school setting.

Transition IEPs

The concept of transition was discussed earlier in the chapter and is the focus of Chapter 6. Once the child reaches age fourteen, if not earlier, the IEP must indicate what courses the child must take to achieve his or her post-graduation goals. Once the child is sixteen, if not sooner, the IEP must indicate what transition services are needed to prepare the child for leaving school. The IEP must also address interagency responsibilities, meaning that it must indicate who besides the school will provide transition support. The post-graduation goals must be measurable.

Age of Majority

The **age of majority** is the age at which a person becomes a legal adult. In many states, including Florida, the age of majority is eighteen. In some states, including Florida, beginning at least one year before the student reaches the age of majority, the IEP must indicate that the student has been informed of those rights that will transfer to him or her at the age of majority.

Skill 6

Evaluate the role and function of system-wide models of support for assisting all students, including students with exceptionalities, in accessing the general education curriculum and achieving high expectations.

Curricular issues are discussed throughout this book, particularly in Chapter 3. Assessment is the focus of Chapter 2. This section provides information on the roles of the child study team, the assessment team, and the IEP team, particularly with respect to assessment procedures and decision-making. IDEA requires that an assessment team consider referrals, and if the assessment team judges that a child has a disability and is eligible for special education and related services, an IEP team must be convened in order to generate an IEP. IDEA does not have specific requirements for the child study team.

Pre-Referral

In some states and school districts, evaluation intended to determine if a student is eligible for exceptional student education and related services does not take place until a team has worked with the general education teacher and determined that the problems the child is experiencing cannot be readily resolved in the general education setting. This team may be referred to as a "child study team" or with some other label, depending on the state. Such teams are not required by IDEA but rather by the laws of particular states. In Florida, prior to referral for evaluation, the following activities must take place:

- Convening of two or more conferences pertaining to the student's area(s) of concern

- Review of anecdotal records or behavioral observations by the student's teacher and at least one other person (showing that the area of concern has arisen in more than one situation)

- Screening for sensory deficits (e.g., hearing problems) that may be responsible for the student's area(s) of concern

- Review of educational records, including achievement data and social, psychological, and medical information

- Review of attendance records and investigation into causes for excessive absenteeism, if any

- Implementation of two or more general interventions or strategies, along with the use of pre- and post-intervention measures to evaluate their effectiveness

If the child study team determines that general education interventions or strategies are not successful, the team initiates an exceptional student education referral. An assessment team then reviews the referral and conducts an evaluation. (The terms "evaluation" and "assessment" are often used interchangeably. In this chapter, the term "assessment" will be used for measurements that help determine whether a child has a disability and is eligible for exceptional student education and related services. Thus, tests are a form of assessment, as are certain observations recorded by teachers. The term "evaluation" will be used in this chapter for the more inclusive process by which the assessment team examines various assessments and other information and comes to a determination as to the child's eligibility.)

Evaluation

Either parents or school professionals such as teachers or child study teams may request that a child be evaluated for a disability, at no cost to parents. Parental consent is required before the evaluation can be made on an individual basis. (Consent is not required for school-wide assessments such as vision and hearing screenings.) The purpose of the evaluation is to determine eligibility for special education services.

IDEA requires a team approach to evaluation. Each evaluation is planned and carried out by an **assessment team** consisting of at least one professional qualified to conduct individual diagnostic assessments of children, as well as a general education teacher (one of the child's own teachers, if applicable), and the parents. When creating an evaluation, the assessment team should consider the results of prior testing and other assessments, input from parents and teachers, and other pertinent information about the child's background.

Briefly, the assessment team will engage in the following activities:

- Review the referral.

- Review background information.

- Develop an evaluation plan indicating what tests and other forms of assessment will be used to evaluate the child.

- Share the evaluation plan with parents and obtain consent.

- Administer assessments to the student.

- Evaluate the results of assessments, along with other available information, to determine whether the student has a disability, and if so, what exceptional student education and related services he or she needs.

- Generate a written report of findings.

- Meet with parents to determine eligibility.

The tests and other assessments used by the assessment team must meet a number of criteria. Following are some key examples:

- The assessments must not be racially or culturally biased.

- The assessments must be administered in the student's native language and/or in some other suitable medium (e.g., sign language).

- The assessments must be technically sound (as discussed in Chapter 5).

- The assessments must be administered by trained individuals in the way that was intended by the creators of the assessments.

IDEA specifies that eligibility for exceptional student education and related services cannot be based on the results of a single test or any other single form of assessment. The assessment team must always consider multiple assessments and other sources of information before making a decision about whether the student has a disability and is eligible for exceptional student education and related services.

If the parents disagree with the results of the evaluation, they may request an **Individual Educational Evaluation (IEE).** Mediation and due process hearings are also options if parents cannot resolve their differences with the assessment team concerning the outcome of the evaluation.

If the assessment team determines that the child has a disability and is indeed eligible for exceptional student education and related services, the results of the team's evaluation are shared with the IEP team and used to inform the development of the IEP, as described earlier in this chapter.

The SETT Framework

The information-gathering and decision-making activities of the assessment and IEP teams are guided by the requirements of IDEA and other federal and state laws. In addition, some teams rely on a systematic process for gathering information and making decisions about students. For example, within the Florida Department of Education, the Bureau of Exceptional Education and Student Services discusses the use of the **SETT Framework.** The acronym "SETT" stands for student, environment, tasks, and tools—four areas of inquiry that guide teams seeking to identify supports and services for students with disabilities. Following are some of the questions an IEP team might ask about each area:

- Regarding the student, what are his or her strengths and special needs? What are the student's goals and expectations? What does the student need to do that is currently difficult or impossible for him or her to do independently?

- Regarding the environment, how can the student's current physical and instructional arrangements be characterized? What types of materials and support are currently available? What are the attitudes and expectations of educational staff, family, and others? What are the specific concerns regarding the student's access to physical and instructional environments?

- Regarding the tasks, what activities normally occur in the student's instructional environment, what activities support the student's curricular goals, and what are the critical components of these activities? How could these activities be modified to accommodate the student's particular needs? What strategies could be used to facilitate the student's active engagement in these activities?

- Regarding the tools, what tools should be considered when developing instruction for the student, and how might these tools be tried out in the environments in which they are ordinarily used? How could differentiated instruction enhance the student's performance? What other accommodations and services does the student need? Does the student have significant cognitive impairment that requires modifications to the curriculum?

Support for Children of Ages Three to Twenty-One

As noted earlier, the IEP must contain a description of support that the student will receive in order to achieve the annual goals specified in the IEP. Several types of support are available through schools for children ranging from three to twenty-one years of age:

- **Exceptional Student Education** is instruction designed to meet the particular needs of a child with a disability, at no cost to parents.

- **Related services** are those services that students with disabilities need in order to benefit from special education. If the child uses a wheelchair, for example, the school must ensure that the child can ride the bus and enter the school building. Another example would be counseling or psychological services provided to a child who is classified as emotionally disturbed.

- **Supplementary aids and services** are those that students with disabilities need in order to participate in general education to the greatest extent possible. Such aids and services help fulfill the LRE requirement of IDEA. An example would be audio recorded books for students with visual impairments. Arranging for a qualified individual to shadow a child with autism when that child is in the general education classroom would be another example.

- **Program modifications** consist of changes made to the general education experience that would benefit the educational progress of a particular student with disabilities. An example would be allowing a child with ADHD to walk around quietly in the back of class at specified times each day.

- **Supports for school personnel** consist of training, materials, and other resources made available to teachers and other staff. An example would be professional development workshops designed for teachers to help them work with children who have particular types of disability.

Support for Infants and Toddlers

The services described above are provided through the school system. For infants and toddlers (birth through age three), IDEA requires that **early intervention services** be provided in natural settings such as the home or a child care center. States have some latitude in determining eligibility for these services and in the nature of services provided. However, all states have a State Interagency Coordinating Council (SICC) that performs functions such as helping identify and coordinate the efforts of agencies that provide early intervention services. In addition, a service coordinator works with each family to ensure that the services described in the IFSP are obtained.

Placement

Earlier in this chapter the LRE requirements of IDEA were discussed. Following are some of the scenarios in which these requirements could be met:

- The student spends the entire school day in the general education classroom. Neither the student nor the teacher(s) receive special services. Of all conceivable scenarios, this represents the least restrictive environment possible. An example would be a student with ADHD who is taking medication that allows him to function in the regular classroom without attentional impairments.

- The student spends the entire school day in the regular classroom with no special services, but one or more teachers are provided with consultation services that would help them provide a better classroom experience for the student. An example would be a blind student whose teacher receives instruction from an outside expert on the use of audio recorded materials, braille, and so on.

- The student spends the entire school day in the regular classroom and receives instruction part or all of the day from an exceptional student education (ESE) specialist. An example would be a student with dyscalculia who receives math instruction in class from a specialist.

- The student spends the majority of the school day in the regular classroom but receives exceptional student education services outside the classroom for part of the day. An example would be a student with an oral language impairment who meets with a speech therapist outside class each day. In this example, the student is only removed from the general education classroom for speech therapy.

- The student spends the majority of the school day in an exceptional student education (ESE) class within the school, and some time each day in the general education classroom and/or with general education students in social settings. An example would be a student with intellectual disabilities who is educated in an exceptional student education (ESE) class but joins peers for lunch and recreational activities. In this example, the student would not benefit from the general education curriculum but can experience social benefits from integration with peers.

- The student spends the entire school day in a special class within the school or within a special school. An example would be a student with severe autism who could not benefit from the academic or social experience of the general education environment.

- The student spends the entire school day in a live-in residential setting or hospital, or at home. An example would be a student who has medical needs that cannot be served in the regular school setting.

Accommodations

Florida state law defines *accommodations* as changes that are made in how students with disabilities access information and demonstrate performance. These changes help students with disabilities function in the contexts of instruction and assessment.

Accommodations can be classified into four types. This approach to classification cross-cuts the classification systems of support and placement discussed earlier in this section.

- **Presentation accommodations** change the format of information presented in the classroom. An example would be the supplementary aids provided to students with visual impairments, such as audio recorded books, braille texts, large-print texts, magnification tools, and so on.

- **Response accommodations** change the format in which students can respond to classroom tasks such as assignments and tests. An example would be allowing students with visual impairments to take tests using a brailler (a braille keyboard), to dictate their test responses to a scribe, to provide oral responses, and so on.

- **Setting accommodations** change the locations or conditions of the educational environment. An example would be allowing students with visual impairments to sit where they can best hear the teacher, to use specialized lighting or light filters, to sit especially close to a natural light source, and so on.

- **Scheduling accommodations** change the timing and scheduling of classroom tasks such as activities and tests. An example would be allowing students with visual impairments to have extended time on tests, to take breaks that prevent eyestrain, to schedule tests according to the availability of a scribe, and so on.

The four types of accommodations are not exclusive. An individual student might receive one, some, or all of these accommodations depending on need. For example, a child with a severe reading-related disability might be provided with classroom texts that have large fonts, wide margins, extra space between the lines, and so on (presentation accommodations). This child might be allowed to provide oral responses to assignments that other students must complete in written format (response accommodations). The child might be permitted to sit close to the teacher, so that it is relatively easy for the teacher to assist with certain reading tasks (setting accommodation). Finally, the child may be allowed extra time on written tests (scheduling accommodation).

Florida's Bureau of Exceptional Education and Student Services notes the following guidelines for accommodations:

- Accommodations should facilitate the student's ability to demonstrate knowledge and skills.

- Accommodations should not give the student an unfair advantage or undermine the validity of a test. Accommodations should not change the nature of the competency being tested.

- Accommodations for the Florida Standards Assessments, or FSA, must be highly similar or the same as accommodations the student uses in classroom instruction and assessment.

- Accommodations must be necessary for the student to demonstrate his or her knowledge or skills.

Skill 7

Apply effective methods of communication, consultation, and collaboration with students, parents, caregivers, and all other stakeholders, including those from culturally and linguistically diverse backgrounds, as equal members of educational teams.

In this section, various means of communication, consultation and collaboration will be reviewed. Specific attention will be given to culturally diverse individuals and their interaction with children with disabilities.

Teachers strive to establish partnerships with parents to support student learning. Strong communication is fundamental to this partnership and to building a sense of community between home and school. In these changing times, teachers must continue to develop and expand their skills in order to maximize effective communication with parents.

Positive parent-school communications benefit parents. The way schools communicate and interact with parents affects the extent and quality of parents' home involvement with their children's learning. For example, schools that communicate bad news about student performance more often than recognizing students' excellence will discourage parent involvement by making parents feel they cannot effectively help their children.

Parents also benefit from being involved in their children's education by getting ideas from school on how to help and support their children, and by learning more about the school's academic program and how it works. Perhaps most important, parents benefit by becoming more confident about the value of their school involvement. Parents develop a greater appreciation for the important role they play in their children's education.

Principles of Effective Communication

- Accept parents' statements and respect parents' point of view.
- Listen actively and respond to the parents.
- Question effectively and speak plainly and use-open ended questions.
- Show the parents their child's improving performance.
- Stay focused on the purpose of a child's educational program and progress.

Teachers and Other School Personnel Should:

- Recognize that all families are different.
- Understand that emotions exhibited by parents of children with disabilities regarding the child are complicated and varied.
- Acknowledge that parents of children with disabilities have additional roles and stressors.
- Make parents feel welcome.
- Show respect to the parents.
- Think of parents as equal partners in ensuring that their children are successful in school.
- Value parents' participation (of whatever level).
- Communicate with families regularly and in a variety of ways.
- Provide parents with meaningful information about their child's school performance.

Understanding and Respecting Cultural Differences

- Many families live in low income and poverty.

- Practitioners should understand that parents are life educators and know a child better than anyone else.

- Families from culturally diverse backgrounds tend to be family-oriented.

- Some may hold idiosyncratic ideologies and practices about the cause of disabilities.

- Educational system may be intimidating to the family.

Skill 8

Use effective methods for coaching and supporting paraprofessionals, tutors, and volunteers to assist students with exceptionalities across settings.

In this section the role and methods of coaching and supporting paraprofessionals in the field will be reviewed. Paraprofessionals are extremely valued as they impact the success of many exceptional student education programs in Florida.

Paraprofessionals are essential work force members of early intervention and school programs. Identified through a myriad of titles and job descriptions, paraprofessionals' roles and responsibilities have evolved along with the need for increased instructional supports for diverse learners. The number of students with disabilities in general education classrooms has increased significantly and paraprofessionals often play key roles to ensure the successful provision of supports and services in general education. Moreover, as the needs of the children and students are becoming more complex, the skills required of paraprofessionals are expanding. Traditionally, paraprofessionals have been undervalued in their roles as service providers. As paraprofessional roles and responsibilities continue to grow, systems must work diligently to ensure high-quality personnel and services.

Several comprehensive, validated training programs designed specifically for paraprofessionals are now available for districts to purchase and use in individual classrooms, small group sessions, or large in-service workshops. While instructional formats vary, the content in the programs is generally based on a core curriculum that focuses on the specific skills paraeducators must have to work with children and youth of different ages, who have different levels of disabilities, and with different learning needs. Content areas may include:

- Roles and responsibilities of paraprofessionals.

- Ethical issues for paraprofessionals.

- Instructional strategies.

- Behavior management practices.

- Basic academic skills (i.e., reading, writing, and math).

- Observing and recording student performance.

- Teaming and communicating with students, teachers, parents, and other colleagues.

- Health issues.

- Working with students with disabilities.

Skill 9

Determine the purposes and functions of professionals, advocacy organizations, and agencies relevant to educating students with exceptionalities.

This section provides information about a few of the many organizations that provide information, materials, and other resources of interest to parents, educators, and administrators who are involved either personally and/or professionally in the education of students with disabilities.

National Organizations

- The **U.S. Department of Education (ED)** maintains a website devoted exclusively to IDEA. This website includes the full text of IDEA, summaries of IDEA and cross-references to other pertinent legislation, discussions of recent trends in research and practice, training materials, resources for schools, and a variety of other information of relevance to families, educators, administrators, and researchers.

- The U.S. Department of Education's **Office of Special Education and Rehabilitative Services (OSERS)** offers programs, services, and a variety of resources that promote inclusion, equity, and opportunity for students with disabilities, the OSERS website contains information of relevance to families, educators, administrators, and researchers.

- The **National Dissemination Center for Children with Disabilities** provides the full text of IDEA and information about this law, as well as information about other legislation that pertain to students with disabilities, about the characteristics and management of specific disabilities, about research-based best practices in special education, and about other topics of relevance to families, educators, administrators, and researchers.

- The **Council for Exceptional Children (CEC)** provides information pertaining to the education of students with disabilities, special education legislation and advocacy, careers and professional development opportunities in special education, scientific and professional trends, and other topics of relevance to families, educators, administrators, and researchers.

- The **American Educational Research Association (AERA)** is one of the largest professional and scientific organizations that supports research pertaining to children with disabilities. Within the AERA, the Special Education Research Special Interest Group (SER-SIG) promotes and disseminates research on children with disabilities and issues related to their education.

- **The National Association of Special Education Teachers (NASET)** is an example of a professional organization with a common interest in the education of children with disabilities. NASET provides special education professionals with information about policy and research, professional development and career opportunities, and other resources.

Local Organizations

- IDEA requires that every state maintain a **Parent Training and Information (PTI)** center, which provides information to parents about IDEA, special education services, and parent organizations as well as other local groups of interest.

- Parents may also receive information from the **Child Find coordinator** working within a particular school district or county. As noted earlier in the chapter, Child Find provisions in IDEA require that children who may have disabilities be identified and evaluated.

Organizations in Florida

- Within the Florida Department of Education, the **Bureau of Exceptional Education and Student Services** administers special education programs, coordinates services to students with disabilities statewide, and provides information pertaining to legislation, policies and procedures, best practices in special education, resources for parents and educators, and so on.

- Florida's **State Advisory Committee for the Education of Exceptional Students (SAC)** is a group appointed by the Commissioner of Education to provide policy guidance concerning exceptional education and related services. SAC annual reports and other information can be found on the Florida Department of Education website.

- Florida's **Department of Children and Families** provides information and resources of relevance to children with disabilities and their families.

- The **Florida Developmental Disabilities Council** provides information and engages in advocacy on behalf of individuals with developmental disabilities and their families.

Skill 10

Determine the factors associated with disproportionality in exceptional student education.

This section specifically addresses the disproportionality in exceptional student education and what can be done to appropriately identify individuals receiving exceptional student education services.

The disproportionate representation of racial and ethnic minorities in special education and the inequities in educational opportunities are among the most critical issues faced by the U.S. public school system in the past 30 years. In general, disproportionate representation, or disproportionality, refers to the over- or under-representation of a given population group often defined by racial and ethnic backgrounds, but also defined by socioeconomic status, national origin, English proficiency, gender, and sexual orientation in a specific population category.

A child's race and ethnicity significantly influence the child's probability of being misidentified, misclassified, and inappropriately placed in special education programs. Research shows the relationship between race and ethnicity and other variables for students' placement in exceptional student education classes. Variables such as language, poverty, assessment practices, systemic inequities, and professional development opportunities for teachers have been cited as factors that play a role in disproportionate representation.

Among the most longstanding and intransigent issues in the field, the disproportionate representation of minority students in exceptional student education programs has its roots in a long history of educational segregation and discrimination. Although national estimates of disproportionality have been consistent over time, state and local estimates may show varying patterns of disproportionality. Several factors may contribute to disproportionality, including test bias, poverty, exceptional student education processes, inequity in general education, issues of behavior management, and cultural mismatch/cultural reproduction.

Factors contributing to disproportionality in exceptional student education include:

1. Test bias
2. Poverty
3. Behavior management
4. Cultural mismatch
5. Identification process
6. Available resources
7. Acclimation in general education
8. Views on diversity

Chapter 1 Practice Quiz

1. Which of the following characteristics is described as one of the symptoms of autism?
   A. difficulty paying attention in social settings
   B. resistance to change in daily routines
   C. lack of interest in mechanical objects
   D. excessive verbalization with others

2. Jason is a hearing-impaired 10th grader whose biology teacher provides him with written versions of the lectures she delivers in class. What type of accommodation does this scenario illustrate?
   A. presentation accommodation
   B. response accommodation
   C. setting accommodation
   D. scheduling accommodation

3. The least restrictive environment requirement of IDEA is closely associated with

   A. assessment.

   B. mainstreaming.

   C. inclusion.

   D. child study teams.

4. A due process hearing might be most appropriate for which of the following situations?

   A. A general education teacher has become frustrated with a student who has ADHD and poor impulse control, and the teacher seeks an outlet for his frustration.

   B. A principal is concerned that a parent brings her child to school late several mornings per week, and the parent has not responded to a note from the teacher.

   C. A special education teacher and a general education teacher disagree about the best approach for helping a intellectually disabled student progress in reading.

   D. A parent disagrees with an assessment team's conclusion that her son has dyslexia, but after meeting with the team and a mediator, no resolution is achieved.

5. Which of the following groups is responsible for setting annual goals for a student with disabilities?

   A. teacher support team

   B. assessment team

   C. IEP team

   D. child study team

6. According to IDEA, on what grounds can a student be considered eligible for special education and related services?

   A. evidence that the student is failing or doing very poorly in two or more classes

   B. evidence that the student has a disability that impairs academic performance

   C. evidence that the student is not achieving his or her potential in school

   D. evidence that the student has limited English proficiency due to country of origin

7. Information about a twenty-month-old's language delay and steps that will be taken to provide support would be found in an

   A. Individualized Family Service Plan.

   B. Individualized Education Plan.

   C. Infant Assessment Plan.

   D. Inter-agency Enrichment Plan.

Explanatory Answers

1. B

Option B is correct because resistance to change in familiar routines is a common symptom among autistic children. Option A is incorrect because although autistic children may not be attentive enough in certain situations, difficulty paying attention is not a symptom distinctive to autism per se. Option C is incorrect because some autistic children show particular interest in mechanical objects. Option D is incorrect because many autistic children exhibit impaired communication with others.

2. A

Option A is correct because presentation accommodations change the format of information presented in the classroom, and the teacher in the scenario has changed the format of her lectures for Jason from oral to written. Option B is incorrect because response accommodations change the format in which students can respond to classroom tasks, but nothing is mentioned in the scenario about Jason's response. Option C is incorrect because setting accommodations change the location of the educational environment, but nothing about such changes is noted in the scenario. Option D is incorrect because scheduling accommodations change the timing of classroom tasks, but no mention is made in the scenario of timing-related changes.

3. C

Although the least restrictive environment (LRE) of IDEA does not guarantee inclusion, it fosters an inclusive environment, and thus option C is the correct answer. Options A and D are incorrect because neither assessment nor the child study team has any particular relationship to the LRE. Option B is incorrect because the LRE prohibits mainstreaming as a general strategy for dealing with students with disabilities.

4. D

Due process hearings are generally a last resort after disagreements involving school personnel and parents cannot be resolved through other means. Thus option D is the correct answer. Options A and B are incorrect because in these scenarios, disagreements between school personnel and parents are not clearly evident. Option C is incorrect because the disagreement does not involve a parent.

5. C

Option C is correct because one of the primary goals of the IEP team is to set annual goals for the student with disabilities. As this is not a primary goal for teacher support teams, assessment teams, and child study teams, the other options are incorrect.

6. B

Option B is correct because according to IDEA, eligibility for special education and related services depends on evidence that the student has a disability *and* evidence that the disability impairs academic performance. Option A is incorrect because academic failure does not necessarily indicate a disability. Option C is incorrect for a similar reason—failure to achieve one's potential does not necessarily imply a disability. Option D is incorrect because limited English proficiency due strictly to country of origin is not a disability.

7. A

Option A is correct because Individualized Family Service Plans are appropriate for infants. Option B is incorrect because Individualized Education Plans are not formulated until after the child is three years old. Option C is incorrect because it pertains to assessment and would probably not include a discussion of steps that will be taken to provide support. Option D is incorrect because this phrase is not standard.

CHAPTER

2

Competency 2: Knowledge of Assessment and Evaluation

This chapter pertains to the use of assessment and evaluation in educational settings. Much of the chapter focuses on the assessment of students who have or who are suspected of having a disability.

Assessment versus Evaluation

In educational settings, **assessment** is the systematic gathering and analysis of information about students in order to make decisions that may benefit their educational experience. The term "assessment" can be used in at least two different but related senses:

- The specific tool used to gather information can be referred to as an assessment. For example, a vision screening, a test of reading fluency, and a state-mandated achievement test are types of assessment.

- The process of gathering information can be referred to as assessment. For example, the administration of a state-mandated achievement test on one particular occasion is an example of an assessment.

Although the terms "assessment" and "evaluation" are sometimes used interchangeably, the following distinction is also made:

- Assessment is an ongoing process of monitoring student learning and identifying areas of strength and weakness. The ultimate goal of assessment is to improve student achievement, and thus it can be considered a formative activity.

- Evaluation is the determination of what students have already achieved. The goal of evaluation is to judge the extent of student achievement, and thus it can be considered a summative activity.

To illustrate the distinction described above, the assessment of a particular student's spelling ability could be carried out by examining the student's essays, homework assignments, spelling tests, and other written work created throughout the semester in order to determine whether the student is progressing as expected. Evaluation would be illustrated by the assigning of a grade to a spelling test at the end of the semester. As this example illustrates, assessment and evaluation are closely intertwined.

Skill 1

Determine the purposes and characteristics of different types of assessments and the appropriate use.

In this section you will read about the various purposes of assessment for students who have or may have a disability. Assessment is carried out in order to answer questions such as the following:

- What is the extent of student progress in particular areas?

- Which students need extra support?

- In what areas do particular students need extra support?

- Which approaches to providing extra support are likely to benefit a particular student?

- Is the extra support being provided to a particular student effective?

- Is a particular student eligible for special education services?

- Are the special education services being provided to a particular student effective?

Assessment data is gathered in order to address one or more of the questions above. In order to evaluate the data properly, teachers must consider the timing and purpose of the assessment, the appropriate interpretation of assessment results, and, of course, the nature of what is measured by the assessment. These considerations are discussed further in this section as well as later in the chapter.

Purposes of Assessment

A distinction can be made among five types of assessments in terms of when they are administered and what purpose they serve (i.e., the kind of information they are intended to provide about students):

- **Screening** assessments are administered to all students in a particular group, such as a grade or a school. Screening is typically carried out at the beginning of the school year, as in the example of a vision screening administered to all incoming kindergarten students. The goal of screening is to identify, as early as possible, students who may need extra academic support. Screening may also be carried out on an individual basis, as when a teacher observes the classroom behavior of a student who may be experiencing an emotional disturbance.

- **Pre-referral** assessments are administered to individual students before formally referring them for special education. Such assessments typically provide more information than what can be obtained through screening. When a student is struggling in some respect, pre-referral assessment can be used to determine which instructional modifications are likely to help the student, and whether these modifications are successful (thereby allowing a formal referral for special education to be avoided in some cases). Pre-referral assessment can also be used to document the need for formal referral for special education, and may then become part of the student's IEP (see Chapter 1 for definition).

- **Diagnostic** assessments are administered to individual students who may need extra support. In some cases, diagnostic assessments are used because screening has suggested the presence of a disability (in which case the diagnostic assessment may function as a pre-referral assessment). In other cases, the diagnostic assessment is used because the student has already been referred for special education and more information is needed. Diagnostic assessments provide a more in-depth understanding of a child's skills and instructional needs than screening assessments do. The goal of a diagnostic assessment is to determine areas of strength and weakness for a particular student. In some cases, the assessment is also designed to identify the nature of the student's disability. The assessment used may be a standardized test, but significant decisions about the student (e.g., determination of eligibility for special education services) will consist of information gathered from several sources. For example, a student who is suspected of having a receptive language limitation may be administered the Peabody Picture Vocabulary Test (PPVT-IV), a standardized test of receptive vocabulary. In addition, school records, teacher observations, parent interviews, and other sources of information may be considered in determining to what extent, if any, the student has a receptive language impairment.

- **Progress monitoring** assessments are used to determine whether an individual student's progress is adequate. Progress monitoring is conducted frequently over some finite period of time, and it often focuses on one specific academic area (e.g., reading fluency) or behavioral dimension (e.g., impulse control). The actual assessments used could be informal or formal and administered either before or after participation in special education services. Examples of progress monitoring include the curriculum-based measurement approaches discussed at length under Skill 6 below.

- **Outcome** assessments are used to determine the extent of student achievement at the end of the school year or other significant time period. Outcome assessments fall under the heading of evaluation, as defined at the beginning of this chapter. A well-known example of outcome assessment would be the state-mandated achievement tests that students of certain grade levels must take in specified content areas at the end of the academic year.

Assessment information must be interpreted in light of whether screening, pre-referral, diagnosis, progress monitoring, or outcome evaluation was the original purpose of the assessment. Each type of assessment tends to yield a different type of information that is used for a somewhat different purpose.

Skill 2

Apply the legal requirements and ethical principles regarding assessment of students with exceptionalities.

The assessment of students with disabilities is expected to adhere to federal and state law as well as to the recommendations of professional organizations. This section introduces some of the legal and ethical requirements for the assessment of students with disabilities, particularly those requirements that are specified in IDEA.

IDEA and Assessment

In Chapter 1, IDEA was introduced as the federal law that governs the education of children with disabilities. IDEA specifies the following requirements with respect to the assessment of students who have or who are suspected of having disabilities:

- School officials must notify parents prior to any assessments over and above those that are routinely administered to all students. Parental permission is required prior to beginning these assessments. [In this section, the term "parents" will be used as shorthand for "parent(s) or guardian(s)."]

- The assessments must be conducted by an interdisciplinary team that includes at least one teacher or educational professional who is knowledgeable about the student's suspected disability.

- Assessments must be carried out on an individual basis.

- Assessments must consist of more than one test or criterion for determining eligibility for special education services, and for determining placement.

- Assessment materials must be nondiscriminatory with respect to the student's racial and cultural background, and the assessments must be administered in the student's primary language or mode of communication.

- Assessments must be empirically validated for the purpose for which they are used, and they must be administered by individuals trained in their administration.

- Test protocols must be adhered to unless it is necessary to make accommodations for a particular student.

- For children between birth and three years of age, assessment must take place in "natural" environments such as the home or day care center.

Confidentiality and Assessment

IDEA, FERPA, and related federal laws protect the confidentiality of assessment results and other educational records. Following are some of the legal requirements pertaining to confidentiality:

- Parents may examine assessment results and other records, and if they request explanations of these materials, the school must comply. Parents may request that the records be amended if they feel the records are inaccurate, are misleading, or violate the child's privacy.

- Generally, the school must obtain parental consent before disclosing assessment results and other records containing personally identifiable information about the child. (Personally identifiable information either names an individual directly or could be used by someone else to infer the individual's identity, location, and/or contact information.)

- Only parents and specific school personnel (e.g., teachers, educational specialists, and administrators) may have access to assessment results and other records. The school must document all instances in which records were examined; documentation must include information about when and why the records were examined, and who conducted the examination.

Assessment Accommodations

As noted in Chapter 1, IDEA requires that the assessment of students with disabilities, like other educational activities, be carried out in the least restrictive environment. IDEA also requires that students with disabilities be included in the state-mandated assessments of achievement used for accountability purposes. If possible, students with disabilities will participate in these assessments with no change to the test protocol. When a particular student cannot do so without additional support, the school will provide **accommodations,** or adjustments to the way the assessments are administered. Some of the guidelines for assessment accommodations set forth by the state of Florida are discussed in Chapter 1 under Skill 7, along with a list of the major types of accommodation that support students with disabilities. Following are concrete examples of each type.

Presentation Accommodations

Presentation accommodations involve changes to the format of information presented in the assessment. Examples include the following:

- increased sized of font and response bubbles

- increased spacing between items

- highlighting of key phrases in instructions

- administration of assessment through a sign-language interpreter

- administration of assessment by audio recording

- administration of assessment through tactile formats (e.g., Braille)

Presentation accommodations such as those listed above may be needed if a student has a visual or auditory impairment, a medication-related impairment in processing written text, or a reading disability, to name just a few examples.

Response Accommodations

Response accommodations involve changes to the format by which the student provides responses to the assessment. Examples include the following:

- use of a scribe to record student responses
- use of audio recording for student responses
- provision of response forms with added cues
- allowing students to use a computer to record responses
- allowing students to take notes prior to response
- allowing students to mark answers without filling in bubbles

Response accommodations such as these may be needed if a student has a physical or cognitive impairment that prevents the student from using a writing implement, for example, or from shifting between a test booklet to a response form.

Setting Accommodations

Setting accommodations involve changes to the location and/or conditions of the assessment. Examples include the following:

- preferential seating for student during assessment
- administration of assessment to small groups in separate settings
- administration of assessment to individuals in separate settings
- administration of assessment under conditions of special lighting or acoustics
- administration of assessment in a location with minimal distractions

Setting accommodations such as those noted above may be needed if a student has a severe attentional problem, a perceptual impairment, or a tendency to engage in behaviors that are highly distracting to others, for example.

Scheduling Accommodations

Scheduling accommodations involve changes to the timing and scheduling of assessments. Examples include the following:

- allowing the assessment to be completed on separate occasions
- allowing the assessment to be completed at a particular time of day
- allowing the order of assessment components to be varied
- allowing frequent breaks during assessment
- allowing consumption of specific foods during assessment
- allowing extended time for the assessment

Scheduling accommodations such as these may be needed if a student has a medical condition that requires distributed testing, extreme anxiety with respect to certain kinds of test content, and so on.

Selection of Accommodations

Accommodations should be provided for assessment if they are routinely provided to the student for instructional purposes. Accommodations are not used to give students with disabilities an unfair advantage, but rather to help them express their knowledge and skills on assessments. For example, on a writing test, providing a student with a scribe would not be appropriate if the test is intended to measure handwriting skill. However, if the purpose of this particular test is to gauge students' verbal expression, and a student has a physical impairment that makes handwriting difficult, then the provision of a scribe is appropriate and would not give the student an unfair advantage.

The preceding example illustrates the importance of considering what an assessment is intended to measure before determining what accommodations, if any, are appropriate. The most important considerations in the selection of an assessment are the student's needs and the ways in which the student's disability are likely to affect performance.

Skill **3**

Identify measurement concepts (e.g., reliability and validity), characteristics, and uses of norm-referenced and criterion-referenced assessments for students with exceptionalities.

This section focuses on the types of assessments that are commonly used in educational settings, including those that can be used with students who have or who are suspected of having a disability.

A distinction can be made among norm-referenced, criterion-referenced, individual-referenced, and performance-based assessments. These four types of assessments differ in how the results for individual students should be interpreted.

Norm-Referenced Assessment

A **norm-referenced assessment** provides results for an individual student that are related to **norms,** or results obtained from the student's peer group. "Norming" an assessment involves administering the assessment to a large sample and then recording the distributions of scores along dimensions such as age or gender. Most norm-referenced assessment results indicate the individual's performance level compared to others of the same age. An example of a prominent norm-referenced assessment would be the Wechsler Intelligence Scale for Children (WISC-IV). The screening, pre-referral, and diagnosis assessments noted earlier sometimes consist in part of norm-referenced tests.

Norm-referenced assessments are **standardized,** meaning that their administration and scoring is both predetermined and consistent. Owing to standardization and norming, scores on norm-referenced tests can be expressed in a familiar format such as percentile ranking. A child whose WISC-IV score represents the 64th percentile has scored higher than 63% of children of the same age who have also taken this test.

Care is needed in the use and interpretation of norm-referenced assessments among students who have or are suspected of having a disability. A student's disability may prevent that student from expressing the true extent of his/her knowledge or skills, as in the example of a student with normal intelligence whose score on an intelligence test is low owing to a visual impairment, to dyslexia, to the side effects of some essential medication, and so on. In this example, the student's abilities are underestimated by the assessment results owing to some disability that affects test performance but not the student's actual abilities. A different problem arises when low performance on an assessment accurately reflects the student's capabilities but misleadingly implies the presence of a disability. A student who obtains an extremely low percentile ranking on a specific assessment may simply be weak in the area being assessed. (Alternatively, the student may fail to understand the instructions, find the test format unfamiliar, lack interest in performing well on the assessment, and so on.)

Criterion-Referenced Assessment

Whereas a norm-referenced assessment compares an individual's scores to the scores of his or her peer group, a **criterion-referenced assessment** compares the individual's performance to some predetermined standard, or criterion. Examples of prominent criterion-referenced assessments include the "high stakes" achievement tests that all states administer in order to monitor student progress, such as the Florida Standards Assessments (FSA). Like norm-referenced assessments, most criterion-referenced assessments are standardized in terms of how they are administered and scored.

Some criterion-referenced assessments are simply used to determine whether or not each student has met a predetermined criterion, an example being the vision screening administered at the beginning of the school year to all students. Others, such as the FSA, allow for more fine-grained evaluations of student performance. For example, FSA Reading and Math scores can be converted into Achievement Levels ranging from 1 to 5, with each level indicating how well the student has mastered the Florida Standards for each content area at a particular grade.

Whereas the screening, pre-referral, diagnostic, and progress monitoring assessments introduced above may or may not consist of criterion-referenced tests, outcome assessments are almost always criterion-referenced. Evidence of a disability may include falling below some criterion on a criterion-referenced assessment and/or an especially low percentile ranking on a norm-referenced assessment. However, as with norm-referenced assessments, caution is needed in the use and interpretation of criterion-referenced assessments among students who have or who are suspected of having a disability. A student may fail to meet some criterion owing to a disability that impairs test performance but does diminish the underlying ability being tested. Moreover, a student may fail to meet some criterion owing to an academic weakness, unfamiliarity with the test, lack of motivation, and so on, rather than the presence of a disability.

Individual-Referenced Assessment

An **individual-referenced assessment** is used to compare an individual's score at one point in time with the same individual's score at some other point or points in time. Rather than being compared to a normative sample or to some predetermined standard, the individual is compared to him- or herself. Whereas most norm-referenced and criterion-referenced assessments consist of standardized tests, individual-referenced assessments may or may not be standardized. Progress monitoring assessments are often individual-referenced. An example of such an assessment would be the **running record** that teachers use to track the progress of students in areas like reading. A running record records a student's performance across multiple administrations of the same task. If the teacher is interested in a student's oral fluency, for example, the teacher might keep a running record of the details of the student's performance when reading a particular passage on different occasions, so that those aspects of fluency that improve, decline, or stay the same from occasion to occasion can be recorded.

Performance-Based Assessment

Norm- and criterion-referenced assessments typically require students to choose among a predetermined set of options (as in, for example, a multiple-choice test). These assessments yield objective scores, as do many individual-referenced assessments. For a **performance-based assessment,** the student must exhibit some behavior or create some product requiring integration of knowledge and skills. Although guidance may be given, students do not simply choose among pre-set options, and thus their behavior or product may need to be evaluated subjectively. Examples of performance-based assessments include:

- a performance (e.g., performance of a musical piece)

- a demonstration (e.g., demonstration of a lab procedure)

- an essay (e.g., a position paper on conservation)

- a project (e.g., a collage)

- a portfolio (e.g., a collection of student work during the semester)

Performance-based assessments are becoming increasingly popular as supplements or alternatives to traditional norm- and criterion-referenced tests, and in some cases they are particularly well-suited for the assessment of students with disabilities, as discussed further under Skill 6 which comes later in this chapter.

Skill 4

Determine the purpose and requirements for participation of students with disabilities in the statewide assessment program and available accommodations, waivers, and exemptions.

In this section you will read about the importance of having accommodations, waivers, and exemptions for students with disabilities participating in statewide assessment programs.

If an eligible student with a disability needs a specific accommodation, even though it is available to all students as a global setting or embedded tool in the online system, the IEP team or Section 504 planning team should document the need for the accommodation in the student's plan. This will ensure that students have access to needed accommodations, even if they transfer to another school or district that uses a different assessment program.

Making Decisions about Statewide Assessment Accommodations

The IEP or Section 504 plan team makes decisions about accommodations for an individual student with a disability when they evaluate the impact of the student's disability and need for accommodations in classroom instruction and assessment activities. The content and format of the statewide assessments are important considerations in the decision-making process. The following guidelines are recommended for making decisions about accommodations for statewide assessments.

1. Accommodations should facilitate an accurate demonstration of what the student knows or can do.

2. Accommodations should not provide the student with an unfair advantage or interfere with the validity of a test; accommodations must not change the underlying skills that are being measured by the test.

3. Accommodations must be the same or nearly the same as those needed and used by the student in completing classroom instruction and assessment activities.

4. Accommodations must be necessary for enabling the student to demonstrate knowledge, ability, skill, or mastery. The IEP team or the Section 504 plan team should determine which accommodations the student needs, if any. The student's needs and types of accommodations must be documented in the student's IEP or Section 504 plan.

Examples of Accommodations

1. Test Features and Computer-Based Accommodations in the TDS (Testing and Disability Services). The TDS platform allows all students to make choices in the global test settings for color contrast and print size. The default setting for the screen color combination is black text on white background and standard print size. All students may select a different color combination: black text on blue, black text on light blue, black text on magenta, yellow text on blue or white text on black. All students may also choose to enlarge the print size to 1.5X, 1.75X, 2.5X, or 3X. These settings are maintained throughout the test session.

2. Text-to-speech and masking are computer-based accommodations for eligible students with disabilities that must be assigned by the test administrator in the system prior to the test administration. Text-to-speech provides an audio presentation of the items (questions) and answer choices for all tests. However, text-to-speech is not enabled on the passages included in FSA ELA Reading Component and FSA ELA Writing Component assessments. Masking allows the student to cover any area of the test page to temporarily hide information that might be distracting.

3. Paper-based versions of the computer-based tests are available in regular print, large print, one-item-per-page, and contracted and uncontracted Braille as an accommodation if the student with a disability is unable to take the test on a computer. However, a student cannot use a paper-based version of the test when taking the assessment on the computer, because the 4 computer-based tests have interactive components that cannot be demonstrated on the paper-based tests, and therefore the test items are not identical.

4. Hardcopy reading passage booklets and writing passage booklets are available in regular-print and large-print versions for eligible students with disabilities to use as they take the FSA ELA Reading Component or FSA ELA Writing Component assessment on the computer.

5. Keyboard commands can be used by any student to navigate between test elements (pages and items/questions), features and tools using a desktop, laptop, or Chromebook. Keyboard commands are not available for touchscreen keyboards used on tablets.

6. Embedded Online Tools The FSA tests include universal tools available in all tests and subject-specific tools available in certain tests, such as mathematics.

7. Line Reader highlights a single line of text with blue. The line remains highlighted until the student clicks on a different line or uses the arrow key.

8. **Zoom In, Zoom Out** increases and decreases the size of all of the text and graphics within a single test page. Five levels of magnification are available on all pages, and zoom settings persist across test pages.

Waivers

A student with a disability may also request a waiver of the use of assessment results for receiving a course grade or a standard diploma.

Exemptions

An exemption from participation in a statewide assessment may be requested for an extraordinary circumstance or condition.

Skill 5

Interpret and apply the results of formal, informal, and performance-based assessments to address specific needs of students with exceptionalities.

This section introduces **alternative assessments,** which can be defined as assessments that are not standardized, norm-referenced, or based on multiple-choice response formats. Alternative assessments are often defined in terms of student expression, in the sense that they are based on behaviors, products, and other forms of expression that are not captured in traditional assessments.

Traditionally, educational assessment relied heavily on standardized tests such as the state-mandated group achievement tests used to determine how well students have mastered curriculum standards. Although such tests continue to be used and to provide useful information, a number of criticisms have been raised about their format and content. Criticisms of these tests include the following:

- Recall and rote learning is valued over critical reflection.
- The knowledge being tested is trivialized by reducing it to a multiple-choice format.
- Test-takers are required to choose among pre-determined options rather than constructing solutions.
- Arbitrary time limits are imposed on test completion.
- The test structure implies that there is only one correct solution to each problem.

As a result of these and other criticisms, educators have shifted toward the inclusion of alternatives to group-administered achievement tests and other traditional approaches to assessment. In this section you will read about some of these alternative assessments. (A prominent example of alternative assessment, the performance-based assessment, is discussed above under Skill 3.)

Observational Assessment

An **observational assessment** yields descriptions of student behavior in natural settings. In many cases, the goal of observational assessment is to describe behavior as objectively as possible, without making inferences about underlying thoughts, motives, feelings, expectations, and so on. In some cases, the observer comments on the student's apparent state of mind as well. Following are some examples of observational assessment methods:

- **Checklists** are used to note the presence or absence of specific behaviors (e.g., talking out of turn, interrupting, leaving one's seat at inappropriate times, making unnecessary noises, and other disruptive behaviors).

- **Rating scales** are used to note the extent to which a behavior is expressed (e.g., the extent of engagement in class activities, as indicated by participation in group work, interaction with teacher and peers during class discussion, and so on).

- **Duration records** are used to note the amount of time the student spends engaged in a particular behavior (e.g., talking to another student when it is understood to be inappropriate to do so).

- **Time-sampling records** are used to note the number of times the student engages in a particular behavior during a particular time period (e.g., tapping a pencil or pen during math class in a manner that may be disruptive).

- **Anecdotal records** are used to record narrative descriptions of behavior in particular settings (e.g., the student's behavior during one class period).

Ecological Assessment

An **ecological assessment** focuses on student functioning in different environments. The goal of the assessment is to identify environments in which the student functions with greater or lesser difficulty, to understand what contributes to these differences in functioning, and to draw useful implications for instructional planning. An example of ecological assessment would be the observation of a mildly autistic student in class, in the cafeteria, on the playground, and in other school settings, in order to better understand the situations in which the student experiences conflict with peers.

Authentic Assessment

An **authentic assessment** provides descriptions of student performance on real-life tasks carried out in real-world settings (or simulations of real-world settings). Authentic assessment is based on the assumption that the purpose of learning is not simply to do well on tests but also to acquire knowledge and skills that can be more broadly applied to life situations. Thus, the goal of authentic assessment is to determine how well a student performs when the knowledge and skills acquired in class are applied to meaningful tasks. An example of an authentic assessment would be a description of how accurately and effectively students maintain a bank account in their mathematics class. Although an actual account is not created, the activity is "authentic" in the sense of allowing students to apply mathematical skills to the management of money in a simulated real-life context.

Authentic assessments can take on many forms. For example, students may be assessed by means of a **rubric,** or a guide to the evaluation of student work that provides definitions of different levels of performance. Whether used for authentic assessment or for some other type of assessment, rubrics have a number of advantages, including the following:

- Rubrics provide students with guidance as to what is expected of them and how their work will be evaluated.

- Rubrics can provide useful feedback to students at a variety of levels.

- The creation of rubrics pushes teachers to clarify their standards of evaluation.

- The use of rubrics helps assessment be more reliable—i.e., more consistent over time and across students.

Portfolio Assessment

A **portfolio** is a collection of work produced by a student over time. The goal of portfolio assessment is to gauge student effort, progress, and achievement through examination of many different kinds of work that the student has produced in a particular class or related to a specific theme. For example, in an elementary language arts class, a portfolio that will be examined at the end of the year might include materials such as the following:

- A list of books that the student has read along with his or her personal reactions to the books

- A collection of tests and homework assignments

- Transcripts of story retells produced by the student

- Audio-recordings of the student reading selected passages out loud
- Drafts and final version of critical reviews created by the student
- Drafts and final version of an original story created by the student

Alternative Assessment and Students with Disabilities

Alternative assessments are appropriate for use with general education students as well as with students with disabilities. Alternative assessments can supplement the evaluation of student progress through traditional forms of assessment. In some cases, alternative assessments should be used in place of traditional ones.

Most students with disabilities can participate in assessments such as the state-mandated achievement tests used for accountability purposes, if they are given appropriate modifications and accommodations. However, some students, such as those with severe cognitive impairments, will require alternatives to traditional assessments. These students are not expected to master the state curriculum standards, and thus the traditional achievement tests are not appropriate measures of progress.

Generally, students with disabilities who do not participate in regular assessments must be provided with alternatives. The alternative assessments should be aligned with the instruction provided to each student, and should be as similar as possible to the content of state and district assessments. Documentation of student performance and how performance is evaluated should be recorded.

Alternative Assessments in Florida

In Florida, the IEP team determines whether a student with a disability should participate in the Florida Standards (FSA). In making this determination, the IEP team is expected to address the following questions:

- Is the student unable to master the curriculum standards (i.e., the Florida Standards), even with accommodations?
- Are the student's cognitive limitations the main reason for his or her inability to master the curriculum standards?
- Is the student participating in a modified curriculum based on mastery of Access Points (i.e., key concepts in the Florida Standards that are expressed with reduced levels of complexity)?

- Does the student require extensive direct instruction in academic, vocational, domestic, social, and leisure activities?

- Is the student unable to function effectively and independently in a variety of settings?

A "yes" response to all five questions indicates that the student should not participate in the FSA tests but rather must participate in the **Florida Alternate Assessment,** a performance-based alternative assessment of student mastery of Access Points. The Florida Alternate Assessment is administered to students individually. The results with respect to each academic area (reading, mathematics, writing, and science) are reported on a scale of nine performance levels representing three score categories:

- Students who score at the lowest three levels ("emergent") are developing basic knowledge and skills but require cueing or prompting in order to express them.

- Students who score at the middle three levels ("achieved") are acquiring specific knowledge and skills and can express them with moderate success.

- Students who score at the highest three levels ("commended") have mastered and generalized specific knowledge and skills.

Skill 6

Analyze assessment data to identify student needs and evaluate student progress in acquiring, generalizing, and maintaining skills across settings.

As noted under Skill 1, progress monitoring is a commonly used approach for assessing individual student progress. This approach serves a number of purposes:

- Progress monitoring helps determine the extent to which instruction is generally effective, both overall and in specific areas.

- Progress monitoring helps determine the extent of each student's progress, both overall and in specific areas.

- Progress monitoring helps indicate how to modify instruction or provide other support for students whose progress is inadequate.

There are many different approaches to progress monitoring. Some of these approaches were discussed earlier in the chapter (e.g., under Skill 5). This section focuses on a form of progress monitoring known as curriculum-based measurement.

Curriculum-Based Measurement

Curriculum-based assessment (CBA) provides information about student mastery of the general education curriculum. Such assessments are typically criterion-referenced. A prominent example of CBA developed for use in special education is **curriculum-based measurement (CBM),** an approach to monitoring student progress that is relatively sensitive to changes in performance over time. CBM is based on the collection of samples of student performance on a specific task or test. Samples are obtained frequently (e.g., one to three times per week) and the tests are brief (e.g., 1 to 5 minutes).

As an approach to progress monitoring, CBM has a number of advantages:

- CBM can be carried out relatively quickly and easily, with minimal disruption to daily routines.

- By means of CBM, student progress can be monitored with respect to a variety of basic academic skills (e.g., reading fluency, reading comprehension, spelling, mathematical calculation, and so on).

- Because CBM is standardized (i.e., test administration, format, and scoring is the same from time to time) test performance can be readily compared across multiple instances of testing.

- The results of CBM are relatively easy to understand.

- The frequency of CBM testing allows teachers to quickly discern the impact of instruction and instructional changes on student performance.

To illustrate how CBM works, the following is a summary of how oral reading fluency might be monitored:

- The teacher or examiner works with the child on an individual basis.

- Once per week, the student is asked to read each of three passages out loud for one minute apiece.

- The student's score for each passage consists of the number of words read correctly and fluently minus the number of words read incorrectly.

- Clear rules are used to define correctly and incorrectly read words. For example, self-corrected words and repeated words are considered to have been correctly read. Substituted words and words that have not been read after three seconds are considered to have been incorrectly read.

- The median (i.e., middle) score across the three passages constitutes the student's fluency score for the week.

- Weekly fluency scores are plotted on a graph which is then examined to determine the trajectory of student progress over time.

Studies have shown that CBM is a reliable and valid approach to progress monitoring. With respect to the assessment of students who have, or who are suspected of having, disabilities, CBM offers a number of advantages, including the following:

- The quickness and ease of CBM administration and the nature of what is tested allows CBM to be readily used for the screening of all students as well as the progress monitoring of individual students with disabilities.

- The frequency of CBM administration allows lack of progress in particular areas to be quickly identified.

- The frequency of CBM administration and the nature of what is tested allow teachers to quickly determine the impact of instructional modifications.

- The standardization of CBM tests and the specificity of the results allow CBM to be a useful tool in IEP planning (see Chapter 1 for discussion of the IEP). That is, short- and long-term goals in the IEP can be expressed in terms of CBM scores.

Chapter 2 Practice Quiz

1. Brief, weekly tests of a student's oral reading fluency best represent which type of assessment?
   A. diagnostic
   B. outcome
   C. screening
   D. progress monitoring

2. Jimmy is an emotionally disturbed second-grade student who spends the entire school day in the general education classroom. Jimmy often shouts, cries, and engages in other distracting behaviors when he is frustrated. At the same time, Jimmy is receptive to cueing from the teacher and quickly settles down if he feels that his frustration has been noted. Which of the following is a setting accommodation that would be most suitable for Jimmy when he participates in the state assessment?

   A. A private room should be made available for Jimmy.

   B. Jimmy should be allowed to have extended time on the assessment.

   C. Jimmy should be seated as close as possible to the teacher.

   D. A scribe should help Jimmy record assessment responses.

3. A particular assessment reveals that Marisa has performed at the 37th percentile for her age group in reading comprehension. What type of assessment was used?

   A. norm-referenced

   B. criterion-referenced

   C. individual-referenced

   D. performance-based

4. During the second week of school, a teacher notices that the medication one of her students takes every day for a medical condition impairs the student's energy and concentration, and that as a result, the student needs frequent breaks during instruction and assessment. The teacher believes that the student's low performance on tests administered at the beginning of the year is not indicative of how well the student will function in class, because those tests were administered without breaks. What type of validity is the focus of the teacher's concerns?

   A. content

   B. concurrent

   C. predictive

   D. construct

5. An IEP team learns from anecdotal reports that a student with both hearing and speech impairments is performing well in some academic and social contexts while struggling in others. What type of assessment is most likely to help the team determine the extent of the student's difficulties and develop a plan of action for him?

   A. standardized assessment

   B. ecological assessment

   C. authentic assessment

   D. portfolio assessment

6. Which of the following is true of curriculum-based measurement (CBM)?

   A. CBM is primarily a form of outcome assessment.

   B. CBM cannot be used for screening purposes under any circumstances.

   C. CBM works best as a tool for preferral assessment.

   D. CBM is a reliable and valid approach to progress monitoring.

Explanatory Answers

1. D

Brief, weekly tests of a specific academic skill exemplify progress monitoring, and thus option D is the best answer. Although progress monitoring tests could be part of screening, diagnosis, or outcome assessment, such tests are not typical of these forms of assessment, and thus options A, B, and C are incorrect.

2. C

Option C is correct because the extent of accommodation is minimal, and close proximity to the teacher will facilitate the use of cueing to manage Jimmy's distracting behavior, as it seems to during classroom instruction. Option A is incorrect because the conditions of assessment should be as similar as possible to the conditions of instruction, and Jimmy always participates in the general education classroom. Option B is incorrect because it does not represent a setting accommodation. Option D is incorrect for the same reason that Option A is incorrect; in both cases, the conditions of assessment are very different from the conditions of instruction.

3. A

Option A is correct because norm-referenced assessments yield scores that can be converted to percentile rankings within age group. Options B, C, and D are incorrect because scores on these assessments are not usually expressed as percentile rankings.

4. C

Option C is correct because the teacher is concerned that for this particular student, low test performance does not predict impaired functioning in class. That is, the teacher is concerned that for this particular student, the tests have limited predictive validity. Options A, B, and D are incorrect because the teacher is not directly concerned about these other forms of validity.

5. B

Option B is correct because ecological assessment would allow the student to be observed in different settings and perhaps clarify which settings are problematic for the student and why he struggles in those settings. Options A, C, and D are incorrect because they are unlikely to provide relevant information.

6. D

Option D is correct because CBM has been shown to be a reliable and valid form of progress monitoring. Although CBM scores can be used as outcome measures, this is not their primary purpose, and thus option A is incorrect. Option B is incorrect because CBM can be used for screening purposes. Option C is incorrect because although CBM can be used for pre-referral assessment, it cannot be said to be "better" for pre-referral than for other purposes.

CHAPTER 3

Competency 3: Knowledge of Instructional Practices in Exceptional Student Education

In this chapter you will read about the selection and implementation of instructional methods and strategies that are widely used in the education of general education students as well as students with disabilities.

Skill 1

Select reliable sources of evidence-based instructional practices and interventions.

The Every Student Succeeds Act (ESSA) implemented December 10, 2015, has a history of equal access to education. ESSA reauthorizes the 50-year-old Elementary and Secondary Education Act (ESEA), the nation's national education law and longstanding commitment to equal opportunity for all students. The Elementary and Secondary Education Act (ESEA) was signed into law in 1965. ESEA provided federal grants to state educational agencies to improve the quality of elementary and secondary education.

Prior to ESSA implementation, the No Child Left Behind (NCLB) Act (2001) put in place measures that exposed achievement gaps among traditionally under-served students and their peers and spurred an important national dialogue on education improvement. The NCLB, represented a significant step forward for our nation's children in many respects, particularly as it shined a light on where students were making progress and where they needed additional support. The law was scheduled for revision in 2007, and, over time, NCLB's prescriptive requirements became increasingly unworkable for schools and educators. Parents, educators, and elected officials across the country recognized that a strong, updated law was necessary to expand opportunity to all students.

In 2012, states were granted flexibility regarding specific requirements of NCLB in exchange for rigorous and comprehensive state–developed plans designed to close achievement gaps, increase equity, improve the quality of instruction, and increase outcomes for all students.

ESSA includes provisions that will help to ensure success for all students and schools.

- Advances equity for America's disadvantaged and high-need students.

- Requires that all students in America be taught to high academic standards that will prepare them to succeed in college and careers.

- Ensures that vital information is provided to educators, families, students, and communities through annual statewide assessments that measure students' progress toward those high standards.

- Helps to support and grow local innovations, including evidence-based and place-based interventions developed by local leaders and educators.

- Sustains and expands this administration's historic investments in increasing access to high-quality preschool.

- Maintains an expectation that there will be accountability and action to effect positive change in our lowest-performing schools.

The Every Student Succeeds Act (ESSA) of 2015 and the No Child Left Behind Act (NCLB) of 2001 require that instructional practices also be informed by scientifically-based research. That is, educational theories, informal anecdotes about teaching and learning, and common sense, are not considered sufficient bases for instructional practice. IDEA (which is discussed at length in Chapter 1) is closely aligned with ESSA and NCLB with respect to the role of scientifically based research in instruction. In this section you will read about what the phrase "scientifically based research" refers to and how to identify such information.

Characteristics of Scientifically Based Research

Scientifically-based research (SBR) is distinguished by a number of characteristics:

- SBR relies on systematic, empirical methods. The word "empirical" means based on observation. SBR can thus be distinguished from theorizing, speculation, traditional beliefs, anecdotal evidence, and so on.

- SBR relies on rigorous data analysis that justifies the conclusions that are drawn. That is, SBR consists of more than just casual observation. Data must be collected as well as carefully analyzed and interpreted.

- SBR relies on methods that yield consistent data across measures and studies. SBR is grounded in replication, meaning that results should not be trusted or applied in educational settings until they have been demonstrated more than once across different approaches to measurement and different investigations.

- SBR relies on clear, detailed reports of studies in peer-reviewed journals, books, and other sources, or reports that are approved by panels of independent experts. Because replication is critical, clear and detailed reportage is important as well.

Preferred Research Designs

Although many types of designs are used in scientific research, ESSA, and IDEA indicate a preference for experimental or quasi-experimental research designs. An **experimental** design is an approach to gathering data that reflects several characteristics:

- Participants are randomly assigned to groups. For example, a researcher who wishes to know whether the use of a new self-monitoring strategy improves children's reading fluency may randomly assign some children to receive training in the new self-monitoring strategy. These children are referred to as the experimental group (or the intervention group). Through random assignment other children may be chosen to receive literacy instruction as usual. These children are referred to as the control group (or the comparison group).

- Pre-test and post-test data are collected. In the example given above, reading fluency would be measured for the members of both groups before and after the experimental group receives training in the new strategy. If the reading fluency of the experimental group improves more than the reading fluency of the control group from pre-test to post-test, we can conclude that use of the new self-monitoring strategy positively affects children's fluency.

A **quasi-experimental** design is like an experimental design except that there is no random assignment to groups. Rather, existing groups are used. In the previous example, a quasi-experimental design would be represented by the use of one classroom as the experimental group and another classroom as the control group. Although the researcher might randomly select these classrooms, the children who are part of each classroom cannot be randomly chosen. Rather, each classroom constitutes an existing group.

Reliable Sources of Scientifically-Based Research

Reliable sources of scientifically-based research that can influence instructional practice include the following:

- peer-reviewed books and journals
- the websites of state education agencies, such as the Florida Department of Education website
- the websites of the U.S. Department of Education
- other websites sponsored by the U.S. government, which can be identified by means of the .gov suffix in their addresses

The **What Works Clearinghouse (WWC)** is an example of a U.S. government website that provides information about scientifically based research of relevance to instructional practice. The WWC is part of the Institute of Education Sciences, which is the research arm of the U.S. Department of Education. The goal of the WWC website is to provide educators with instructional techniques and strategies that have shown to be effective through scientifically based research (as defined above).

Skill 2

Apply appropriate instructional approaches, strategies, and materials based on assessments of the student's educational needs (e.g., grade-level standards, academic and functional performance, effect of exceptionality).

This section introduces the use of assessment information as a means of guiding instruction for all students, including those with disabilities. Extended discussion of assessment can be found in Chapter 2.

As noted in Chapter 2, assessment can be defined as the gathering and analysis of information about students in order to make decisions that may benefit their educational experience. One of the many purposes of assessment is to learn more about students' strengths and needs in order to plan appropriate instructional approaches for them.

Following are some of the questions that assessment can help answer in the process of instructional planning:

- What knowledge and skills have students acquired?

- What gaps are there in students' learning?

- What misconceptions do students have?

- What specific content or skills are particularly challenging for students?

- How well are students integrating and applying new knowledge and skills?

- How do students learn, reason, draw conclusions, solve problems, and so on?

- To what extent do certain topics interest or motivate students?

These questions pertain to general education students as well as students who have, or who are suspected to have, a disability. Each question can be asked about entire classrooms, specific groups of students, or individual students. As discussed at length in Chapter 2, teachers use both formal and informal assessments in order to address these and other questions. In addition, both formative and summative assessments are used.

Formative Assessment

Effective teachers continually plan and modify instruction based on assessments that provide feedback about student understanding, motivation, interest, and so on. **Formative assessment** refers to this process of obtaining feedback that informs instructional plans and modifications. Following are some examples of teachers using formative assessment as a basis for modifying instruction:

- At the end of a review session, a math teacher poses questions to students about a particular mathematical operation. If the students answer incorrectly, the teacher revisits key aspects of the review. If the students answer correctly, the teacher proceeds to a more advanced topic.

- During class discussion, a science teacher takes notes on student understanding of a particular topic. If misconceptions are expressed but not addressed during the discussion, the teacher explicitly addresses them in a subsequent discussion.

- While grading student homework, an English teacher makes note of how accurately and consistently a particular student with dyslexia uses punctuation. The teacher then decides how much emphasis to place on punctuation in specialized instruction developed for this particular student.

Formative assessments such as those described above tend to be informal and provide qualitative information, although sometimes they may yield quantitative scores. In most cases, the assessments are relatively "low stakes," in the sense that their main purpose is not to judge student performance but rather to monitor student progress and to identify ways that instruction can be improved overall or tailored to specific students.

Formative assessment is particularly important when modifying instruction for students with disabilities. Whereas an experienced teacher may have a general sense of which instructional techniques, strategies, and materials will be effective with general education students, each student with disabilities has unique strengths and needs, and is therefore likely to benefit from highly specific instructional modifications.

Summative Assessment

Summative assessment is the process of evaluating student achievement at the end of an instructional period. Examples of summative assessment data include the following:

- scores on a quiz administered by the teacher at the end of an instructional unit

- grades on a student's report card

- scores on a "high stakes" state achievement test administered at the end of the school year

Although a conceptual distinction can be made between formative and summative assessment, both influence instructional planning. A key difference is that the time between assessment and instructional modification tends to be shorter for formative assessment. Whereas the results of summative assessment are obtained at the end of an instructional period, some formative assessments can be administered during instruction and yield results that have an immediate impact (as in the example of the teacher who modifies instructional content based on student responses to simple questions).

Assessment and Response to Intervention

The ongoing role of assessment in instruction and intervention is illustrated by the educational process known as **response to intervention (RTI)**. Through RTI, students who are at risk for academic problems, whether or not they have disabilities, are identified, and their progress is repeatedly assessed. Evidence-based interventions are provided to these students, and the content and intensity of the interventions are adjusted as needed. The three levels of intensity, or tiers, are as follows:

- In Tier 1, students who have been identified as at-risk receive additional, targeted instruction for several weeks.

- In Tier 2, students who have not responded sufficiently to Tier 1 interventions receive more intensive, longer-lasting interventions.

- In Tier 3, students who have not responded sufficiently to Tier 2 interventions receive still more intensive, individualized interventions.

Students who do not respond sufficiently to Tier 3 interventions will probably be referred for evaluation for disability status, although referral may take place at any time. Assessments are integral to RTI as a means of understanding student response to each tier of interventions.

Skill 3

Choose effective instructional strategies to promote a student's generalization of knowledge and skills across content areas, curriculum, and settings.

This section presents information about how instruction can promote the learning and application of skills across a variety of academic and non-academic settings. Systematic instruction is discussed first as a general strategy for promoting the acquisition, generalization, and maintenance of both knowledge and skills among all students. Then, instruction for students with disabilities that pertains to functional skills (i.e., skills that support independent functioning in real-life domestic, occupational, and social settings) is discussed.

Goals for Learning

With respect to learning, three of the most fundamental goals of instruction are acquisition, maintenance, and generalization:

- **Acquisition** refers to the initial learning of new content or skills. Instruction begins with a focus on acquisition, and the purpose of many instructional strategies is to help students with the initial learning process.

- **Maintenance** refers to the recall of what has been learned. Successful acquisition does not guarantee that new information will be maintained, because it is relatively easy to forget what one learns as time passes and newer content and skills are learned. Thus, instructional strategies are needed that will help promote maintenance.

- **Generalization** refers to the application of what has been learned to new situations. Just as acquisition does not guarantee maintenance, so maintenance does not guarantee generalization. In other words, students may be able to learn and remember new content and skills yet fail to generalize what they have learned to new situations. Thus, instructional strategies are also needed to help students transfer what they learn beyond the original context in which it was learned.

As is evident from these definitions, students cannot benefit much from instruction unless acquisition, maintenance, and generalization all take place. An effective approach that supports these processes, particularly when learning specific skills, is systematic instruction.

Systematic Instruction

The phrases "systematic instruction," "explicit, systematic instruction," and "direct instruction" are used in many different senses, and are sometimes treated interchangeably. Generally, **systematic instruction** involves breaking new knowledge or skills into small elements and then presenting them to students in a sequence from simple to complex. Systematic instruction is grounded in five types of activities: planning, review, presentation, guided practice, and independent practice.

Planning

Prior to engaging in instructional activities, the teacher selects the knowledge or skills that will be presented, divides the new content into manageable elements, and decides on the appropriate sequence with which the new material will be introduced. For example, a math teacher who is developing a unit on long division will plan a sequence in which simple division problems are discussed first, and then long division problems with no remainders are studied before problems in which the solutions contain remainders.

Review

The teacher begins each instructional unit by reviewing what was previously learned, and discussing connections between prior learning and the current unit. The purpose of what will be learned in the new unit is also explicitly discussed with students. For example, a math teacher who is introducing long division to students will review simple division problems, and then provide explanations and examples illustrating the need for long division.

Presentation

In the presentation phase, the teacher explains and perhaps also models the new knowledge or skills that students are to learn. The knowledge or skills are broken down into small components and presented in a sequence from simple to complex. Examples of presentation include the following:

- A math teacher introduces the elements of long division to students, first through graphic means and then using numerical examples.

- A language arts teacher who wants her students to memorize a particular poem recites the poem and encourages students to notice her phrasing and expression as they follow along in the text.

- A social studies teacher interacts with a student while others listen. The teacher structures the conversation so that a key idea is articulated and discussed. The teacher then describes the key idea in a subsequent discussion.

- A chemistry teacher introduces a new formula and, using this formula, solves two problems on the board as students watch. While solving the problems, the teacher explicitly notes how each part of the formula is being applied.

- A music teacher briefly analyzes a particular passage and then plays the passage for students as they listen.

Guided Practice

In the guided practice phase, students are given the opportunity to practice, under the supervision of the teacher, what was presented to them in the demonstration phase. During this time the teacher will provide feedback to students, indicating when they are expressing their new knowledge or skills correctly, and correcting them when mistakes occur. The goal of guided practice is to facilitate the acquisition of new knowledge and skills. Guided practice contributes to maintenance as well and can also provide opportunities for generalization under the guidance of the teacher. Examples of guided practice include the following:

- After a mathematics teacher has explained long division, students are asked to summarize the correct procedures for solving simple long division problems and are given opportunities to solve problems. Corrective feedback is provided if the procedures are summarized or applied incorrectly.

- After a language arts teacher has recited a poem, students are given the opportunity to recite the poem while looking at the written text as little as possible. The teacher provides corrective feedback with respect to students' accuracy as well as their phrasing and expression.

- After a social studies teacher has interacted with a student in front of the class, indicated which elements of the interaction correctly reflect an important idea, and then reiterated the idea, students are asked to respond to similar questions and given the opportunity to restate the idea. The teacher provides corrective feedback.

- After a chemistry teacher has used the same formula to solve two problems on the board, students are asked to solve similar problems that also require the application of this formula. Errors are corrected by the teacher.

- After a music teacher has performed a particular passage for students and discussed some of the key elements, students are asked to perform the passage. The teacher provides corrective feedback on students' performances.

Independent Practice

Following guided practice, students are given further opportunities to practice what they are learning. During the independent practice phase, students practice without supervision from the teacher. Teachers may still continue to provide students with feedback on their performance, but practice takes place independently. The goal of independent practice is to facilitate acquisition and maintenance of new knowledge and skills, and in some cases to provide opportunities for generalization. Examples of independent practice include the following:

- After students have solved long division problems under their math teacher's guidance, they receive a homework assignment that contains long division problems.

- After students have practiced reciting a poem for their language arts teacher, they work together in groups on reciting the poem with good phrasing and expression, and with minimal reliance on the written text.

- After students in a social studies class have learned a new concept by observing and then participating in interactions with the teacher, they are asked to write a short essay paraphrasing and critically evaluating the idea.

- After students have received support from their chemistry teacher in solving problems that require the use of a particular formula, they take a short, informal quiz that tests their ability to apply the formula to a variety of problems.

- After students have performed a particular passage for their music teacher, they are asked to continue working on the passage at home prior to the next class.

Assessment in Systematic Instruction

Although not a separate phase, systematic instruction includes an assessment component, as teachers regularly monitor their students' acquisition, maintenance, and generalization of new knowledge and skills, particularly during the guided and independent practice phases (see discussions under Skill 1 in Chapter 2).

Academic versus Functional Skills

Academic skills are critical to functioning in daily life, but mastery of these skills does not guarantee that a person will be able to function independently. For example, knowledge about the nutritional content of different foods, although critical to survival, does not guarantee that a person can independently prepare a healthy meal. In contrast, **functional skills** allow a person to function independently in real-life domestic, occupational, and social settings. Functional skills include, for example, the ability to select, purchase, and cook nutritionally beneficial foods.

Functional Skills and Students with Disabilities

Functional skills are an integral part of the general education curriculum. In addition, for a student with a disability, the IEP team must make decisions about the kinds of functional skills that should be supported and the extent of support, particularly if the nature of the disability prevents full mastery of general education curricula.

Once they have graduated from school, students with disabilities may find it challenging to function independently in domestic, occupational, and/or social settings. For this reason, the IEP team may need to develop and oversee means of supporting the functional skills of these students. In order to do so, the IEP team will need to address a number of critical questions.

The first question for the IEP team is whether a functional curriculum needs to be developed for the student, particularly as the time of graduation nears. Such a curriculum may be needed if the following conditions are observed:

- The student has significant difficulties with learning and transfer.
- The student seems well below peers in skill development.
- The student spends relatively little time participating in the general education curriculum.

Other questions for the IEP team pertain to the details of the student's life after graduation. For example:

- Where might the student live?
- What kind of work does the student hope to do?
- Who might the student associate with?
- What kinds of support might others provide to the student?

When considering these questions, the IEP team will need to monitor the extent to which the student's planned educational experience is aligned with post-graduation goals, and whether progress toward those goals has been adequate or will require some adjustment to the support currently being provided to the student.

Systematic Instruction and Functional Skills

Systematic instruction has been shown to be an effective method of teaching functional skills to students with disabilities. Characteristics of systematic instruction that contribute to its effectiveness in this regard include the focus on specific skills or components of skills, the sequencing of skills in order of increasing complexity, the creation of opportunities for student practice, and the provision of teacher guidance throughout the learning process.

Skill 4

Identify the characteristics and purposes of the core curriculum, supplemental programs, and intensive interventions as they relate to language arts and mathematics in a multi-tiered system of supports.

This section briefly discusses instructional methods that can be used to integrate communication-related skills across the curricula.

Explicit and Systematic Instruction

Systematic instruction was introduced earlier in this chapter under Skill 3. The phrase "explicit and systematic" instruction can be used to indicate systematic instruction in which new information is presented explicitly by the teacher (as opposed to being presented by modeling, discovered through student inquiry, acquired by passive observation, and so on). To reiterate, systematic instruction is grounded in the following activities:

- planning
- review
- presentation
- guided practice
- independent practice

Scaffolding

Scaffolding refers to direct support given to students during the learning process by a teacher or some other experienced individual. Scaffolding can consist of verbal support (e.g., giving a hint) or physical support (e.g., guiding a student's hand as the student writes a particular letter). The extent of scaffolding varies widely depending on student need. Following are some examples in which the extent of scaffolding is relatively minimal:

- A teacher periodically looks over the shoulder of a student who is working independently on a project and offers a brief comment or suggestion.

- A teacher briefly summarizes the main theme of a passage before asking students to read the passage independently.

- A teacher briefly models the correct approach to solving a particular type of mathematics problem before students complete a worksheet containing this and other types of problems.

In the following examples, the extent of scaffolding is much greater:

- A teacher sits with a student who is working on a project and reiterates instructions and expectations, offers specific directives about what to do next, and provides corrective feedback.

- Before asking students to read a passage independently, a teacher summarizes the main theme of the passage and then reads the passage aloud, pausing to emphasize how particular details contribute to the theme.

- A teacher models and thoroughly explains the correct approach to solving a particular type of math problem, and then supervises guided practice before asking students to complete a worksheet that only contains the same type of problem.

As these examples imply, scaffolding can be provided to groups of students or tailored to an individual student. The extent of scaffolding provided to a student with a disability depends on the nature and severity of the disability.

Modeling

Modeling refers to the process by which the teacher demonstrates whatever students are intended to learn, and students then attempt to mimic what they have observed. Modeling can take place with or without explanation, and either prior to or following students' first attempts to demonstrate their learning. Modeling can contribute to a variety of instructional goals, including the following:

- mastery of specific behaviors (e.g., the formation of a particular letter during a handwriting lesson)

- application of problem-solving strategies (e.g., using the Internet to conduct research on a particular question)

- development of reasoning skills (e.g., making inferences from story events about the motives of key characters)

Integrating Communication-Related Skills

In order to achieve instructionally effective integration of communication-related skills across the curricula, the individual skills (reading, writing, speaking, listening, viewing, researching) must be connected in a meaningful way. One way to achieve meaningful connections is to ensure that instructional activities require the integration of different skills for some common purpose. For example, consider a simple activity in which the teacher reads students a short story and then asks the students to write down their favorite part, share what they wrote with a partner, and engage in discussion. In this activity, listening, writing, reading, and speaking are integrated in a purposeful way.

The use of thematic units is another effective method of promoting integration of both curricular content and the practice of communication-related skills. Involvement in a thematic unit gives students opportunities to read, hear, research, and view content related to instructional themes, as well as to discuss and write about what they and their classmates are learning.

Skill 5

Apply techniques for differentiating, accommodating, and modifying classroom instruction to meet the educational needs of individual students with exceptionalities.

This section describes how the differentiation and modification of instructional methods, strategies, and materials can be carried out by teachers in order to meet individual student needs. (The differentiation, accommodation, and modification of assessment are discussed in the next chapter.)

Differentiated Instruction

Differentiated instruction refers to the individualization of instruction within the general education setting. The purpose of differentiated instruction, or differentiation, is to meet the educational needs of each student. Not all students have the same needs in school settings generally or in particular classes. Rather, students have different needs owing to their backgrounds, abilities, preferences, interests, and so on.

Assessment is necessary in order to determine how particular aspects of instruction should be differentiated for individual students, and to monitor the success of specific differentiation strategies. In addition, as discussed in Chapter 6, assessment itself may need to be differentiated for some students.

Although differentiated instruction is a student-centered approach, it does not apply strictly to individuals but also to particular groups of students. Differentiation is carried out flexibly and with a degree of fluidity because groups will be formed and reformed according to shifting instructional needs.

According to a prominent analysis, four aspects of instruction can be differentiated: content, process, products, and learning environment.

Differentiation of Content

The content of what is taught can be differentiated on the basis of what students know and what they are capable of learning. For example, when introducing concepts that are required learning according to state curriculum standards, the teacher may need to present material in greater depth to students who have already mastered the concepts, whereas background information will need to be provided to students who do not have knowledge that is prerequisite to learning these concepts. An English language learner may require simplification of the language through which new content is presented, although the student may be expected to engage in the same extent of critical thinking about the content as his or her classmates. In contrast, a student with an intellectual disability who also requires simplification of new content may be expected to engage the content in a very concrete way, as opposed to engaging in the higher-level thinking that is encouraged among other students. The teacher's specific approach to differentiating the content in this case would depend on the nature and severity of the student's disability.

Differentiation of Process

Teachers must sometimes differentiate the process, or the activities by which individual students learn. For example, in light of differences in learning styles, the teacher may give students the option of visual as opposed to auditory presentation of certain materials. An English language learner might benefit from having both visual and auditory materials, along with extra support from the teacher in understanding these materials and carrying out specific activities based on their content. In the case of a blind student, visual presentation of materials will not be an option, and differentiation of process will be reflected in the use of Braille texts, tactile materials, audio presentations, and other non-visual formats to facilitate the instruction of this student.

Differentiation of Products

Differentiation may be needed for the products of learning, i.e., the tests, reports, projects, performances, and other means by which students demonstrate how well they have mastered the content of instruction. For example, the teacher may allow students in a math class to demonstrate their mastery of key geometric concepts through construction of a three-dimensional model, a two-dimensional drawing, or a narrative description of how such a model or drawing could be constructed. An English language learner might benefit from creating a model or drawing rather than providing a narrative description, or if evaluated in such a way that narrative is required, given extra time and support to produce the narrative. In the case of an autistic student with a keen interest in visual patterns, differentiation of products would be reflected whenever a teacher modifies the regular classroom evaluations so that the student could express his or her learning through drawings and other two-dimensional representations.

Differentiation of Learning Environment

Differentiation can be applied to various aspects of the learning environment, including the physical layout, the use of space, the distribution of materials, the ambient lighting, and so on. For example, an English language learner might benefit from sitting close to the teacher or to a student who is verbally gifted, so that the teacher or student can easily provide language-related support on occasion. A student with a medical problem who needs to leave class periodically might benefit from being in a seat that allows easy access to the door. Students who are especially sensitive to distraction and/or especially likely to create distractions for other students may be seated away from windows and from other students who seem likely to create distractions, and in some cases they may be asked to complete individual work in a quiet area near the teacher. For these students, differentiation of environment is reflected in any way the teacher modifies the seating arrangements in the classroom.

Specific Strategies for Differentiation

Through differentiation, teachers modify various aspects of instruction to better meet the needs of individual students, groups of students, and/or entire classes. Generally speaking, instructional practices should be modified as little as possible in order to meet student needs. Minimal changes should be attempted first, and only if they are not successful should teachers proceed to more substantial changes. In the most extreme case, new materials, activities, procedures, and/or tasks are substituted for existing ones. Before these substitutions take place, teachers should attempt to modify existing elements of instruction. The following discussion illustrates some of the relatively minor changes that can be made.

Modification of Instructional Materials

One of the simplest approaches to the adaptation of instruction is to modify instructional materials through changes that make the material more suitable for particular students. Following are examples of relatively minor changes that can make task requirements more accessible:

- Task instructions can be restated, expanded, simplified, presented in more than one format, or otherwise changed in order to clarify the nature of the task and the expectations for performance. For example, a student with a hearing impairment might benefit from written instructions that are delivered to other students orally. A student with a visual impairment or with a learning disability such as dyslexia might benefit from the addition of oral instructions to an assignment in which the instructions are also presented in writing. A student with a specific intellectual disability might benefit from a brief, simplified summary of the instructions and expectations associated with a particular task.

- Prompts can be added to a task in order to highlight key information in the task, provide further details about expectations for performance, or otherwise provide students with guidance. For example, a student with a disability that results in attentional problems might benefit from the addition of arrows, underlining, or other graphics that demarcate key information in a text. A student with a specific intellectual disability might benefit from oral reminders to examine particular details in written materials, or to follow a particular sequence of steps in solving a problem.

Modification of Instructional Activities and Procedures

Instructional activities and procedures can be modified to meet the needs of individual students. Many such modifications are possible. For example, following are some examples of relatively minor changes that can be helpful when a student consistently makes the same kind of error:

- Additional instructional time can be devoted specifically to the area in which errors are consistently observed. For example, a young student with a speech impairment might benefit from extended discussion of strategies for articulating phonemes that many students struggle with initially but he or she finds especially challenging. A student with an intellectual disability who consistently leaves out a step during long division might benefit from additional explanations of the importance of each step.

- Additional practice can be encouraged in the area in which errors are consistently observed. The additional practice can be guided or independent, or a combination of the two. Practice can be increased for familiar activities; in addition, the teacher may incorporate new activities in order to maintain student interest. For example, the students described in the previous bullet item might benefit from additional practice with articulation and mathematical problem-solving activities.

Modification of Instructional Tasks

The requirements of instructional tasks can be modified in accordance with student needs. Many kinds of task-related modifications are possible. For example, here are just a few of the relatively minor changes that can reduce the difficulty of a task:

- The number or complexity of task demands can be decreased, the amount of time required for the task can be lessened, or the task requirements can be modified in some other way to make it less difficult for the student. For example, during a group activity, a student with autism might benefit if required interactions with other students are scripted and minimized. A student with an intellectual disability might benefit from a simplified version of a task that all students complete.

- The criteria for successful performance on a task can be relaxed. That is, the teacher can indicate that in order to meet some benchmark, the amount of work required of a student, the accuracy of the work, and/or the speed with which the work must be completed will be reduced. Thus, a student with a speech or language impairment might be given more latitude in a task requiring an expressive reading of a poem. A student with a mild visual impairment might be allowed extra time to complete a task that involves visual processing.

Differentiation may involve just one type of modification to instruction, as in the case of a student with mild hearing impairment who is given certain materials in visual form. In many cases, differentiation involves more than one type of modification. For example, a student with an articulation disorder might benefit from extra discussion of strategies for articulating difficult phonemes, extra guided practice with articulation of those phonemes, and reduced demands for tasks and assessments involving oral communication.

In this section you will read about methods of communication, consultation, and collaboration for the many people who are involved in the education of students who have, or who are suspected to have, a disability.

The Team Approach

A team approach to the identification and support of students who have or may have a disability is required by federal and state law, and thus team approaches strongly inform the education of these students. The three types of teams that are most prominent are the pre-referral team, the assessment team, and the IEP team.

- The purpose of the **pre-referral team** is to help students who are struggling in the general education setting before referring them for special education assessment. The pre-referral team obtains information about the student's strengths and weakness, designs and oversees the implementation of interventions, and evaluates the results of the interventions. If the interventions are successful, referral may not be needed, and the student may be able to function in the general education classroom with the support of teachers who provide some extent of differentiation. If the interventions are not successful, referral for special education assessment will be made. (Pre-referral assessment is discussed further in Chapter 2.)

- The purpose of the **assessment team** is to evaluate the referral and then design, implement, and summarize the results of the assessment. The assessment team takes the lead in determining whether the student has a disability and, if so, what educational supports are needed. (Further details about the composition and activities of the assessment team are discussed in Chapter 2.)

- The purpose of the **IEP team** is to use the results of assessment along with other information to create, implement, and monitor the effectiveness of an individualized education plan for the student. (Further details about the composition and activities of the IEP team are discussed in Chapter 2.)

The creation, composition, and responsibilities of the assessment and IEP teams are mandated by IDEA, while pre-referral teams are legally required in some but not all states. Pre-referral requirements according to Florida state law are summarized in Chapter 1 under Skill 5.

Team Characteristics

The various teams that serve children who have or may have a disability reflect a number of distinctive characteristics:

- The teams are composed of individuals from a variety of backgrounds who each contribute an important perspective on the student's needs. The teams are multidisciplinary, in the sense of being composed of both general and special educators as well as other professionals. In the case of the IEP team, parents and perhaps even the student himself or herself will be included. (The legal requirements for team composition are summarized in Chapter 1.)

- The teams serve multiple purposes. In particular, information-seeking, planning, implementation, monitoring, and evaluation are part of the activities carried out by each team.

- Because the teams are multi-disciplinary and multi-purpose, open communication and a collaborative spirit are critical to their effectiveness. Communication is necessary not only within teams but also between teams and school administrators such as principals as well as parents.

Skill 6

Apply flexible grouping strategies (e.g., academic, behavioral, social) for specific instructional activities.

This section concerns classroom management and student grouping strategies that promote the achievement of instructional objectives.

Classroom management can be defined as whatever a teacher does to ensure that the classroom environment is positive and allows instructional objectives to be achieved. Following are some of the dimensions that are critical to the development and maintenance of a positive classroom environment:

- the physical layout of the classroom (e.g., the arrangement of students' desks)

- the types and distribution of materials (e.g., worksheets)

- the allocation of time (e.g., the amount of time spent on a particular hands-on activity)

- the establishment of class rules and routines (e.g., the rules for use of the restroom)

- the monitoring of student behavior (e.g., monitoring students during group work)

- the imposition of discipline (e.g., dealing with a student who has broken the rules)

Effective Classroom Management

Effective classroom management results when a teacher attends to the dimensions as described above and makes modifications wherever appropriate. Most classroom management strategies pertain to the management of space, time, or behavior — that is, the physical environment of the classroom, the use of time during class, and the management of student behavior. These are not wholly independent dimensions. For example, student behavior is affected by the layout of the classroom and the teacher's use of time. Misbehavior is more likely when desks are located too close together and there is a substantial amount of "down time" while the teacher prepares instructional activity.

Physical Environment

Effective classroom management depends on creating a physical environment that is clean, safe, minimally distracting, maximally engaging, and most conducive to instructional activities. To take just one example, to the greatest extent possible, desks and chairs should be arranged so that:

- students are not sitting so closely to each other that physical contact is inevitable.

- both the teacher and the students can move throughout the room with minimal disruption.

- the teacher can maintain eye contact with students at all times.

- areas used for group work are as separate as possible from individual desks.

Use of Time

Effective classroom management depends on using time efficiently so that maximal time is devoted to the pursuit of instructional objectives, while minimal time is spent on discussing classroom procedures, transitioning between activities, clarifying behavioral expectations, and dealing with undesirable behaviors. (Discussing procedures, transitioning, and so on, are essential to classroom management, but teachers should avoid spending more time on them than necessary.) For example, the following strategies promote effective time management in the classroom by minimizing the loss of instructional time:

- Teachers should come to class each day fully prepared for all lessons, activities, and transitions, so that minimal class time is spent getting ready for each.

- Teachers should provide students with clear explanations of the purpose, instructions, and expectations for each activity, in advance, so that minimal time is spent on merely reiterating this information during the activity.

- Teachers should keep track of time and modify activities accordingly so that instructional objectives can be achieved and time is not lost completing activities on a subsequent day that were intended to be completed the previous day.

- Teachers should delegate some work to aides and volunteers (if available) and to students (as appropriate to their age and capabilities) in order to reduce the amount of time needed to prepare for instructional activities.

- Teachers should describe and discuss classroom rules, routines, and expectations clearly, at the outset of the year, so that throughout the year minimal time will be needed to reiterate key points.

Student Behavior

Effective classroom management depends on keeping students engaged and attentive, confident about learning, clear about what is expected of them, and consistently on-task, while helping them avoid negative emotional states, tuning out, becoming distracted, or engaging in disruptive behaviors. Following are just a few of the strategies that teachers use to promote positive classroom behaviors while discouraging negative ones:

- Setting reasonable expectations for classroom behavior, and making sure that students understand those expectations, helps promote positive student behavior. If students understand clearly what is expected of them, they will be less likely to engage in undesirable behaviors owing to confusion about the nature of the expectations or a sense that the expectations are inconsistent. As noted earlier, teachers should take time at the beginning of the year to clarify rules, routines, and expectations, and then to reiterate key points as needed depending on student age and level of comprehension.

- Paying close attention to what is happening in the classroom helps teachers understand the basis of both positive and negative behaviors. By noticing both the antecedents and consequences of a disruptive behavior, for example, the teacher will gain more insight into why the student is engaging in the behavior. Through such insights the teacher will be better prepared to deal with the behavior.

- Using differentiation (discussed earlier under Skill 5) helps teachers structure activities for individual students so that the students are appropriately challenged and neither feel bored by overly easy work nor frustrated by overly difficult work. Differentiation also helps promote good teacher-student relationships and allows teachers to interact with individual students in a way that encourages positive behaviors while discouraging negative ones.

- Modeling desirable behaviors, and responding positively to desirable behaviors, can promote further expression of those behaviors.

- Responding effectively to undesirable behaviors helps discourage those behaviors. Undesirable behaviors can be ignored if they constitute minor violations of the rules and are of short duration (e.g., a student who talks out of turn once, without receiving any response from his or her neighbor). When undesirable behaviors are more serious, longer in duration, or likely to spread or otherwise continue to be disruptive to other students, the teacher will need to intervene as soon as possible. Chapter 4, which focuses on classroom behavior, includes more information about the various strategies that can be used to deal effectively with undesirable behavior.

Grouping Strategies

When teachers organize students into groups for instructional purposes, decisions must be made about the size and the composition of the groups.

- **Homogeneous groups** of students are similar to each other in some respect. Most commonly, homogeneous grouping is carried out in order to ensure that students of the same ability level work together. This practice enables differentiation, in the sense that students who have been placed in more skilled groups can receive more challenging tasks, and/or less teacher scaffolding, than students in less skilled groups.

- **Heterogeneous groups** of students are different from each other in some important respect. For example, the teacher can ensure that each group consists of at least one of the highest and lowest performing students in the class. In this way, low-performing students can benefit from modeling and other guidance provided by more advanced peers, while high-performing students can benefit from the challenge of taking on an instructional role.

Other approaches to grouping are sometimes used. For example, the composition of groups can be randomized through techniques such as counting off. In such cases, what is essential to the teacher is that students work in groups; the range of interests and ability levels represented in each group is not critical.

Regardless of group composition, teachers need to be flexible, so that groups can be formed and reformed depending on instructional needs.

Classroom Management and Students with Disabilities

The principles of classroom management discussed in this section apply to general education students as well as to students with disabilities. For example, being aware of why a particular student is exhibiting a particular undesirable behavior will help the teacher respond appropriately to the behavior, regardless of whether or not the student is thought to have a disability. In the case of a student with a disability, the undesirable behavior may or may not be related to the disability. For example, a student with an intellectual disability may repeatedly talk out of turn because his disability makes it difficult for him to remember when he should avoid talking. Alternatively, this student may repeatedly talk out of turn because the work assigned to him is too easy and he is bored (a response that any student is prone to exhibit when insufficiently challenged).

The presence of students both with and without disabilities in the same classroom can pose a unique challenge for classroom management, for any one or more of the following reasons:

- Students without disabilities have stereotypes or other misconceptions about their disabled peers that are sometimes expressed by teasing and other forms of overt discrimination.

- Students without disabilities may view their disabled peers with anxiety or distrust, or with an extent of curiosity that is distracting.

- Students with certain disabilities may miss social cues or engage in behaviors that their non-disabled peers find distracting or offensive.

- Students with disabilities may feel anxious about the possibility of being rejected or judged negatively, by their non-disabled peers.

Following are some of the strategies that teachers can use to promote the social acceptance of students with disabilities and to help students with and without disabilities develop more positive attitudes toward each other.

- Teachers should reflect on their own attitudes toward each student with a disability, in order to determine whether they themselves are engaging in stereotyping or in treatment of students that is not called for in each particular case. For example, a teacher might tend to isolate an emotionally disturbed student more than necessary, in the interest of preventing the student from becoming frustrated. Because the decision of the IEP team to allow the student to participate in the general education classroom indicates that the student should be treated like his classmates to the greatest extent possible, the teacher may need to reconsider how much the student needs to be sheltered from situations that create frustration.

- As appropriate, teachers can provide the class with information about a student's disability. The purpose of doing so is not to put the student "on display," but rather to provide the class with information that can dispel prejudices and other misconceptions, and to indicate what, if anything, the class might do to support the student. In some cases, this information can be provided before a student with disabilities joins the general education classroom. Such information is relevant not only to students but also to their parents.

- Students with disabilities can be provided with information that helps them adjust to the general education classroom. For example, if a student's social skills are much less advanced compared to peers, social skills training both before and after joining the general education classroom can be of benefit to the student.

This section briefly considers some of the instructional strategies that facilitate understanding of text features and text structure.

Text Features

Text features are elements added to a text that facilitate the reader's comprehension. Examples of text features include the following:

- a table of contents
- a heading or subheading
- a figure or table
- a timeline
- an index
- a glossary

Instruction and Text Features

Following are some of the instructional strategies that help students recognize and make use of text features when they read, and to incorporate text features appropriately into their own writing:

- Students should be explicitly taught the names and purposes of each text feature and presented with examples of each.

- Students should be given opportunities to practice locating text features in meaningful texts, and deriving useful information from these features.

- Students should be given opportunities to add text features to enhance plain text that is provided to them.

- Students should be given opportunities to practice creating text features to accompany their own writing in useful ways.

Text Structures

Text structures consist of the ways that information is organized in a text. Examples of text structures include the following:

- A sequential structure presents information in chronological order.

- A compare and contrast structure presents a contrast among ideas, things, events, or people.

- A cause and effect structure presents one or more causes followed by one or more outcomes.

- A problem and solution structure introduces a problem and then presents one or more solutions.

Instruction and Text Structures

Following are some of the instructional strategies that help students understand text structures in written texts, and to make use of these structures effectively in their own written work:

- Students should be explicitly taught the names and characteristics of each text structure and presented with examples of each. Instruction should focus on one text structure at a time.

- Students should be taught that certain words may signal particular structures. For example, words like "next" and "then" may indicate a sequential structure, words like "because" and "as a result" may indicate a cause-and-effect structure, and so on. Although these signal words are not infallibly linked to particular text structures, students should be taught that such words are possible indicators of particular structures.

- Students should be given opportunities to discuss text structures in meaningful texts, and to analyze the structures in these texts through discussion and representational means such as graphic organizers.

- Students should be given opportunities to practice writing texts that reflect each structure. Through writing, students will not only improve in their ability to express themselves using these structures but will also become more sensitive to the presence of these structures in the texts they read.

Skill 7

Use criteria for selecting and utilizing print and non-print media for instructional use to match student needs and interests.

This section pertains to criteria for the selection and evaluation of print and non-print media for instructional use.

Teachers cannot choose instructional materials freely, of course. Textbooks are likely to be pre-determined, and teachers have limited budgets for the purchase of additional materials. In particular, the cost and accessibility of both print and non-print media typically must be taken into consideration when teachers select media for classroom use. Constraints on cost and accessibility will vary from district to district and media item to media item. This section assumes that a teacher has some flexibility in the selection of print and non-print media for instructional purposes.

Following are some of the questions teachers should ask when considering a particular media item for use in the classroom:

- Is the level of difficulty suitable for the students? This is a question about the content of the media item and, in the case of electronic media, about the technological expertise required to use the item.

- How well can the content promote instructional objectives? This is a question about alignment between the content and both curricular standards as well as specific lesson plans.

- Is the content likely to be meaningful and engaging for students? This is a question about the extent to which the content matches student interests, the extent to which the content is culturally relevant, and—in the case of digital materials— the extent to which use of the materials is interactive.

- To what extent does the material allow differentiation? This is a question about the extent to which the complexity of the material varies (so that students of different ability levels can be served), and about the extent of variety in the content (so that instruction can be tailored somewhat to students with differing experiences and interests).

Skill 8

Analyze characteristics of specialized instructional approaches for students with significant disabilities.

In this section you will read about general education and alternate standards for curricular content. **Content standards** indicate what knowledge and skills students at particular grades are required to master in particular subject areas. **Achievement standards** indicate how students should demonstrate mastery of the knowledge and skills identified in the content standards. Because achievement standards are discussed in Chapter 2, the focus in this section is on content standards.

General Education Content Standards

All states are legally required to specify curricular content and student achievement standards for K–12 public school settings. In Florida, the content standards are known as the Florida State Standards. These standards indicate curricular content in these subject areas:

- Dance
- English Language Arts
- English Language Development
- Gifted
- Health Education
- Mathematics
- Music
- Physical Education\
- Theatre
- Science
- Social Studies
- Special Skills
- Visual Art
- World Languages

Beginning with the 2014–2015 school year, all K–12 schools began implementing the Florida Standards. Education leaders across Florida improved our academic content standards, creating new expectations for what students need to know and be able to do. The Florida Standards are designed to ensure that ALL students reach their greatest potential. These standards were a result of the alarming numbers of ill-prepared college students in need of remedial courses, and the growing skills gap in our workforce, as compared to other workers in the global economy. According to these standards, exceptional education students should be challenged to excel within the general education curriculum.

Alternative Content Standards

The Florida Standards Alternate Assessment (FSAA) is designed for students whose participation in the general statewide assessment program (Florida Standards Assessments, Statewide Science Assessment, Next Generation Sunshine State Standards End-of-Course Assessments) is not appropriate, even with accommodations. The FSAA measures student academic performance on the Access Points (FS-AP) in Language Arts, Mathematics, Science, and Social Studies. Access Points are academic expectations written specifically for students with significant cognitive disabilities.

Beginning in 2016–2017, the FSAA program includes two assessment components. The FSAA Performance Task (FSAA-PT) designed to assess students at three levels of complexity and results reported through achievement levels. In Florida, alternative content standards are reflected in the *Access Points for the Sunshine State Standards*. Access Points were developed for the benefit of students with the most extreme cognitive disabilities. Each Access Point is written at three levels of complexity: participatory, supported, and independent.

- Students functioning at the participatory level have significant difficulties with learning and transfer. As adults they will probably be dependent on others for most or all of their daily needs.

- Students functioning at the supported level can learn and transfer new knowledge with support. As adults they will require supervision and support from others but can also develop skills that will promote a degree of independence.

- Students functioning at the independent level can learn and transfer independently, with minimal support. As adults they can function independently with little support from others.

Chapter 3 Practice Quiz

1. Which of the following best illustrates formative assessment?

   A. a standardized achievement test administered at the end of the school year as per state requirements

   B. a mid-term exam administered to students in order to evaluate the extent of their learning during the first half of the semester

   C. a quiz administered during the first week of class that is not graded but rather used to guide instructional planning

   D. a test administered at the end of an instructional unit intended to determine how well students mastered unit content

2. Which of the following is the correct sequence of activities in systematic instruction?

   A. review, presentation, guided practice, planning, independent practice

   B. planning, presentation, review, independent practice, guided practice

   C. review, presentation, guided practice, planning, independent practice

   D. planning, review, presentation, guided practice, independent practice

3. Mary, a high school sophomore, experienced a traumatic brain injury in childhood that resulted in significant cognitive impairments. Mary is unable to participate in the general education curriculum without substantial modifications to the curriculum and other forms of support, and her ability to learn and apply curricular content does not exceed that of most third graders. When Mary's IEP team conducts its first meeting of the year, which of the following should be one part of the meeting?

   A. The IEP team should discuss how to support Mary's academic skills this year, with the understanding that instruction in functional skills can be emphasized in subsequent years.

   B. The IEP team should review the goals for Mary's life following graduation, and evaluate the extent to which progress has been made toward the realization of those goals.

   C. The IEP team should review Mary's academic progress thus far, and determine how best to prepare her to take the state achievement test without accommodations for her disability.

   D. The IEP team should discuss the education of students with traumatic brain injury, using Mary's case as a guide for the development of broader principles of instructional support.

4. Which of the following concepts is illustrated by the math teacher who allows a mildly-autistic student to quietly draw and fold paper while the teacher is lecturing, so long as the student appears to learn from the lectures?

   A. differentiation

   B. independent practice

   C. scaffolding

   D. modeling

5. Bill is a student with multiple disabilities who is frequently off task, frustrated, and disruptive without frequent guidance from the teacher. Which of the following is the most appropriate seating arrangement for Bill during regular, whole-class activities?

   A. Bill should sit in the back of the room, away from other students who might distract or be distracted by him.

   B. Bill should sit next to a well-behaved student, so that he can learn better behavior through modeling.

   C. Bill should sit close to the teacher, so that the teacher can monitor his behavior and readily intervene.

   D. It does not matter where Bill sits, because he will be prone to frustration and disruptive behaviors no matter where he is.

6. Which of the following best illustrates heterogeneous grouping in a math class?

   A. The teacher ensures that each group of students consists of one student who scored a grade of A on the previous test, along with one student who scored lower than a grade of C.

   B. The teacher ensures that each group of students consists of individuals who scored the same letter grade on the previous test.

   C. The teacher ensures that each group of students consists of one student who scored a grade of B on the previous test.

   D. The teacher ensures that each group of students is randomly chosen by means of a counting-off procedure.

7. An elementary school student asks her teacher in front of the class why one of her classmates, who has a speech impairment, "talks funny." How should the teacher respond?

   A. The teacher should explain that the student's question is rude, and that in the future the class should avoid teasing the student with the impairment or otherwise discussing the topic.

   B. The teacher should reply that students must ask their classmate directly why he "talks funny," rather than spending class time discussing the topic, and that they should feel free to ask the student any question about the impairment.

   C. The teacher should provide a brief explanation, ask the student with the impairment to pronounce certain phonemes in order to illustrate the disability, and then develop a thematic unit on speech impairments.

   D. The teacher should provide a brief, factual answer, comment favorably on some distinctive personal characteristic of the student with the impairment, and discuss how the class is more interesting owing to each student's distinguishing characteristics.

Explanatory Answers

1. C

Option C is correct, because the assessment is being used to inform instruction rather than as a means of evaluating students (e.g., by assigning their performance a score). Options A, B, and D are all incorrect because they reflect summative assessment; in each case, students are evaluated at the end of an instructional period and their performance is scored.

2. D

Option D presents the correct order of activities in systematic instruction. Options A, B, and C all present incorrect orderings.

3. B

Option B is correct, because Mary will be graduating soon and is likely to need domestic, social, and occupational support. Option A is incorrect because consideration of functional skills should not be delayed, especially given that Mary is unlikely to be able to function on her own without substantial support. Option C is incorrect because if Mary is not receiving the general education curriculum without modifications, she should not participate in the state achievement test without support such as accommodations. While Option D represents a worthwhile discussion, the primary concern of the IEP team must be for Mary's future.

COMPETENCY 3: KNOWLEDGE OF INSTRUCTIONAL PRACTICES IN EXCEPTIONAL STUDENT EDUCATION

4. A

Option A is correct, because the teacher is engaging in a differentiation of the teaching process in order to accommodate the student's particular needs. Although the student may be "practicing" representational skills, Option B is incorrect because the student is not engaging in independent practice of what is being taught, as would take place during systematic instruction. Option C is incorrect because the teacher is not directly supporting the student's learning but rather simply relaxing one of the class rules pertaining to attentiveness. Option D is incorrect because the student is not copying the teacher's actions.

5. C

Option C is correct, because sitting near the teacher gives the teacher easy access to Bill and increases the likelihood of him or her helping Bill without disrupting class activities. Option A is incorrect because it makes it more difficult for the teacher to reach Bill, either physically or through eye contact; moreover, isolation from other students may create social problems. Although Bill may be able to learn more appropriate classroom behavior through modeling, Option B is incorrect because it is not likely that progress will be made in a short period of time. Option D is incorrect because the teacher should not give up trying to help Bill, and in any case an appropriate choice of seating for him can help minimize distraction for other students in the class.

6. A

Option A is correct because the groups will be relatively heterogeneous with respect to math achievement. Option B is incorrect because the groups will be relatively homogeneous. Options C and D are incorrect; it is not clear that the process of group assignment will result in heterogeneity.

7. D

Option A is incorrect because the teacher's response would not help increase the students' understanding or appreciation of the student with the impairment, but rather may contribute to distance between this student and the rest of the class. Option B is incorrect for similar reasons. Option C is incorrect because the teacher's actions would place too much attention on the student with the impairment, when it is not clear that such attention is welcomed or would contribute to instructional objectives. Option D is correct because the class would be provided a simple account for a characteristic that is already apparent to them, while promoting acceptance of the student with the impairment by helping the students view diversity (in the most general sense) in a positive way.

Competency 4: Knowledge of the Positive Behavioral Support Process

This chapter concerns the assessment, design, and implementation of positive behavioral supports for all students, including students with disabilities.

Broadly, **positive behavior support (PBS)** is an evidence-based approach to promoting desirable behaviors while discouraging undesirable ones. PBS is based on the assumption that problem behaviors cannot be effectively addressed unless their causes are understood. Knowledge about the causes of problem behaviors informs the development of interventions in which the goal is to replace these behaviors with more desirable ones. Successful intervention may require modifications to the student's educational environment rather than an exclusive focus on changing the problem behaviors directly. What constitutes "desirable" behaviors, as well as the methods by which those behaviors are encouraged, must be acceptable to the community, to parents, and to the students themselves.

PBS is implemented in a tiered fashion, with preventative measures established at the school level, increased support available to students who exhibit behavioral problems, and behavioral intervention plans developed by IEP teams for individual students whose behavior is most problematic.

Skill 1

Identify and choose appropriate prevention and intensive intervention strategies for students who display challenging behaviors.

In this section you will read about the selection and evaluation of proactive interventions that foster desirable behavior.

Three-Tiered Approach to Positive Behavior Support

Positive behavior support systems are proactive, in the sense that they attempt to prevent problem behaviors before they occur, and to address problem behaviors before their severity intensifies. This proactive emphasis is illustrated by a three-tiered system of implementation:

- The first tier consists of school-wide preventative measures such as making behavioral expectations clear to everyone present at the school, creating a system of positive reinforcements for desirable behavior, establishing consequences for undesirable behavior, maintaining consistency in the handling of undesirable behavior, and so on. First-tier efforts are largely focused on prevention.

- The second tier consists of additional support available to students who have not responded to first-tier measures and currently exhibit problem behaviors. Supports such as mentoring, social skills training, friendship clubs, simple behavior plans, and so on, are provided in the hopes of avoiding more serious consequences such as suspension or expulsion.

- The third tier consists of interventions created for individual students whose problem behaviors are most severe. In the case of a student with a disability, a behavior intervention plan will be created, monitored, and evaluated by the IEP team on the basis of a functional behavior assessment, as described in the next section.

Preventative Strategies

At the classroom level, the teacher can use a variety of strategies that address problem behaviors in a proactive way, in the sense of attempting to prevent their occurrence or reducing the likelihood of their persistence. Following are examples of some simple preventative strategies:

- The teacher should communicate behavioral expectations to students. Classroom rules should be explained clearly and concretely on the first day of class, for example, accompanied by demonstrations by the teacher and opportunities for student rehearsal as appropriate.

- The teacher should create a structured environment in which rules, routines, and procedures are consistent and clear. At any given time, students should know what they are supposed to be doing.

- The teacher should come to class fully prepared. Transitions between activities should be carefully planned, for example, so that transition time is minimized and expectations for students during the transition are clear.

- The teacher should continually monitor student behavior, making note of and responding appropriately to both desirable and undesirable behaviors.

- The teacher should create an atmosphere in which students focus on responding to positive behaviors rather than judging negative ones. Instead of "tattling," for example, students can be encouraged to recognize peers who engage in positive classroom behaviors.

- The teacher should implement specific strategies for promoting desirable behaviors—not only at particular moments but throughout the school year. Positive reinforcement (discussed under Skill 5 below) should be the typical incentive for desirable behaviors rather than threatening to punish students for failing to exhibit those behaviors. For example, if the teacher uses the opportunity for the class to receive a special privilege at the end of the year as an incentive for positive behavior, the teacher could create a system in which "points" are given for good behavior rather than deducted for bad behavior.

Reactive Strategies

Through positive behavior management, teachers engage in strategies for preventing problem behaviors rather than simply reacting to misbehavior punitively. However, preventative measures can only reduce the incidence of misbehavior to a greater or lesser extent rather than preventing it altogether. A proactive approach to behavior management thus includes strategies for implementing swift and appropriate responses to problem behaviors when they arise.

When responding to a problem behavior, the teacher should maintain a positive classroom atmosphere by selecting the minimal response that prevents the behavior from reoccurring. Following is a typical list of strategies ranging in order from the most minimal to the most intensive; typically, if one strategy is unsuccessful, the teacher will proceed to the next one:

- The most minimal response to misbehavior is to ignore it. Minor misbehaviors such as talking out of turn or groaning during silent reading can be ignored if they are one-time occurrences and do not spread.

- The most minimal responses to a student who is misbehaving include nonverbal cues such as looking at the student, frowning at the student, and/or moving closer to the student. Nonverbal cueing can be carried out while the teacher continues to address the class, or while the class continues to work independently, and thus other students may not even notice that cueing has taken place.

- If nonverbal cueing is ineffective, the teacher might resort to brief verbal cues that do not identify the student directly (e.g., "We're all paying attention now, right?"). Here too, regular class activities may not be disrupted if the student responds quickly to the verbal cue.

- The teacher might offer brief verbal cues directed specifically at the student, such as saying the student's name, or quietly asking the student to cease the problem behavior. Disruption to class activities is likely to be minimal if the student quickly responds to the cue.

- Interrupting regular classroom activities in order to explicitly address the problem behavior should be considered a last resort. Doing so may be necessary if the student is unwilling or unable to respond to brief verbal cues.

Skill 2

Distinguish the various concepts and models of positive behavior support.

In this section you will read about concepts and models of positive behavior management that are widely used in educational settings with all students, including those who have disabilities.

The goals of positive behavior management are to promote desirable classroom behaviors while discouraging undesirable ones using methods that respect individual students. These goals can be more readily achieved through an understanding of the general processes by which behaviors are learned and subsequently modified. Two such processes are modeling and reinforcement.

Modeling

Modeling, also known as observational learning, refers to learning that takes place by imitating someone else's behavior. The term "modeling" also refers to the demonstration of the behavior by the individual being modeled. Thus, a teacher might "model" a particular behavior that the students learn through "modeling."

Modeling reflects an explicit approach to instruction when explanations about how to perform the behavior are provided, or when prompts are given (as when a teacher says, "Do what I do" and then performs some action while students watch). Modeling can also be implicit, as when a teacher expresses disagreement with a student's ideas in a positive and tactful way that is later reflected in students' interactions with each other. In this example, the teacher models a socially appropriate way of disagreeing with another person's ideas, but she does not describe or otherwise call attention to what she models.

Substantial learning takes place through explicit as well as implicit modeling. However, teachers cannot rely exclusively on modeling as a means of promoting desirable behavior in the classroom. Teachers must also explicitly discuss behavioral expectations with students and respond to both desirable and undesirable behaviors that students exhibit.

Reinforcement

The likelihood of a particular behavior continuing to occur is influenced by the outcome of the behavior. This outcome is referred to as the **reinforcer.** A child who tries grapes for the first time and discovers that they taste pleasantly sweet is likely to eat grapes in the future in order to once again experience their sweet taste. In this example, eating grapes is the behavior, and sweet taste is the reinforcer. A child who touches a hot stove and experiences pain may not touch the stove again because the child has discovered that touching the stove (behavior) leads to pain (reinforcer).

Positive Reinforcement

Positive reinforcement occurs when a behavior is followed by a desirable outcome that makes the behavior more likely to occur. For example, when a teacher praises a student for completing an assignment neatly, praise may serve as a positive reinforcer that increases the likelihood of the student completing future assignments neatly. Other examples of positive reinforcement in educational settings include the following:

- a special privilege granted for being helpful to classmates

- a positive note sent to parents regarding good classroom citizenship

- a special award given for effort

In order for positive reinforcement to be effective (i.e., cause a behavior to be exhibited more frequently), the following conditions must be met:

- The student must consider the reinforcer to be positive. Students vary widely in what they consider desirable; thus the teacher must consider each student's interests and abilities when selecting positive reinforcers. The opportunity to select and read an extra book would be viewed very positively by some students, for example, while others would consider it a form of punishment.

- The student must understand what behavior is being reinforced. Thus, telling a student that she did a "good job" on her writing assignment will not be as effective as a more specific statement such as "I like how neat your writing is this time."

Negative reinforcement

Negative reinforcement occurs when a behavior is followed by the removal of an undesirable outcome, and the removal of that outcome makes the behavior more likely to occur. For example, when a teacher points out to a student that his handwriting on a homework assignment is sloppy, the teacher's comment is a negative reinforcer that makes it more likely the student will complete future assignments neatly. By doing his work neatly, the undesirable outcome (i.e., the teacher's negative comment) will be removed. Other examples of negative reinforcement include the following:

- frowning at a student who is slow to begin an activity

- warning a student to follow a particular instruction on homework assignments

- sending a note to parents commenting on inconsistency in following the classroom rules for polite interactions with peers

As with positive reinforcement, negative reinforcement will not be effective unless the student truly considers the reinforcer to be negative, as well as understanding what behavior is being reinforced. Frowning at a student who is slow to begin an activity will not constitute negative reinforcement if the student enjoys adult attention regardless of whether the attention is positive or negative. Moreover, even if the student does view the frown as a negative reinforcer, noticing the frown will not induce him to act more promptly in the future unless he understands that the frown was specifically elicited by his slowness. In such a case, the teacher may need to include a brief verbal explanation.

Punishment

Punishment occurs when a behavior is followed by an undesirable outcome that makes the behavior less likely to occur. For example, when a student loses recess privileges for throwing objects in the classroom, the loss of recess privileges is a punishment that makes it less likely the student will continue to throw things in class. Although negative reinforcement and punishment both consist of undesirable outcomes, negative reinforcement makes a behavior more likely to occur, while punishment makes a behavior less likely to occur. Thus, teachers can use negative (and positive) reinforcement to promote desirable classroom behaviors, while using punishment to discourage undesirable classroom behaviors. However, as noted earlier in this chapter, punishment is not intended to be a major element in positive behavior support systems.

A distinction can be made between positive and negative punishment. Positive punishment involves the introduction of an undesirable outcome, while negative punishment (also known as **response cost**) involves the loss of a desirable outcome. For example, requiring a student to redo an assignment or to complete an extra assignment would be examples of positive punishment, while loss of recess privileges would be an example of negative punishment.

Behavior Management Strategies

Principles such as modeling and reinforcement are the foundation of a variety of specific behavior management strategies that teachers can use to address problem behaviors exhibited by students. Some of these strategies are based on additional instruction provided to students in order to foster behavioral change, two prominent examples being training in social skills and anger management. Other behavior management strategies consist of modifications to the student's environment.

Social Skills Training

Social skills training focuses on providing students with skills that benefit their interpersonal relationships and communication with others. Examples of social skills that can be enhanced through behavioral training include the following:

- how to establish and maintain friendships
- how to effectively communicate one's needs
- how to listen to and cooperate with others
- how to recognize and respond to conflict with others
- how to deal with frustration, loss, and other negative outcomes
- how to deal with being bullied or neglected

Anger Management Training

Anger management training focuses on providing students with skills that help them to avoid situations that create anger, to deal with their anger when it is experienced, and to manage conflict with others. Following are some of the strategies that may be provided in anger management training:

- Relaxation techniques can help students reduce the likelihood of becoming angry as well as the severity of anger when it is experienced.

- "Self-talk" strategies can help students monitor their responses in different situations, so that they can manage their own anger in its early stages, as well as reframing social situations in more positive ways so that the severity of their anger (or the likelihood of their becoming angry in the first place) is diminished.

- Social skills training (see above) in areas such as conflict resolution can help students avoid conflict and develop positive verbal strategies for dealing with conflict when it is inevitable.

Behavioral Instruction

Regardless of whether behavioral instruction focuses on social skills, anger management, or some other behavioral strategy, instruction may reflect a sequence such as the following:

- Initially, the teacher engages in **task analysis** or the division of what is to be learned into small components. Components are introduced separately; once students have mastered one component, they proceed to the next one. **Chaining** refers to the teaching of complex behaviors whose components are linked sequentially.

- Instruction begins with the teacher describing to students what behavioral skills they will be learning.

- The teacher models the behaviors of interest for students. Explanations are provided as appropriate.

- Students are given opportunities to practice the desired behaviors, and the teacher provides feedback on student performance. Because students may not exhibit the desired behavior perfectly at first, the teacher may use **shaping,** or a process of reinforcing behaviors that are successively closer to the desired behavior, until that behavior is finally achieved.

- As students practice the behaviors of interest, the teacher may provide **prompts,** which are cues or hints for appropriate action. Because the goal of instruction is for students to exhibit the behaviors independently, prompts are lessened and then completely withdrawn through a process of **fading.**

- To the greatest extent possible, the teacher will provide students with opportunities and support for **transfer,** or the generalization of the new behaviors to different people, places, and materials.

Environmental Modifications

Positive behavior management may focus on directly changing student behavior, as described above, on modifying the student's environment so that behavioral change is elicited, or on a combination of the two. The term "environment" is used in a broad sense here to include both the physical and the social environments in which learning takes place. Following are some of the ways in which the student's environment can be modified to reduce the incidence of a particular problem behavior:

- A positive reinforcer for the problem behavior can be removed. For example, a student who deliberately breaks his pencil points because he enjoys using the pencil sharpener can be told that in the future he will not be allowed to use the pencil sharpener after engaging in this behavior. In this example, use of the pencil sharpener had been a positive reinforcer for the student's pencil-breaking behavior. (In the interest of avoiding a punitive atmosphere, the teacher might add that the student will be allowed to sharpen his pencils once per day, at a designated time.)

- A negative reinforcer for the problem behavior can be removed. For example, a student with an intellectual disability who is shouting in class because she fears that the teacher will think she is weak if she does not speak up for herself can be reassured that the teacher knows she is strong. In this example, the prospect of seeming weak had been a negative reinforcer for the student's shouting behavior.

- A positive reinforcer for a desirable alternative to the problem behavior can be introduced. For example, a student with an emotional disturbance who slouches, deliberately slips out of his chair, and makes noises during morning announcements can be told that if he sits up straight and quietly listens to the announcements, he can subsequently help the teacher pass out materials to the class. In this example, helping the teacher is a positive reinforcer intended to promote the desirable behavior of quiet attentiveness to morning announcements. (A key assumption here is that this particular student enjoys helping the teacher with class activities.)

- A token economy can be introduced that includes a positive reinforcer for a desirable alternative to the problem behavior, along with a response cost for that behavior. For example, a student with autism who sometimes mimics a statement from the teacher rather than responding meaningfully can be given a token each time he responds meaningfully, while losing a token each time he mimics the teacher. The tokens can be subsequently traded in for a privilege that the student desires.

- The teacher can modify his or her own behavior. For example, through conversations with a student who sometimes covers his ears when the teacher talks to him, the teacher may discover that the student feels threatened whenever the teacher speaks in unpleasant tones, or stands too close to him when providing critical feedback. Upon reflection, the teacher may discover ways to modify her tone of voice and proximity to the student that make the student feel less threatened, yet do not interfere with instructional and classroom management practices.

- The teacher can modify the behavioral expectations for the student. For example, a student with a traumatic brain injury who quickly becomes agitated by class work she finds challenging can be allowed a short time to put her head down, or walk around the back of the classroom quietly, if such strategies prove effective at helping her to calm herself.

- The teacher can modify the physical characteristics of the classroom or the student's placement in it. For example, a student with autism who is easily provoked to disruptive behavior by innocuous movements and sounds originating from nearby students can be seated in the front row of the classroom, at one end of the row, in order to minimize the number of students seated in close proximity to him.

Skill 3

Analyze the legal and ethical issues pertaining to positive behavior support strategies and disciplinary procedures for students with exceptionalities.

This section briefly introduces some of the legal and ethical bases of contemporary approaches to behavioral management and discipline in school settings.

Traditional Approaches

Traditional approaches to addressing misbehavior in school settings relied heavily on punitive measures ranging from verbal reprimands to the most extreme disciplinary measures of suspension and expulsion. Punishment was considered an essential deterrent for undesirable behavior, as well as an effective approach to dealing with misbehavior once it had occurred. Along with concerns about the actual effectiveness of such approaches, ethical concerns have been raised regarding the impact of punishment on students as well as the fairness with which punishments were traditionally administered. Concerns have also been raised about overreliance on suspension and expulsion as methods of addressing misbehavior among students with disabilities because these practices create further isolation from the general education population.

IDEA and Positive Behavior Support

In contrast to traditional approaches to behavior management and discipline, IDEA recommends the use of positive behavior support as a means of reducing problem behaviors in school settings, thereby minimizing the role of punishment, encouraging the respectful treatment of students, and reducing the need for suspension or expulsion as disciplinary strategies. The use of positive behavioral-management strategies as a means of avoiding suspension or expulsion reflects IDEA's fundamental emphasis on inclusion (see Chapter 1 for discussion).

IDEA and Manifestation Determination Review

When a student with a disability has a behavioral problem that interferes with his or her own learning or that of other students, IDEA requires that the IEP team explore the need for positive strategies, supports, and interventions to address the problematic behavior. In particular, the IEP team will need to conduct a functional behavioral assessment in order to identify the causes of problem behavior and to then develop an intervention.

Recurring and/or extreme misbehavior may result in a student being removed from his or her regular educational placement through suspension or through placement in an alternative educational setting. When such behaviors occur, the IEP team must involve school administrators and parents in a **manifestation determination review** in order to determine whether the misbehavior is a manifestation of the student's disability, or whether it resulted from the school's failure to appropriately implement the IEP.

If the conclusion of the manifestation determination review is that the misbehavior is indeed related to the student's disability, the IEP team must conduct a functional behavior assessment for the purpose of developing a behavioral intervention plan (a description of the problem behavior and the strategies by which it will be addressed). If a behavioral intervention plan already exists, the IEP team must meet in order to review and possibly revise the plan. Functional behavior assessment and behavior intervention plans are discussed in detail in this chapter under Skill 5.

If the conclusion of the manifestation determination review is that the misbehavior is not related to the student's disability, the student may be disciplined in the same way that students without disabilities are disciplined in the particular school. A functional behavior assessment may still be conducted as appropriate.

Skill 4

Interpret individual and group data to apply interventions that increase positive behavior.

This section briefly introduces data collection strategies that can be used to assess the behavior of all students, including students with disabilities.

Data Collection by Teachers

Teachers encourage desirable classroom behaviors in order to maintain a positive classroom environment and to help students develop good habits and social skills. For example, teaching students how to disagree with each other's ideas in a respectful way serves the dual purpose of helping maintain a positive classroom environment and helping students develop a social skill of great importance both within and beyond the classroom.

In order to encourage desirable classroom behaviors while discouraging undesirable ones, teachers need information about students' current behavior, particularly if a student is struggling in some respect or has a disability that seems to manifest in problem behaviors. A variety of strategies, both indirect and direct, are available to teachers for obtaining information about student behavior:

- Indirect assessment can be used to obtain information about behavior without directly observing the student. For example, a teacher who is concerned about a particular student's social awkwardness may interview the student, as well as parents, other teachers, educational specialists familiar with the child, school administrators, and so on. If the student has a disability, data previously gathered by the IEP team is likely to be considered as well. Although these strategies can yield essential information, direct observation of the student in social settings such as the classroom would be needed in order for the teacher to be fully informed about the extent and possible causes of the student's awkwardness.

- Direct assessment is used to obtain information about student behavior through first-hand observations of the student. For example, as discussed in Chapter 5, teachers can use observational assessments to obtain descriptions of student behavior in natural settings such as the classroom. The observational assessments (checklists, rating scales, duration records, and time-sampling records) all rely on direct observation, as does simply observing a student in an informal way.

Regardless of the specific approaches to gathering data that are used, it is critical for the teacher to develop a system for recording the data, so that student behavior can be monitored over time and changes can be more readily understood.

Data Collection by the IEP Team and Others

The IEP team, as well as educational professionals who are not part of the team, will typically use a combination of direct and indirect assessments as a basis of learning more about the behavior of a student with a disability. As discussed below under Skill 5, the IEP team may also need to conduct a functional behavior assessment, a flexible, inclusive approach to the evaluation of behavior that relies on direct observation and usually incorporates indirect approaches as well.

Skill 5

Interpret the essential elements of a functional behavior assessment and measure the effects of the behavior intervention plan through data collection strategies.

This section provides a detailed introduction to the functional behavior assessments and behavior intervention plans mentioned at several points in this chapter.

Functional Behavior Assessment

As noted under Skill 1, IDEA requires that a functional behavior assessment be conducted if the IEP team has concerns about the behavior of a student with a disability, or if the student has engaged in extreme misbehavior that would result in suspension or removal from the current educational setting for more than 10 days. Functional behavior assessments can also be conducted with students who exhibit problem behaviors but have not been identified as having a disability.

Functional behavior assessment (FBA) consists of strategies for determining what causes and sustains problem behaviors, and for developing interventions that might best address those behaviors. FBA is based on the assumption that behavior serves specific purposes in specific situations. When a student misbehaves, the misbehavior serves some particular purpose, and intervention is not likely to be effective unless this purpose is understood.

The need for understanding the purpose of a problem behavior is illustrated by the fact that the same behavior may serve different purposes for different students. For example, one student who repeatedly talks back to the teacher may do so because he resents the way the teacher treats him, while another student may exhibit the same behavior because she is seeking peer approval. Clearly a different remedy is needed for each student. The first student needs to develop a more effective and appropriate way of expressing concerns about the teacher, while the second student needs to learn more appropriate ways of seeking approval from peers. In short, the intervention that will be most suitable for each student is different because the causes of their misbehavior are different, even though the same sort of misbehavior is expressed in each case.

For students such as those described above, FBA would address questions about how to describe the problem behavior, where and when the problem behavior is observed, what the underlying cause of the behavior seems to be, and what interventions are most likely to be effective.

Description

Descriptions of problem behavior in FBA should consist of concrete, specific statements rather than vague summations. For example, rather than stating that a student is "rude," a description of the problem behavior might be "the student talks back to the teacher during one-on-one interactions initiated by the teacher." Judgments about the student's character, hypotheses about the causes of the problem behavior, and predictions about future behavior should be avoided in these descriptions.

Context

FBA requires the gathering of information about contextual influences on the problem behavior. That is, information is needed about when, where, and under what conditions the problem behavior is exhibited, and about what contextual factors seem to increase or diminish the frequency and intensity of the behavior. In order to obtain such information, the student will need to be observed in different contexts. Conversations with the student, and perhaps also parents and other adults, will be helpful as well.

Although IDEA specifies when FBA must be conducted, the law does not indicate which methods of assessment should be used. Generally, information is needed about the antecedents as well as the consequences of the targeted behavior in order to understand its causes. For example, regarding a student who repeatedly talks back to his teacher, it might be noted whether the student talks back to just one particular teacher, to all teachers, or to all adults generally. It might also be noted whether the student is more likely to talk back when peers are present, and if so, how these other students respond. If the student's tendency to talk back seems relatively independent of context, an interview might be needed with the student to determine whether he is aware that talking back is considered inappropriate, and whether he is capable of more appropriate exchanges if motivated to do so and not distracted by anger or some other strong emotional state.

Cause

FBA yields hypotheses about the underlying cause of a problem behavior—i.e., informed guesses about what purpose or purposes the behavior serves for the student. Talking back to the teacher, for example, might reflect one or more of the following causes:

- resentment toward authority figures
- concerns about one particular teacher
- insecurity about the ability to succeed academically

- lack of knowledge about appropriate interaction with others

- poor impulse control

- a need for more attention from adults

- a need for approval from peers

The list presented above is not exhaustive. The fact that there are so many possible causes for the same behavior highlights the importance of multiple approaches to gathering data, including both observation of the student as well as conversation with the student about his or her thoughts and feelings.

Although there are many possible specific causes for a problem behavior, the IEP team will need to be particularly cognizant of the distinction between skill deficits and performance deficits. A student who exhibits a problem behavior because he or she does not know how to perform the desired behavior has a **skill deficit.** A student who knows how to perform the desired behavior but chooses not to, or is incapable of doing so owing to anger, frustration, or some other condition, has a **performance deficit.** The difference between these two types of deficits has important implications for intervention.

Intervention

FBA also yields hypotheses about which interventions might reduce the incidence or intensity of the problem behavior. These interventions will be closely related to hypotheses about the underlying cause of the behavior, and will include suggestions for "replacement behaviors," or behaviors that are likely to serve the same purpose as the problem behavior. In short, emphasis is placed on changing the behavior rather than the purpose that it serves. A student who talks back to the teacher because he seeks approval from peers must learn effective strategies for gaining approval rather than being expected to give up the desire for approval. In this example, the strategies for gaining peer approval that might be taught to the student during an intervention are the replacement behaviors for the undesirable behavior of talking back to the teacher.

Behavior Intervention Plan

The IEP team uses information from the FBA to develop a **behavior intervention plan (BIP)**, which describes the behaviors that are to be changed as well as the intervention strategy or strategies for effecting change. The focus of these interventions is not on controlling the problem behaviors but rather on fostering positive replacement behaviors.

Content of BIP

IDEA requires that the following elements be described in the BIP:

- the targeted problem behavior
- the types and effectiveness of interventions that have been tried already
- the interventions that will be used
- the specific goals of the interventions
- the approach to evaluating the effectiveness of the interventions
- the plan for reviewing the success of the interventions
- the plan for disseminating intervention results and other information to parents
- the plan for supporting the student if his or her behavior reaches crisis proportions

Other information is recommended for inclusion in the BIP but is not required. This information includes, for example:

- a summary of student strengths
- a statement regarding the purpose of the problem behavior
- a description of the positive replacement behavior

Success of BIP

An intervention proposed in the BIP is most likely to achieve long-term success if the following conditions are met:

- close alignment between intervention and cause of problem behavior
- close alignment between intervention and the student's strengths and needs
- choice of replacement behaviors most likely to receive environmental support
- choice of least intrusive and least complex intervention
- choice of intervention most acceptable to those responsible for implementing the plan
- choice of intervention most acceptable to the student
- choice of intervention with greatest systemic support

Chapter 4 Practice Quiz

1. Under which of the following conditions would a functional behavior assessment be legally required for a student with a disability?

    A. The student exhibits rude and intolerant behavior toward classmates throughout the school year.

    B. The student commits an act of aggression that would ordinarily result in a two-week suspension.

    C. The student leaves school early one afternoon without informing anyone of his destination.

    D. The student complains of diminishing intellectual functioning that impairs his ability to learn.

2. At the end of a lesson in November, Mrs. Smith announces that it is time for recess. The students rush noisily toward the door as Mrs. Smith admonishes them to line up and be quiet. As the students begin to form a line, pushing and shoving each other, Mrs. Smith asks them to settle down. During this time, Mark, an emotionally disturbed student, begins to get agitated. He pleads with Mrs. Smith to be first in line, and when she refuses, he throws a tantrum. Mrs. Smith is now struggling to deal with Mark's tantrum and with the rest of the class, who are still engaging in some pushing and shoving while they wait. What appears to be lacking in Mrs. Smith's approach to classroom behavior management?

    A. Mrs. Smith should have anticipated that Mark would throw a tantrum. She should have proactively told him that he would not be first in line.

    B. Mrs. Smith should remind the class of all procedures for lining up properly. Then, she should have announced that anyone who wants to be first in line could be first.

    C. Mrs. Smith should have used a different approach when announcing recess that day. She should have had students line up one at a time when she called their names.

    D. Mrs. Smith should have already established routines for transitioning to recess. She should not have had to do more than remind students of the routines.

3. At which tier is the approach to positive behavior management most proactive?

    A. first tier

    B. second tier

    C. third tier

    D. fourth tier

4.   Which of the following would be the most appropriate description of problem behavior in a functional behavior assessment?

   A.   Juan is an angry young man.

   B.   Juan frequently exhibits verbal hostility toward classmates, and he sometimes gets into physical fights with them.

   C.   Juan feels threatened by his peers and so he often interacts with them in a hostile manner, picking fights with them on occasion.

   D.   Juan responds to criticism from peers with verbal and physical aggression because he has learned these patterns of response from his father.

5.   Which of the following is NOT a required part of a behavioral intervention plan?

   A.   a list of all suitable interventions for the student

   B.   a summary of the goals of the proposed intervention

   C.   a description of how intervention results will be evaluated

   D.   a discussion of how intervention results will be communicated to parents

6.   Which of the following most clearly illustrates the removal of a negative reinforcer for a problem behavior?

   A.   A student who is whining about the difficulty of an assignment is told by his teacher that if he continues to whine, he will lose his chance to participate in the creation of a Presidents' Day poster by the entire class.

   B.   A student who is arguing about an assignment because he considers it unfair is told by his teacher that he should express his concerns in a more tactful way, so that the teacher will be more likely to take those concerns seriously.

   C.   A student who is complaining about an assignment because he hopes to be disciplined and avoid completing the assignment is told by his teacher that if he continues to complain, he will be disciplined but still have to do the assignment.

   D.   A student who is refusing to complete an assignment because he wants more attention from the teacher is told by the teacher that if he does not complete the assignment, he will receive a zero and have no chance to raise the grade.

7. Sally is a student with a traumatic brain injury who sometimes pushes, hits, or otherwise touches other classmates inappropriately. Sally's teacher reminds her at the beginning of a group activity that as long as Sally keeps her hands to herself during the activity, Sally will receive a gold star at the end of class. Assuming that Sally would like to have a gold star, which of the following does the teacher's comment represent?

   A. positive reinforcement

   B. negative reinforcement

   C. positive punishment

   D. negative punishment

Explanatory Answers

1. B

Option B is correct because IDEA requires that a functional behavior assessment be conducted when a student with a disability engages in behavior serious enough to merit suspension. Options A and C are incorrect because neither of the particular behaviors would be sufficient to require a functional behavior assessment unless the IEP team is concerned about the behavior. Option D is incorrect for similar reasons, and because the student's complaint pertains to cognitive functioning rather than behavior.

2. D

Option D is correct because by November the routines for transitioning to recess should be established. Students should be able to line up appropriately with minimal reminders, at most, concerning the routines. Option A is incorrect, because it is not clear that Mrs. Smith could have anticipated a tantrum, and in any case it would be inappropriately punitive to tell him, without further explanation, that he could not be first in line. Option B is incorrect, because by November students should not need a full review of the procedures for lining up; moreover, telling students that anyone can be first in line is likely to create a disturbance as students clamor to be first. Option C is incorrect because even if the amount of time needed to call students to the line individually on that day could be justified, the fact that students were so unruly suggests that the key problem is failure to establish routines for transitioning to recess.

3. A

Option A is correct because first tier support is provided to all students, including those who have not exhibited problem behavior. Options B and C are incorrect because the second and third tiers consist of support provided to students who have already exhibited behavioral problems. Option D is incorrect because there is no "fourth tier."

4. B

Option B is correct because it presents a clear, concrete description of the problem behaviors. Option A is incorrect because the description is vague. Options C and D are incorrect because they include interpretations of the causes of Juan's behavior, rather than focusing exclusively on the behavior.

5. A

Option A is correct because there is no requirement that all suitable interventions be listed in the behavioral intervention plan. Options B, C, and D are all incorrect because the inclusion of each is required by IDEA.

6. C

Option C is correct, because in this scenario, the problem behavior is complaining and the negative reinforcer had been the prospect of completing the assignment. The student had been complaining in hopes of not having to complete the assignment. Option A is incorrect because it illustrates negative punishment (i.e., response cost). Option B is incorrect because it illustrates explicit instruction. Option D is incorrect because it illustrates negative reinforcement (by completing the assignment, the student will avoid a grade of zero), but there is no removal of a negative reinforcer.

7. A

Option A is correct because the gold star would serve as a positive reinforcer. Option B is incorrect because the gold star is not a negative reinforcer. Options C and D are incorrect because punishment is not indicated.

CHAPTER 5

Competency 5: Knowledge of Multiple Literacies and Communication Skills

This chapter introduces some basic information about the development of language, reading, and communication. Impairments in these areas are described, as are strategies for enhancing their development among all children.

Skill 1

Identify language development and the components of language structure.

In this section you will find information on the components of language structure, followed by a description of typical patterns of development. The information presented in this section is informed by an important distinction between receptive and expressive language.

Receptive versus Expressive Language

Receptive language refers to the ability to understand language, while **expressive language** refers to the ability to express oneself using language.

Receptive language, or comprehension, includes the ability to understand speech, written text, and/or the elements of a sign language. Expressive language, or production, includes the ability to speak, write, and/or sign.

Receptive and expressive language each rely on somewhat independent skills. As a result, a child may have impairments in either type of skill without necessarily experiencing difficulties with both. For example, children who stutter have an expressive language impairment but their receptive language may be normal. In contrast, children with hearing impairments have a receptive language impairment yet may not experience difficulties expressing themselves. A child who is deaf, however, may experience impairments in both receptive and expressive language.

Throughout normal development, receptive language tends to be superior to expressive language. That is, at any given age, children's ability to understand language is superior to their ability to express themselves. Children understand more vocabulary, more grammar, more pragmatic rules, and so on, than may be evident in their speaking and writing.

Components of Language

Language consists of a number of components, or systems, that play an essential role in communication. The components discussed here include phonology, semantics, grammar, pragmatics, and orthography.

Phonology

Phonology refers to speech sounds. Each **phoneme** in a language consists of a distinct sound used to distinguish spoken words in the language. For example, the word "sick" consists of three phonemes–/s/, /i/, and /k/. The word "six" consists of four phonemes—/s/, /i/, /k/, and /s/. The English language contains about 45 phonemes. Although infants with normal hearing are competent from an early age at discriminating between phonemes, children initially find it challenging to analyze and explicitly identify such differences (as discussed under the topic of Phonological Awareness later in this chapter). Thus, phonological development in oral language consists of the growing ability to analyze and identify language sounds, as well improvement in the production of these sounds.

Semantics

Semantics refers to the meanings of parts of words, words, sentences, and larger units. Vocabulary acquisition is an important part of semantic development, involving changes in both expressive and receptive language. Over time, children learn new words as well as a deeper understanding of the words they already know, including the knowledge of how a word's meaning may shift to a greater or lesser extent from context to context.

Grammar

Grammar refers to the rules that govern the structure of language. Grammar can be further divided into two systems of rules, syntax and morphology.

- **Syntax** pertains to rules governing the placement of words in phrases, clauses, and sentences. Native speakers of a language understand many syntactic rules. In English, for example, when a boy enters the classroom it is acceptable to say "Steve is here now" or "Steve is now here," but it is incorrect to say "Steve here is now." When a person says "In my hand there is a miniscule . . . ," the listener knows that the word that comes next must be a noun. If the listener does not know what the word "miniscule" means, once the speaker has completed the sentence, the listener will at least understand that "miniscule" is an adjective describing a characteristic of the object in the speaker's hand.

- **Morphology** refers to rules governing the use of **morphemes**, the smallest parts of words that contribute to meaning. In English, for example, the verb "learn" takes on somewhat different meanings depending on whether we refer to someone as "relearning," "unlearning," "learning," or "having learned," because the prefixes "re-" and "un-" and the suffixes "-ing" and "-ed" each modify the basic meaning of the verb. These prefixes and suffixes are morphemes. Other examples of morphemes include the letter "s" (e.g., when placed at the end of a word to create a plural) and the word "book" (as used in words such as "bookmark," "bookshelf," and so on). Grammatical development is reflected in increasing mastery of the rules of syntax as well as morphology. As with semantic development, the acquisition of grammar is reflected in changes in both expressive and receptive vocabulary.

Pragmatics

Pragmatics can be defined as whatever contributes to meaning over and above the literal meanings of the words that are used. Many different kinds of pragmatic cues contribute to meaning. Following are just a few of the many examples:

- Contextual information often provides important clues to meaning. For example, in the sentence "Jackson searched for the bug," the word "bug" will be interpreted differently depending on whether Jackson has been previously described as afraid of insects or as a professional spy.

- Differing tones of voice often convey important differences in meaning. For example, the sentence "Why don't you visit me?" can be construed as an invitation or a complaint depending on the speaker's tone and phrasing.

- When language is used in a figurative way, as in the case of metaphor or analogy, the intended meaning of a phrase differs from the literal meaning. For example, the sentence "This classroom is like a jungle!" does not mean that the classroom literally resembles a jungle in the sense of being filled with trees and wild animals. Rather, the speaker intends to call attention to the messiness of the classroom, the chaotic behavior of the students, or some other detail.

- There are many conventions governing word choice in communicative contexts, such as how much information to convey, or what level of formality is needed. For example, students are expected to address their teachers somewhat differently from the way they speak with each other. The casual style in which they speak with each other may be inappropriate when addressing a teacher, just as the comparatively polite language used to address a teacher may seem stilted when talking with a peer.

As with semantic and grammatical development, children's growing knowledge of pragmatics is reflected in both expressive and reflective language changes.

Orthography

Orthography refers to the system of representing oral language in writing. Rules of orthography pertain to spelling, punctuation, capitalization, use of hyphens, and so on. In English, for example, children must learn the Roman alphabet and then the many rules governing letter–sound correspondences. As children learn these rules (and their many exceptions) their spelling abilities develop, and changes can be observed in both expressive and receptive language skills.

Sequence of Language Development

Normal development of expressive and receptive language proceeds somewhat predictably. Although there is much variation among children in rate of development, language- and communication-related disabilities may be indicated when a particular child lags far behind peers in rate of acquisition.

To illustrate those aspects of language development that are predictable, the following is a short list of a few of the milestones of receptive and expressive language development that can be observed from birth through age 3:

- Birth to 3 months (receptive)—Turns head toward sounds; responds to familiar voices

- Birth to 3 months (expressive)—Coos; gurgles; smiles; produces different cries for tiredness, hunger, pain

- 4–7 months (receptive)—Responds to own name; distinguishes among people

- 4–7 months (expressive)—Laughs; babbles; expresses emotion vocally

- 8 months–1 year (receptive)—Understands simple words, commands, gestures

- 8 months–1 year (expressive)—Imitates speech sounds; uses gestures such as pointing; may begin to talk

- 1 year–2 years (receptive)—Understands growing number of words

- 1 year–2 years (expressive)—Talks in one- and then two-word phrases; produces growing number of words

- 2 years–3 years (receptive)—Participates more actively in conversations

- 2 years–3 years (expressive)—Speaks intelligibly; expresses a range of emotions, desires, comments, questions

Skill 2

Distinguish characteristics of communication disorders and the impact on academic achievement and functional skills.

In this section, you will read about different types of communication deficits and the interventions that are appropriate for children who experience these deficits.

Types of Communication Deficits

Children with communication deficits exhibit a wide variety of receptive and/or expressive language symptoms, depending on the nature of the deficit. What these deficits have in common is that the child's communication is significantly poorer in some respect than would be expected for her or his age, and that the deficit interferes with academic performance and/or social communication. The severity of these deficits typically varies from child to child. For some children, the deficit is temporary, while for others it will be lifelong.

Communication deficits can be subdivided into speech impairments and language impairments, two of the categories in Florida's list of disabilities for which a student may qualify for Exceptional Student Services.

Speech Impairments

Speech impairments can be divided into four types: motor speech disorders, articulation disorders, fluency disorders, and voice disorders. These impairments tend to reflect limitations in expressive rather than receptive language skills.

Motor Speech Disorders

Motor speech disorders reflect anatomical or physiological limitations in the physical mechanisms used to produce speech. The two general categories of motor speech disorders are dysarthria and apraxia.

- **Dysarthria** is a weakness or paralysis of the musculature that controls speech, typically resulting from illness or injury. The symptoms of dysarthria vary widely and may include excessively rapid or slow rate of speech, slurred speech, distorted vowels, unmodulated pitch and/or word flow, overly nasal speech, and so on.

- **Apraxia** is an impairment in the ability to translate speech plans into actual speech. Children with apraxia know what they wish to say but their brains do not readily translate planned speech into the necessary movements of lips, tongue, and other parts of the speech apparatus. As a result, these children experience difficulties initiating speech and then producing language sounds. They may appear to be groping as they attempt to form sounds. Their utterances may exhibit abnormal rhythm, stress, and intonation, as well as errors of articulation that are not consistent each time a word is produced. Children with the disorder are aware of their speech errors and may attempt to correct themselves. If the apraxia is not the result of illness or injury, the problem is referred to as **childhood apraxia of speech (CAS).** Along with other symptoms, children with CAS will show language delays and other abnormalities beginning in infancy.

Articulation Disorders

Articulation disorders are reflected in difficulties producing certain speech sounds. The mispronunciations that occur reflect one or more of several types:

- Omissions occur when the child leaves out sounds, as in the sentence "I ha a boo" ("I have a book").

- Substitutions occur when the child uses an incorrect sound in place of the correct one. In such cases, the incorrect sound is usually easier to imitate. An example would be the child who says "wight" when attempting to say "right."

- Distortions occur when the child produces the correct sound but does not articulate it clearly, as in the case of a slight lisp.

Articulation disorders should be distinguished from the errors of articulation that young children make and usually grow out of (and from alternative pronunciations reflecting accents or dialects). Teachers should recognize that articulation errors are common among young children and do not necessarily imply the presence of a disorder.

Fluency Disorders

Fluency disorders are reflected in difficulties with the rhythm and timing of speech. Two prominent examples are stuttering and cluttering:

- **Stuttering** is a problem in which speech is disrupted by involuntary pauses, also known as blocks, as well as repetitions and/or prolongations of sounds, syllables, words, or phrases. Although all people exhibit pauses, repetitions, and prolongations from time to time, these dysfluencies are especially severe in the case of stutterers. The extent of severity varies not only across individuals but also within individuals, in the sense that stuttering is more likely in some situations than in others. Stuttering is typically developmental but may be acquired.

- **Cluttering** is a problem in which speaking rate is unusually fast and/or irregular. Fluency is affected owing to a lack of phrasing, to omissions and/or slurring of syllables, and to other dysfluencies resulting from the high rate of speed. Stuttering and cluttering may occur together, although they are distinct disorders. For example, stutterers tend to struggle, while clutterers produce streams of speech relatively effortlessly. Whereas stutterers typically know what they wish to say but have difficulty expressing themselves fluently, clutterers experience some disorganization or uncertainty in what they intend to say.

Voice Disorders

Voice disorders are manifest as difficulties in producing language sounds of appropriate quality, pitch, and/or loudness. These disorders can be subdivided into phonation disorders and resonance disorders.

- **Phonation disorders** result in excessive hoarseness, raspiness, sudden changes in volume, and/or sudden changes in pitch while speaking.

- **Resonance disorders** result in either too much or too little nasal emission of air while speaking.

Language Impairments

Language impairments can be discerned when children have difficulties in expressing their thoughts, needs or feelings, and/or in understanding what others say. Three of the main types of language impairments are phonological disorders, expressive language disorders, and mixed receptive-expressive language disorders.

Phonological Disorders

Phonological disorders refer to impairments in the ability to distinguish specific phonemes. The extent of impairment is greater than would be expected given the child's age and dialect.

Phonological disorders can be classified as impairments of language rather than speech. Although phonological and articulation disorders may both result in specific mispronunciations, articulation disorders reflect limitations in the ability to produce specific language sounds, while phonological disorders reflect limitations in the ability to distinguish phoneme contrasts. A child with a phonological disorder does not recognize differences between certain phonemes, and as a result may pronounce different phonemes the same. Unlike children with expressive language disorder or mixed receptive-receptive language disorder, the difficulties that children with phonological disorder experience are limited to specific sounds. These children may omit certain sounds, distort the sounds, or substitute one sound for another. Children with phonological disorder do not have impairments in other aspects of oral fluency such as rate, stress, pitch, loudness, and so on.

Expressive Language Disorder

Expressive language disorder, also known as **specific language impairment (SLI),** refers to expressive language abilities that are much lower than expected for age, although mental functioning and receptive language skills fall within the normal range. Expressive language disorders may be developmental and thus noticeable when the child first begins to talk, or they may be acquired as the result of disease or injury to the brain. A child with an expressive language disorder is likely to have difficulty expressing him- or herself with anything more than a few words or simple sentences. Symptoms vary from child to child and may include grammatical errors, difficulty constructing coherent sentences, limited vocabulary, and so on.

Mixed Receptive-Expressive Language Disorder

Mixed receptive-expressive language disorder refers to a disorder in which both receptive and expressive language abilities are affected. As with expressive language disorder, mental functioning falls within the normal range, and the disorder may be developmental or acquired.

Prevention and Intervention

A number of steps can be taken to help prevent speech and language impairments, including attention to signs such as delay or regression, and consideration of risk factors such as hearing impairment, a family history of communication disorders, a medical disorder such as cleft palate, and so on. A child who is suspected of having a speech or language disorder can be screened and then, depending on the results of the screening, evaluated in depth.

If the results of in-depth assessment suggest that intervention is necessary, the intervention can be direct (i.e., focused on the child) or indirect (i.e., focused on parents, teachers, or anyone else who will intervene with the child). Direct interventions in turn can be carried out with the individual child or with small groups of children.

A further distinction can be made between directive and interactive interventions, although most interventions reflect a mix of both approaches.

- **Directive interventions** are structured learning activities in which the professional responsible for the intervention models speech, prompts the child for specific responses, and offers incentives for desired responses. Through these techniques, the professional attempts to develop targeted aspects of the child's communication.

- **Naturalistic interventions** are activities carried out in day-to-day settings in which the professional responsible for the intervention makes use of opportunities for the child to learn. The professional may engage in modeling, prompting, and the use of incentives, but he or she will also allow the child's interests to influence the content of communication with the child.

Skill 3

Identify appropriate assistive technology and alternative communication systems to facilitate communication across all educational settings.

This section describes the use of assistive technologies and alternative communication systems to facilitate communication among children with communication-related disabilities.

Some terms used to describe these systems and technologies can be distinguished. First, the term **assistive technology** refers to any device that maintains or improves the functioning of individuals with disabilities. Discussed in this section are assistive technologies of direct relevance to communication (as opposed to assistive technologies such as wheelchairs and walkers that are not primarily intended to support individuals with communication-related impairments). The term **alternative communication system** refers to any system of communication other than the conventional natural language systems of reading, writing, hearing, and speech. Finally, the term **augmentative and alternative communication** is often used to describe a broader category of methods that includes both assistive technologies and alternative communication systems.

Assistive technologies and alternative communication systems can be classified in terms of the types of students they primarily support. In this section, children with visual impairments, hearing impairments, and speech or language impairments will be discussed.

Children with Visual Impairments

Traditionally, students with visual impairments were supported by the use of tactile symbols, objects, and systems of representation, the most famous of which is the **Braille** system.

Braille is not a language, but a system of raised dots. It is a code that can be used to read many languages such as English and Spanish, and even Arabic and Chinese. Blind and visually impaired children can read braille by touch, and they can create braille texts by means of special devices, including braille typewriters and computers. However, braille does not consist of a simple one-to-one representation of orthographic marks (e.g., letters) as raised dots. For example, braille is based on complex rules governing the use of contractions (e.g., the word "but" is represented with the letter "b," but the note *b* in the musical scale is represented differently). For this and other reasons, mastery of braille is a gradual process.

In recent years, students with visual impairments are being increasingly supported by special computer programs. Following are some examples:

- **Screen readers** read aloud text that is presented on a computer screen, including the main text as well as "extras" such as drop-down menus and dialog boxes.

- **Digital book readers** read books aloud and provide numerous interactive features.

- **Scan/read systems** allow printed materials to be scanned and then read aloud.

- **Screen magnification software** allows the user to magnify all or part of what is presented on a computer screen.

Children with Hearing Impairments

Students who are deaf or hearing-impaired can receive support from hearing technologies, alerting devices, and/or communication supports.

Hearing technologies enhance the volume and quality of spoken language and other sounds. Following are the two primary examples:

- **Assistive listening devices** increase volume as well as minimize the effects of background noise, the acoustics of the surrounding room, and so on. These devices can be used by individuals or groups.

- **Personal amplification devices** such as hearing aids increase the quality of sound for individuals.

Alerting devices are designed to gain the attention of an individual by means of an amplified sound, flashing light, or vibration. Such devices can be used to alert the deaf or hearing-impaired student of an emergency as well as for more routine situations such as the need to move to another part of the classroom.

Communication supports consist of technologies that facilitate communication among students who are deaf or hearing-impaired. Following are some examples:

- Conventional word-processing programs

- Conventional cell phones (with texting capacity)

- Text telephones

- Video conferencing devices and programs

- Closed captioning

- Speech-to-text translators

Finally, **sign language** is an alternative communication system that is used by many children who are deaf or have significant hearing impairments. In American Sign Language (ASL), meaning is conveyed through hand movements, bodily gestures, and facial expressions. However, just as Braille is not a simple one-to-one representation of letters and other orthographic elements, so ASL is not a simple manual representation of English. Rather, ASL represents a distinct natural language, with rules of semantics, grammar, and pragmatics that are largely independent of spoken English.

Children with Speech or Language Impairments

Along with sign language, a number of technologies are available to support children with speech or language impairments. Some of these technologies are *low-tech*, meaning that their use is relatively simple and does not require batteries or electricity, while others are *high-tech* and consist of sophisticated devices. Following are two of the most prominent examples of technologies designed specifically for speech or language impairments:

- **Communication boards** allow students to choose among photos, pictures, or symbols arranged on a board. A communication board could be as simple as a piece of paper containing pictures, in which case the student communicates by pointing to individual pictures. This "low-tech" communication board would be appropriate for a student with impaired speech who has no other disability. An example of a "high-tech" communication board would be one in which images, symbols, and/or text are presented on a computer screen, and the student makes choices by means of shifting his or her gaze. This board would be appropriate for a student who has impaired speech as well as limited mobility and is unable to point.

- **Voice output communication aids** (also known as "speech-generating devices") are devices that produce speech. What they say may be pre-recorded, produced by synthesizers, or both. Students with impaired speech but no limitations in mobility may use a keyboard or touch screen to operate such a device. Students with limited mobility may use movements of head and/or eyes to operate the device.

Skill 4

Determine the sequence of reading development and the critical components of reading proficiency included in the state standards.

This section reviews the typical progression in the development of reading. Incorporated into this review are definitions of the key components of reading development.

As children acquire reading skills, their development can be divided into stages. Following is one of many approaches to describing the stages.

Pre-Reading

Long before children know how to read, they acquire skills and experiences that will contribute to later reading development. They enjoy listening to and retelling stories, for example, and they gradually realize that certain marks in their environment convey stories and other kinds of information. Children see the marks (i.e., words) on signs, in books, and in other places, and they recognize that these printed marks are meaningful to others, even though they do not understand yet how the marks represent spoken words. Thus, young children gradually acquire **concepts of print** such as the concept that the words in a picture book convey stories, and the concept that these words are printed in an orderly, linear way (such that people read from top to bottom, and from left to right).

Learning to Read

In order to enter the "learning to read" stage, children must acquire **alphabet knowledge**, or the ability to name the letters of the alphabet and recognize these letters in print. Also critical to the emergence of reading is the **alphabetic principle**, the understanding that letters represent sounds in systematic and predictable ways. Children's understanding of the alphabetic principle is accompanied by increases in **phonological awareness**, or the ability to consciously recognize, discriminate among, and manipulate language sounds such as phonemes and syllables. Put simply, knowledge of the relationship between spoken and written words (alphabetic principle) supports and is in turn supported by awareness that spoken words are composed of units of sound (phonological awareness).

As children begin to read simple texts, most of their efforts will be devoted to **decoding**, or the sounding out of words. At the same time, high-frequency words (e.g., "you," "the," "and") will start to be recognized automatically and become part of children's growing set of **sight words.** At this stage, reading requires much support from more experienced individuals such as parents and teachers. Support will be essential for progress in decoding, comprehension, and **fluency** (i.e., the ability to read quickly, effortlessly, accurately, and expressively).

Transitional Reading

Once children have mastered the alphabet and many of the rules linking letters and letter combinations to sounds, they can read more fluently and with greater comprehension. During this transitional period, decoding skills become more advanced, and the number of sight words that children automatically recognize continues to grow. These changes allow children to read aloud with greater fluency, and to focus more on the meaning of what they read. Improvements in reading comprehension can now be seen in children's ability to infer meaning from context, make predictions about what will happen next in a story, and discuss what they have read. Most children still need support in all aspects of reading, but they can proceed with less dependence than before on teachers or other experienced individuals.

Reading to Learn

The "reading to learn" stage is marked by improvements in children's decoding skills, increases in the number of sight words they automatically recognize, and a deeper understanding of the reading process and the properties of texts. These changes allow age-appropriate materials to be readily understood. Although children are not yet reading with the same fluency or comprehension as adults, reading skills have progressed to the point that more attention can be paid to content than to the mechanics of reading. The abilities that are well-developed but continue to progress during this stage include the ability to:

- apply knowledge of letter–sound correspondences to difficult words.

- infer meaning from context.

- make predictions about what will happen in a story.

- identify text structures.

- read critically.

- shift between close reading and skimming.

- read with fluency.

- self-correct during reading.

- read independently.

Although the terms and concepts that have been discussed so far are essential to the description of how pre-readers and early readers develop, these are not the only terms and concepts of importance to planning instruction. For example, student **motivation** must be considered as well. It is important for teachers not only to promote reading skills but also to foster a positive attitude toward books and an appreciation of reading among their students. When a student seems reluctant to read, the teacher should consider the source of the student's reluctance. Following are some of the many possibilities:

- The student has poor reading skills or a reading-related disability so that reading is a perpetual struggle for the student.

- The student has a visual impairment or some other problem that is not specific to reading that makes the experience of reading difficult and unpleasant.

- The student has low self-confidence or low self-efficacy with respect to reading so that the student believes he or she will not make progress as a reader or learn much from reading texts.

- The student thinks of reading as a compulsory, class-specific activity and is not aware yet that texts of interest to him or to her can be informative and entertaining.

Skill 5

Apply specialized instructional methods and techniques to address deficits in phonological processing in students with exceptionalities.

As noted earlier, phonological awareness is the ability to consciously recognize, discriminate among, and manipulate language sounds, including syllables, onsets and rimes, vowels and consonants, and phonemes. **Phonemic awareness** can be defined as the ability to consciously recognize, discriminate among, and manipulate phonemes. Thus, phonemic awareness is a subset of phonological awareness—an important subset—because phonemes are the smallest units of sound that contribute to meaning in language. In this section you will read about instructional activities that are used to explicitly and systematically promote the development of phonological and phonemic awareness.

General Instructional Considerations

Phonological and phonemic awareness activities differ in their level of difficulty. Teachers should sequence activities so that the level of difficulty gradually increases and earlier activities provide the foundation for later activities. Generally speaking, the smaller the unit of sound on which an activity focuses, the more difficult the activity is likely to be. For example, it will be easier for young children to repeat a word than to repeat the word without the initial syllable, just as it will be easier for them to repeat a word without the initial syllable than to repeat the word without the initial phoneme.

Phonological and phonemic awareness activities also differ in the complexity of what teachers do with students. The complexity of the activity is largely independent of the difficulty. For example, asking children to repeat a word without the initial phoneme is a very simple activity, but it will be difficult at first for young children to perform successfully. By comparison, asking children to walk around the room in a circle while the teacher says words that rhyme, and to sit down whenever the teacher says a word that does not rhyme, is a more complex activity to organize yet one that would be easier for young children to perform successfully.

In general, the goals of phonological and phonemic awareness instruction are to help develop the following:

- the ability to hear and produce rhymes and alliteration
- the ability to divide sentences into words
- the ability to segment words into syllables, and to build words from syllables
- the ability to segment words into onsets and rimes, and to blend these sounds into words
- the ability to segment words into individual phonemes, and to blend phonemes into words

Following are a few examples of activities that are "simple," in the sense that they consist of nothing more than questions or requests that the teacher poses to students.

Simple Syllable Awareness Activities

- "Say the word *water*. Now say it without the *wa*."
- "How many syllables are in the word *potato*?"
- "I'm going to say the first part of the word *student* and you finish it. Ready? *Stu...*"

Simple Rhyme Awareness Activities

- "Do these words rhyme: *peek, week*?"
- "Which word does not rhyme: *cat, bell, pat*?"
- "Can you tell me some words that rhyme with *call*?"

Simple Phonemic Awareness Activities

- "What sound do you hear at the beginning of *panda*?"
- "What word do these sounds make: *rrr...ooo...mmm*?"
- "How many sounds can you hear in the word *six*?"

Following are a few examples of activities that are more complex, in the sense that they involve more than just verbal exchange between students and the teacher:

"This Old Man"

After students learn the song "This old man," the teacher guides them in singing each pair of lines and identifying the rhyming words (e.g., "one" and "thumb" in the first pair: "This old man, he played one, he played knick-knack on my thumb"). Once students have become familiar with this activity, the teacher might sing the first line of each pair and ask students to recall the rhyming word in the second line. These are phonological awareness activities that help increase student awareness of rhyme.

Word Break

Students are given connector materials such as Lego bricks or beads and told that they will be using them to break words into parts called syllables. The teacher begins by modeling the activity with a multisyllabic word, such as "barking." The teacher divides his or her own materials into two parts and indicates how each part stands for a different syllable ("bar" and "king"). At first the students follow the teacher. Once they have become familiar with the activity, they can make their own guesses as to how to divide words into syllables, and the number of syllables in the words chosen by the teacher can increase. These are phonological awareness activities that help increase children's awareness of syllables.

"I'm Going on a Trip"

The teacher says "I'm going on a trip, and I'm bringing a bird." Children take turns saying the same phrase, but they substitute another object whose name begins with the same sound (e.g., "book," "ball," etc.). When children run out of ideas, the teacher repeats the phrase with an object whose name begins with a different sound. Once children become familiar with this activity, they can try to incorporate what others have said before them. For example, if the teacher says "I'm going on a trip, and I'm bringing a bird," the child who goes first might say "I'm going on a trip, and I'm bringing a bird and a ball." The next child might say "I'm going on a trip, and I'm bringing a bird and a ball and a book," and so on. These are phonemic awareness activities that help increase children's ability to isolate phonemes.

Programs designed to teach reading can be distinguished in terms of their content and their specific role in the classroom. This section describes some of the characteristics and purposes of core reading programs, supplemental reading programs, and intensive intervention programs.

Core Reading Programs

A **core reading program** is the basic program for teaching reading in the general education classroom. Although teachers may use supplementary materials and methods as well, the core reading program is the one that all teachers will rely on to support instruction in all aspects of reading.

A strong core reading program will provide teachers with clear descriptions of the following, at least:

- Program objectives

- Scope and sequence of the program

- How program materials are organized

- How to implement instructional approaches used in the program

- How to manage specific details of program activities

- How to assess student progress in reading

In addition, if implemented appropriately, a strong core reading program will reflect characteristics such as the following:

- Explicit, systematic, balanced instruction in all reading-related skills

- Coherent instructional design

- A variety of texts, instructional approaches, and student activities

- Opportunities for student practice, participation, discussion, and feedback

- Progression from easier to more challenging activities

Supplemental Reading Programs

As the name suggests, **supplemental reading programs** are used to supplement a core reading program. The supplemental program does not replace the core program but rather supports and extends the core.

Typically, a supplemental program focuses on one or two components of reading (e.g., word identification, fluency, etc.). The supplemental program will be needed in a particular school for one of two reasons:

- If evidence suggests that the core reading program is not sufficiently effective or is not providing sufficient support for one component of reading, such as fluency, a supplemental reading program can fill in the gap.

- Individual students who are not performing well with respect to one component of reading may benefit from a supplemental reading program.

Intensive Intervention Programs

Intensive intervention programs are intended to support students with reading difficulties. These programs may focus on one, several, or all components of reading. The goal of these programs is for students to be functioning at grade level. The students who are served by intensive intervention programs may be poor readers, or they may have a reading-related disability of the sort described in the next section.

Response to Intervention

Implementation of supplemental and intensive intervention programs for reading are often carried out within a **response to intervention (RTI)** framework: a school-wide, multi-level approach to identifying students at risk for reading difficulties and other problems, monitoring student progress, and providing interventions to students who need them. RTI frameworks for intervention are discussed at length in Chapter 4.

Experts have not reached a consensus as to how to classify different types of reading difficulties. One point on which all would agree is that there is much variability in reading difficulties from child to child (and that it is more important to identify the reading skills for which a particular child needs extra support than it is to agree on how to label the child). Among children who are labeled as dyslexic, for example, there is much variability in both the nature and the severity of the symptoms.

Dyslexia is considered a learning disability that primarily affects reading. Individuals with dyslexia read at a level much lower than would be expected, given that their intelligence is at least normal. Dyslexia that can be observed in early childhood is called **developmental dyslexia,** while dyslexia that is acquired as the result of disease or injury to the brain is called **alexia.**

Following are some of the symptoms associated with dyslexia. A particular child with dyslexia is likely to exhibit some but not all of these symptoms:

- Difficulty recognizing familiar words
- Inability to decode unfamiliar words

- Difficulty segmenting words into phonemes

- Difficulty identifying or creating rhymes

- Seeing letters or words in reverse

- Seeing letters move or blur

- Dysfluency when reading out loud

- Difficulty following a sequence of instructions

- Poor spelling

- Difficulty learning a foreign language

Along with the symptoms described above, dyslexic children often exhibit characteristics such as a reluctance to read, a high rate of guessing when encountering unfamiliar words in a text, and low academic self-efficacy. These characteristics can be understood since reading is especially effortful and frustrating for these children.

Skill 6

Apply evidence-based instructional methods for increasing reading proficiencies in phonics, word recognition, and fluency that meets the specific educational and functional needs of individual students with exceptionalities.

In this section, evidence-based instructional methods will be reviewed for increasing reading proficiencies in phonics, word recognition, and fluency. Effective readers have access to a variety of processes and skills that contribute to word recognition.

Graphophonemic Knowledge

Graphophonemic knowledge is another word for the alphabetic principle, which was defined under Skill 4 as the understanding that letters represent sounds in systematic and predictable ways. Children's decoding skills develop as they learn more about letter–sound correspondences. They learn about the contributions of individual letters to the sounds of words as well as the contributions of groups of letters. Some letter groups constitute phonological units, or units of pronunciation. Following are examples of phonological units:

- **Digraphs** are pairs of letters that represent a single sound, such as "sh" and "oo."

- **Consonant clusters** are pairs of consonants that appear together in a syllable. Unlike digraphs, they do not represent a single sound. Thus, in the word "charts," the "ch" is a digraph, while the "ts" is a consonant cluster.

- **Syllables** are units of pronunciation containing one vowel sound. Some syllables contain consonants, while others do not. For example, the word "uneaten" consists of three syllables—one containing a vowel sound and a consonant ("un"), one containing a vowel sound but no consonant ("ea"), and one containing a vowel sound and two consonants ("ten").

- **Rimes** are the parts of syllables consisting of the vowel and any consonant that follows. Examples of rimes include "og" in the word "dog" and "ank" in the word "bank." (**Onsets** are the parts of syllables that precede the vowel. In the preceding examples, the onsets are "d" and "b," respectively.)

Other letter groups constitute morphemes, or grammatical units, as discussed under the heading "Structural Analysis."

Structural Analysis

Reading skills progress as children become more aware of morphemes and their role in word meaning. As discussed under Skill 1, morphemes are the smallest units of meaning in a word. There are two types:

- **Free morphemes** can stand alone as words (e.g., the word "fire" serves as a morpheme in words such as "fireworks," "bonfire," and "firefly").

- **Bound morphemes** cannot stand alone as words. Examples of bound morphemes include prefixes such as "re," "anti," and "un," as well as the letter "s," which can be added to the end of a word to indicate plural ("cats"), possessive tense ("John's"), or second person singular tense ("runs").

Structural analysis refers to the reader's use of knowledge about morphemes to help recognize familiar words, pronounce familiar as well as new words, and understand the meanings of new words. For example, a child who encounters the new word "untested" in a story can decode the word more quickly as a result of familiarity with the prefix "un" and the suffix "ed." The child's ability to infer the meaning of the word is also facilitated by knowledge of how this particular prefix and suffix contribute to word meaning. Through structural analysis of the word into a prefix, a root, and a suffix, the child's ability to decode and understand the word is enhanced.

Syntactic Cues

Syntax pertains to rules governing the placement of words in phrases, clauses, and sentences. As children's reading skills progress, they rely increasingly on syntactic clues to recognize familiar words, to anticipate upcoming words in a text, and to infer the meanings of unfamiliar words. For example, consider the following passage:

> The little tiger clambered into the boy's lap. The boy lifted the tiger. Lifting the tiger required all the boy's strength. Laughing, the boy said to himself, "This tiger is so . . .

Syntactic knowledge contributes in distinctive ways to the child's understanding of each sentence in this passage:

- In the first sentence of the passage, the word "clambered" may be unfamiliar to a young reader, but syntactic knowledge will allow the child to recognize that the word is a verb that describes an action by the tiger.

- The second sentence of the passage consists of five words. The syntax of this sentence will inform the child that it is the boy who lifted the tiger. A slight alteration in the order of these five words ("The tiger lifted the boy") would inform the child that it is the tiger who lifted the boy.

- Before the child has finished reading the final sentence of the passage, the child will know that the word or words following the word "so" will describe the tiger, and that the word or words could only represent one of a few grammatical categories (e.g., an adjective or adjectival phrase).

Semantic Cues

Semantics refers to the meanings of parts of words, sentences, and larger units. As they read a text, children make use of background knowledge as well as semantic cues given in the text in order to recognize words, anticipate upcoming words, and infer the meanings of unfamiliar words. For example, in the excerpt about the boy and the tiger presented above, a young reader is likely to infer from knowledge about animals and from the context established by the first sentence that "clambered" is a word that describes movement. Likewise, in the context of this passage, the child is likely to anticipate that the word following "so" in the final sentence will be "heavy" or something comparable in meaning.

In order to promote reading development, teachers should use a variety of instructional methods. The methods chosen should be suitable for the particular reading level of the learners. This section introduces some of the explicit, systematic instructional methods that are used to promote reading fluency in particular. As noted under Skill 5, fluency can be defined as the ability to read quickly, effortlessly, accurately, and expressively.

Practice with High-Frequency Words

Giving children practice with high-frequency words helps these words become part of their sight word vocabulary. The more sight words children can recognize, the more quickly and accurately they can read, and the more attention they can pay to reading with expression. Following are some materials and activities that teachers can use to promote the acquisition of high-frequency words:

- **Word walls** are organized lists of words placed on the wall of a classroom. The words may be arranged alphabetically or organized in some other fashion. The height of the word wall and the size of the words should allow for comfortable viewing from students' desks.

- **Word banks** consist of collections of words stored in one place (e.g., index cards in a small box) that students can use for reading practice, for consultation when writing, and so on.

- **Word games** are structured activities that allow children to make use of words they are learning. For example, in word search games, children are instructed to find particular words in written materials. In illustration games, children draw pictures that illustrate particular words or write sentences in which those words appear.

Repeated and Timed Readings

Repeated readings promote fluency by allowing students to read the same passage more than once. The readings may be performed silently or out loud, alone or in groups. **Timed readings** are repeated readings in which the amount of time spent reading each passage is recorded, and targets are set for subsequent passages. The goal of a timed reading is for the student's reading rate to increase for each subsequent reading of the same passage. For example, after the student chooses a passage of interest, the teacher might read the passage out loud and then discuss with the student what aspects of the reading reflect good fluency. Next, the student reads the passage and the teacher will help record how long the reading took. Following the student's first reading, the teacher might help the student identify words that were unfamiliar or difficult to read. The teacher and student might then choose a target reading rate for the passage, and in subsequent readings of the same passage, the student's progress toward that rate will be recorded.

Read-Alouds

As the name suggests, **read-alouds** involve reading texts out loud to children. Read-alouds benefit many aspects of children's literacy development, particularly when carried out interactively so that children have the opportunity to ask and answer questions, engage in analysis, provide commentary, and so on. Read-alouds contribute to fluency by giving the teacher an opportunity to model fluent reading. Through interactive activities during a read-aloud, students can also practice reading particular phrases, refrains, and short passages with expression.

Choral Reading

Choral reading occurs when an entire class or group of students reads together in unison, with or without the teacher. Choral reading contributes to fluency by giving students opportunities to practice reading out loud. Students who ordinarily feel uncomfortable about reading aloud can do so with less attention being drawn to them. Less fluent readers also have opportunities to hear and copy models of oral fluency in choral reading activities. Following are some of the different kinds of choral reading:

- The entire class, including the teacher, reads a passage together.

- The teacher reads a sentence from a passage, and the entire class repeats the sentence. The teacher then moves on to the next sentence.

- Students divide into groups, and each group reads a different part of a passage (following the order in which the passage was written).

- For texts such as poems, the teacher reads the main parts, and the students read the refrain.

Recorded Books

Recorded books allow students to listen to fluent reading being modeled. Students can listen, read along with the recording, or read the text after hearing part or all of it on the recording.

Skill **7**

Apply evidence-based instructional methods for increasing literacy (e.g., oral language, vocabulary, reading comprehension) in all content areas that meet the specific educational and functional needs of individual students with exceptionalities.

In this section, literacy development in the content area in relation to language, vocabulary and reading comprehension will be reviewed for students with exceptionalities.

Literacy is the ability to use language to communicate and interpret the knowledge and ideas of others, as well as our own. Literacy involves the integration of reading and writing, along with speaking, listening, viewing, and critical thinking in a variety of contexts and for a variety of purposes.

- **The purpose of literacy:** The literacy standards now found in all course descriptions are intended to enhance content area instruction by deepening student learning.

- **Literacy is not an add-on:** Content area teachers should think of literacy strategies as an integral part of their instruction and not an add-on to classroom activities.

- **Text types:** Content area teachers should be using the text types found in their specific disciplines in developing reading and writing tasks. Where possible, authentic texts should be the focus, along with simpler supporting texts when necessary to differentiate instruction.

- **Design tasks with the outcome in mind:** Determine the understandings the student product is expected to demonstrate, create a rubric or other criteria describing this, and then scaffold instruction to guide students through the process.

When supporting students' literacy development in any content area, it is important to:

1. consider what learning strategies students need to use to master the concepts and skills being taught.

2. determine what instructional strategies best fit the context.

3. make sure effective instructional routines are practiced on a regular basis.

Skill 8

Determine and apply strategies for facilitating students' critical-thinking, executive functioning, and metacognition skills.

Even before students have entered the "reading to learn" stage, teachers should provide support for their reading comprehension and critical thinking skills. This section provides information about explicit, systematic instructional methods and strategies that can provide such support. Generally speaking, reading comprehension strategies refer to anything that promotes comprehension before, during, and/or after the reading of a text.

Graphic Organizers

Some of the strategies that support reading comprehension and critical thinking depend heavily on the use of materials. For example, **graphic organizers** are visual representations of concepts and facts as well as relationships between them. Examples of graphic organizers include Venn diagrams, flow charts, cause-and-effect diagrams, story maps, and so on. A **semantic organizer** is a type of graphic organizer consisting of a central concept, to which related concepts are linked by means of branching lines. Graphic organizers can be used to illustrate a sequence of events, to analyze cause-effect relationships, to compare and contrast concepts, and to summarize the connections among related concepts. Graphic organizers support reading comprehension and critical thinking skills by providing visual representations of abstract relationships. After reading a story, for example, students can create a graphic organizer that maps out the relationships among characters, or the sequence of events in the story arranged in chronological order.

Comprehension Monitoring

Unlike graphic organizers, strategies such as comprehension monitoring, support reading comprehension and critical thinking without reliance on physical materials. **Comprehension monitoring** refers to the reader's ongoing awareness of whether the text makes sense or not. Through comprehension monitoring, the reader keeps track of how well he or she understands the text, and makes notes of characteristics such as the following:

- elements of a text that are inconsistent with each other, or with the reader's prior knowledge
- elements of a text that are unclear, ambiguous, or lacking in key information
- elements of a text that are too difficult for the reader to understand
- elements of a text that represent unwarranted conclusions or unexpected events

Comprehension monitoring is a form of **metacognition,** or thinking about one's own knowledge, mental capacities, and thought processes. Examples of metacognition include reflecting on what you have learned from a text and how well you understand it, recognizing the steps by which you drew conclusions from the text, and making note of gaps in your knowledge about the text. Thus, when you read a mystery novel, merely stating that Patricia is the thief is not an example of metacognition. Rather, metacognition would be involved when you state that Patricia is the thief but acknowledge that this conclusion reflects a bias on your part rather than incontrovertible evidence, and that if you just had one more piece of information about Patricia's whereabouts on a certain day, your conclusion might be stronger. In this example, you are not just stating knowledge about Patricia but also commenting on your thought process—on the certainty of what you know and the origins of that knowledge. Another example of metacognition would be your statement that it was easy for you to figure out that Patricia is the thief, because you are a very logical person. Likewise, it would reflect metacognition if you commented that identifying the thief was difficult for you, because logical reasoning is not one of your strengths.

Comprehension monitoring is a form of metacognition in the sense that during reading, the reader is always asking questions such as: How well do I understand? What do I know? What do I not know? To reiterate, cognition would be reflected in a statement by the reader that "Patricia behaved suspiciously on Thursday." Metacognition would be illustrated if the reader were to state "I know that Patricia behaved suspiciously on Thursday, because I have clear evidence to that effect."

Multiple-Strategy Instruction

Because reading is a complex act requiring the simultaneous use of many skills and strategies, teachers are often encouraged to teach students how to use multiple strategies during the reading process. There are a number of frameworks, or sets of strategies, that young readers can use to promote critical thinking and comprehension. An example of such a framework is the **reciprocal teaching** approach. Reciprocal teaching allows students to play the role of teacher and engages them in the conscious use of four strategies during reading:

- **Prediction:** Readers make predictions about what will occur next in a passage, and the extent to which these predictions are confirmed is noted.

- **Questioning:** Readers generate questions about parts of a text that seem difficult or confusing, or about how parts of the text are related to each other or to what the reader already knows.

- **Clarification:** Readers seek clarification about the aspects of different passages that are incomprehensible, confusing, or ambiguous.

- **Summarization:** Readers summarize part or all of the text in a way that captures the main theme or idea without including information of lesser importance.

Initially, teachers support the use of these four strategies through modeling, and through feed-back to students when they ask questions, make statements, and so on. Students may then work together in groups of four, with one student in each group designated as the Predictor, the Questioner, the Clarifier, and the Summarizer. Over time, students increasingly take the lead in carrying out this activity.

A number of other strategies besides the four noted above can support reading comprehension, including previewing a text, making inferences, and visualizing key concepts, events, and individuals. Moreover, there are a number of other frameworks that make use of these strategies. These frameworks share at least two important characteristics: Emphasis is placed on multiple strategy use by students before, during, and/or after reading, and most of the strategies that students use are metacognitive.

Skill 9

Select and use effective instructional methods and supports for teaching writing foundations, the writing process, and purposes of writing to meet specific educational and functional needs of individual students with exceptionalities across all content areas.

In this section, writing foundations, the writing process, and purposes of writing to meet specific educational and functional needs of individuals across all content areas will be reviewed for students with exceptionalities.

Writing Process

Written Language Specialized Instruction includes daily opportunities to write on students' choice of topics. Genre-specific products are taught by classroom teachers, and exceptional student education providers teach, reinforce and provide opportunities to practice a continuous writing process which includes:

- prewriting.
- drafting.
- revising.
- editing.
- publishing.

Writing Foundations and Writing for a Purpose

- Writing about what we learn helps us to understand it better and move it into long-term memory.

- Writing helps us sort out our ideas, share our thinking, document information, remember, and understand.

- Developing a foundation of academic discourse, both in speaking and in writing, allows students to collaborate, learn from others, and find the language to clearly articulate their ideas. In the workplace and in college, students will be expected to express themselves with professionalism.

- Written work provides a window into student thinking (formative assessment). For example: "Explain in one paragraph the process we studied today." The results the students hand you as they head out the door will give a quick and fairly accurate idea of what they have learned and what still needs work.

Skill 10

Apply evidence-based instructional methods for increasing mathematic skills in all content areas that meet the specific educational and functional needs of individual students with exceptionalities.

In this section, mathematical skills for specific educational and functional needs of individuals across all content areas will be reviewed for students with exceptionalities.

Evidence-Based Mathematics Instruction

Specialized math instruction focuses on building computational skills and fluency, problem solving skills and conceptual understanding through systematic, explicit and research-based instructional practices. Formative assessments are used to develop individual targets for students and identify students' strengths and needs. Assessment results guide lesson planning.

Principles of Effective Math Specialized Instruction

- Teachers use explicit instruction to model steps in the process of reaching a solution, and think aloud about the strategies used during problem solving.

- Students are given many opportunities to solve problems using the strategies taught, and receive corrective feedback from the teacher.

- Students verbalize their decisions and solutions to math problems to practice strategies and solidify skills which facilitates self-regulation. Visual representations or graphic depictions of math problems are used by teachers and students to illustrate solutions for math problems.

- Students receive, at a minimum, 20 minutes per day of additional instruction beyond the core mathematics class.

- Well-planned lessons with purposefully selected examples that cover a range of solutions presented in a sequence. Students may need to be taught skills first with concrete examples, then with pictorial representations and finally in an abstract (or symbolic) manner. Sequenced examples are beneficial for initial learning of new skills, and a range of examples supports transfer of new learning to new problem situations.

- Teachers expose students to multiple problem solving strategies which includes talking through problems with students and reflecting on students' attempts to solve problems. Students may be guided in the selection of a strategy.

- Teachers use formative assessment data and feedback on students' math performance to guide them in what to teach (learning targets), when to introduce the next skill, and how to group students.

- Students are given time to work independently and in cooperative learning groups.

- Mathematics vocabulary instruction: problem solving in mathematics requires students to use and understand math language; therefore, vocabulary must be explicitly taught and directly connected to meaningful context.

Chapter 5 Practice Quiz

1. During the first week of kindergarten, Mary's teacher observes that although Mary has no difficulty understanding requests and other verbal information, she has a definite lisp and pronounces the "s" sound as "th." What can Mary's teacher infer from this observation?

    A. Mary should be observed more closely, because she may have a receptive language impairment.

    B. Mary's lisp indicates that she has an articulation disorder and is in need of speech therapy.

    C. Mary's expressive language limitation is likely to create significant challenges to her learning.

    D. Mary may have a speech disorder or she may just need more time to learn how to pronounce "s" correctly.

2. In the word "breaking," what is the "ing"?

    A. a phoneme

    B. a morpheme

    C. a consonant

    D. a digraph

3. Following a head injury, a student experiences some paralysis in his tongue and other areas, resulting in slurred speech and distortions of certain phonemes. Which of the following is the most likely description of his impairment?

    A. dysarthria

    B. phonological disorder

    C. cluttering

    D. resonance disorder

4. When children are taught "The Alphabet Song" (a song in which the letters of the alphabet are sung in order), what do they learn?

    A. alphabetic principle

    B. alphabet knowledge

    C. phonological awareness

    D. phonemic awareness

5. A teacher engages students in an activity in which they compare the written words "sight," "light," "tight," and "fight," in order to call attention to the fact that "ight" makes the same sound in each case. What phase of decoding is the teacher attempting to promote?

    A. pre-alphabetic

    B. partial-alphabetic

    C. full-alphabetic

    D. consolidated-alphabetic

6. A kindergarten teacher reads a familiar passage out loud and asks her students to clap their hands once every time they hear the "b" sound. What skill is this activity intended to promote?

    A. awareness of syllables

    B. phonics

    C. phonemic awareness

    D. structural analysis

7. Which of the following best illustrates metacognition?

    A. reading a text slowly because one finds it enjoyable

    B. misunderstanding the meaning of a difficult passage

    C. asking oneself if the paragraph one just read makes sense

    D. reading a passage out loud at someone else's request

Explanatory Answers

1. D

Option D is correct because lisping could indicate a problem such as articulation disorder, but given Mary's age it might instead simply reflect a temporary difficulty with the pronunciation of one particular sound. Option A is incorrect because Mary's difficulty falls under the heading of expressive rather than receptive language. Option B is incorrect because, as noted, it is not certain that Mary has an articulation disorder. Option C is incorrect because it is implausible that difficulty producing one sound would impair a child's learning experience.

2. B

Option B is correct because a morpheme is the smallest unit of meaning in a word. In this case, "ing" indicates present active tense. Option A is incorrect because "ing" consists of three phonemes. Option C is incorrect because "ing" contains two consonants. Option D is incorrect because a digraph consists of pairs of letters that constitute a single sound.

3. A

Option A is correct because dysarthria is illustrated by speech impairments such as slurring and distortions as a result of paralysis to the musculature that controls speech. Option B is incorrect because phonological disorder is an impairment related to the inability to distinguish specific speech sounds. Option C is incorrect because cluttering is indicated by speech that is too fast and/ or irregular. Option D is incorrect because resonance disorder is indicated by too much or too little nasal flow during speech.

4. B

As "The Alphabet Song" only teaches children the names and sequence of the letters in the alphabet, Option B is the correct answer. Option A is incorrect because the alphabetic principle consists of knowledge that letters represent sounds in systematic ways. Option C is incorrect because phonological awareness pertains to the ability to discriminate among and manipulate language sounds. Likewise, option D is incorrect because phonemic awareness is related to the ability to discriminate among and manipulate phonemes.

5. D

Option D is correct because the consolidated-alphabetic phase involves the understanding of how groups of letters function as units. Option A is incorrect because children have not begun the process of decoding in the pre-alphabetic phase. Options B and C are incorrect because in either phase, any decoding that takes place is carried out letter by letter.

6. C

Option C is correct because the activity helps children develop the ability to isolate specific phonemes in the flow of speech. Option A is incorrect because the "b" sound does not consistently correspond to a syllable. Option B is incorrect because phonics is related to letter–sound correspondences. Option D is incorrect because structural analysis is related to the identification of morphemes.

7. C

Option C is correct because monitoring one's own comprehension is a form of metacognition, or reflecting on one's own knowledge, mental abilities, and thought processes. Options A, B, and D are incorrect because they do not illustrate a conscious reflection of one's own thought process.

CHAPTER

Competency 6: Knowledge of the Transition Process

6

This chapter discusses **transition planning**—the supports and services that are designed to help students with disabilities shift from life in a secondary school environment to adult life in the community.

Transition Planning

IDEA and Transition

IDEA requires that transition planning be coordinated by the IEP team, which includes the student and the parents, and that the student must be invited to any IEP meeting in which transition-related issues are considered. Specifically, IDEA requires that when a student with a disability turns 16, if not earlier, the student's IEP must include a description of goals for employment, education, and other significant dimensions of postsecondary life. These postsecondary goals must reflect two characteristics:

- The postsecondary goals must be measurable, meaning that whether or not they are achieved will be directly observable. For example, "enrolling in business-related courses at the local community college within one year of graduation" would be a measurable goal.

- The postsecondary goals must be based on age-appropriate transition assessments that reflect the student's particular strengths, interests, preferences, and needs.

The IEP must also contain a description of transition services (including courses of study) that will be needed to help the student achieve his or her postsecondary goals. **Transition services** consist of a set of activities that facilitate transition. These services must reflect several characteristics:

- Transition services must be coordinated, in the sense of converging on common goals (e.g., independent living), rather than being separate activities.

- Transition services must be tailored to the individual student— i.e., based on the transition assessments noted above.

- Transition services must be results-oriented and foster the development of academic and adaptive life skills that will help students become engaged in a variety of personal, social, educational, and occupational activities following school. "Results-oriented" means that the transition services must focus on creating improvements in the student's ability to function during postsecondary life.

- The transition services themselves may consist of instruction, community experiences, employment assistance, postsecondary adult living support, and so on.

Postsecondary Goals and IEP Goals

During transition planning, the IEP team will develop specific IEP goals that support the student's progress toward his or her postsecondary goals. For example, if the postsecondary goal is for the student to "enroll in business-related courses at the local community college within one year of graduation," the specific IEP goals might be for the student to have done the following by a certain time:

- accurately summarize the published admissions criteria for the college

- accurately state the admissions deadlines for the college

- identify three business-related courses in the college that the student would be eligible to take, and that would serve the student's stated interests

Skill 1

Determine appropriate programs for career development and career and technical education that meet the needs of individual students with disabilities.

This section discusses the activities that support career development, one of the critical areas of focus in transition planning.

Student knowledge about careers and career-related activities change over time. Four stages of career development that are often discussed include career awareness, career exploration, career preparation, and career placement. These stages overlap somewhat, and the kinds of activities that support one stage tend to support the other stages as well (assuming age-appropriate modifications to each activity).

Career Awareness

During the career awareness stage, students become aware of the purpose of work and of the existence of an increasing number of different types of jobs. During this time they also become increasingly aware of personal interests, strengths, and goals that may be relevant to later work experiences. Activities that support career awareness include the following:

- lessons, instructional materials, and other resources that provide information about different professions

- field trips and classroom visits that provide opportunities to interact with people from different professions

- discussions and activities that promote work-related values such as cooperation and a collaborative attitude

- encouragement to reflect on personal strengths and interests and how they might relate to the performance of certain kinds of jobs

Career Exploration

During the career exploration stage, students become increasingly knowledgeable about the characteristics, social importance, and interconnectedness of different types of jobs. Activities that support career exploration include those described above in connection with career awareness, as well as the following:

- critical reading of autobiographies, biographies, and work-related narratives

- authentic activities with work-related themes

- informal and formal assessments of vocational skills and interests

Career Preparation

During the career preparation stage, students acquire more detailed information about job opportunities and how various educational and vocational training experiences might prepare them for these jobs. As they are now on the verge of graduation, students will need to decide soon whether to work after graduation or to pursue further education or training. Activities that support the career preparation stage include those mentioned in connection with the previous two stages, as well as the following:

- opportunities for interviewing professionals

- opportunities for shadowing professionals in the workplace

- assistance with job search

- assistance with the evaluation of different job opportunities

- instruction in appropriate interview behavior

Career Placement

During the career placement stage, students acquire jobs through their own efforts and with support from the IEP team, school staff, and possibly also community agencies such as the vocational rehabilitation agency. Follow-up efforts will be needed, given that individuals may need additional education or training, and given that their career-related interests and priorities may evolve.

Skill 2

Use results of transition assignments to determine appropriate planning strategies to assist the student, parents, caregivers, and stakeholders in developing postsecondary education, career goals, and post-school outcomes.

This section touches on some of the resources and strategies available to assist students as they transition into postsecondary environments, particularly those involving employment and independent living. Some of these resources and strategies are school-based, in the sense of being provided by the IEP team and others in the secondary school setting, while others are provided by individuals and agencies in the community.

School-Based Support for Transition

School-based resources and strategies that provide transition support to students include the following:

- training in self-determination and self-advocacy
- social skills training
- psychological services
- community experiences
- opportunities for work experience
- vocational guidance
- higher education-related guidance

Individual Support for Transition

Transition can be facilitated by the addition of key community members to the IEP team, or by involving these individuals in the collaborative task of providing support to the student. Following are some of the important roles that can be played by these individual community members:

- role model
- mentor
- informational resource
- service provider
- advocate
- liaison between agencies

As this list suggests, individual community members can play a variety of different roles during the transition process and in supporting postsecondary living.

Agency Support for Transition

Successful transition can also be facilitated by the involvement of community agencies. For example, **independent living centers** are local, nonresidential agencies that help individuals with disabilities lead self-sufficient lives. A specifically work-related example is the **vocational rehabilitation agency,** a federal- and state-funded agency that provides employment-related services to students who qualify. The vocational rehabilitation agency in Florida is the Florida Department of Education's Division of Vocational Rehabilitation. This agency provides services such as the following:

- career counseling and guidance
- résumé development
- postsecondary training and education
- job placement
- job coaching and training
- assistive technology
- supported employment

Supported Employment

Supported employment is a community-based approach to promoting the employment of individuals with disabilities in integrated settings (i.e., those in which a substantial number of employees do not have disabilities) through various kinds of support. For example, in the **Individual Placement and Support (IPS)** approach, supported employment teams housed within community agencies provide coordinated services to individuals with disabilities, beginning with the development of a plan for seeking employment, and continuing with job search assistance, interview training, and on-the-job support.

Coordination of Support

As noted at the outset of the chapter, the school- and community-based resources and strategies used to facilitate postsecondary goals should be coordinated, in part because each individual's goals will tend to be related. An individual with limited mobility, for example, will have transportation needs that include access to stores (in order to achieve domestic living goals) as well as access to the workplace (in order to achieve employment goals). For this individual, the achievement of transportation goals may be related to decisions about place of residence, place of employment, allocation of personal finances, and so on. Thus, transportation needs should not be considered an isolated problem during transition planning.

Skill 3

Select instructional approaches to assist students with exceptionalities to engage in self-determination and self-advocacy practices.

This section introduces the characteristics and promotion of self-determination and self-advocacy skills, both of which are extremely important to an individual's functioning beyond the classroom.

Self-Determination

Self-determination refers to the ability to make choices for oneself. Through self-determination, an individual can function independently. Adaptive life skills depend on general self-determination abilities such as the following:

- the ability to set goals

- the ability to choose actions that will help achieve goals

- the ability to monitor progress toward goals and make adjustments as necessary

Examples of specific self-determination behaviors include:

- choosing what foods to eat

- choosing what clothing to wear

- choosing which service provider to use

- choosing how to budget money

- choosing how to spend free time

- choosing who to establish friendships with

- choosing where to seek employment

- choosing when to seek assistance

- choosing when to reject advice

Promoting Self-Determination

Teachers can use a number of strategies to promote self-determination among students with disabilities, including the following:

- maintain positive expectations for students

- facilitate students' self-esteem

- help students identify their own strengths and interests

- teach students about their own disabilities

- teach students planning skills

- provide students with information about choices

- teach students strategies for obtaining information about choices

- provide students with opportunities to make meaningful personal choices

- provide guidance for students' personal choices

- allow students to make independent choices

- positively reinforce students' planning and choice-making behaviors

- allow for mistakes and negative outcomes for students' choices

Each of the strategies in this list can be supported in multiple ways by the teacher. To take just one example, in order to foster a student's self-esteem, the teacher should engage in a variety of activities such as the following:

- model positive self-esteem

- create opportunities for student success

- encourage increasing student independence

- help the student recognize his or her strengths and achievements

- use praise and other positive reinforcers judiciously

Self-Advocacy

Self-advocacy includes the ability to assert one's own needs and to obtain assistance in meeting those needs. Students with disabilities will use self-advocacy skills in order to meet the kinds of needs that anyone might have (e.g., obtaining a particular product in a store) as well as to meet needs related specifically to their disabilities (e.g., obtaining accommodations for which they are eligible).

Need for Self-Advocacy Skills

Students with disabilities who are weak in one or more adaptive life skill may face significant challenges in school and in their lives beyond school. The support that these students can obtain from people around them may be lacking in some key respect such as the following:

- Parents or school staff may have low expectations for a student's future independence and productivity.

- A student may have little or no awareness of successful role models who share the same disability.

- The student may have limited informational support from parents or school staff whose knowledge of disability rights laws is lacking.

- Parents or school staff may be unable to provide adequate support for the student in some specific respect.

Students with disabilities thus need self-advocacy skills not only as a means of self-expression, but also to help ensure that they can achieve their potential when environmental support is lacking.

Promoting Self-Advocacy

Students' self-advocacy is fostered by the promotion of self-determination, as described above, and by the enhancement of other skills related to the ability to independently assert and gain assistance with one's needs. Following are some examples of how teachers can promote self-advocacy:

- Encourage students to communicate their needs.

- Encourage students to express their ideas, attitudes, and interests.

- Provide guidance to students, as appropriate, for effective communication of needs, ideas, and so on.

- Positively reinforce students for assertiveness and appropriate self-expression.

- Provide students with opportunities for self-advocacy and leadership activities.

- Teach students about the social and occupational experiences of individuals with disabilities.

- Teach students about legal rights and responsibilities pertaining to disabilities.

- Encourage student communication of disability-related needs.

- Teach students how to obtain informational and service-related resources for individuals with disabilities.

Integration of Approaches

As this chapter suggests, teachers can use a variety of specific strategies to promote self-determination and self-advocacy among students with disabilities. In practice, teachers and other educational professionals often use approaches that integrate specific strategies. For example, **person-centered planning approaches** support the transition to life beyond graduation by helping students achieve their goals for the future. A person-centered planning team (including the student), will help the student articulate goals, pursue his or her goals with increasing independence, identify community members and resources that can be of support, find ways to increase the student's participation in the community, and otherwise empower the student to achieve his or her goals and dreams.

Skill 4

Identify and compare resources and strategies that can assist individual students with disabilities to function independently in postsecondary education, home and community living, and employment.

This section includes a brief introduction to instructional procedures for teaching adaptive life skills.

Multiple approaches to assessment are needed to determine the adaptive life skills for which a student needs the most support. Chapter 2 discusses some of the more common types of assessment. Based in part on assessment results, instructional methods for teaching adaptive skills will need to be chosen. A variety of methods are available, and the choice of methods will depend on the types of needs revealed by prior assessment.

Regardless of which instructional methods are used, hands-on activities and modeling will be essential to the learning process, given that adaptive life skills tend to require independent action. Group work and role play will be important too, given the social nature of some adaptive life skills. Finally, authentic activities and community learning will be critical given that adaptive life skills reflect applied knowledge that contributes to functioning in natural settings. These strategies (hands-on activities, modeling, group work, role play, authentic activities, and community learning) are not fully independent of each other, nor do they reflect the same level of analysis in the classification of instructional strategies, but together they illustrate some of the most effective instructional procedures for teaching adaptive life skills.

Hands-on Instruction

Hands-on instruction refers to a broad category of instructional strategies in which students learn by actively applying the knowledge or skills being taught rather than passively listening to the teacher. Hands-on instruction is essential for learning skilled behaviors because mastery of these behaviors requires performing them rather than merely understanding how they are performed. Thus, hands-on activities are central to instruction in adaptive life skills involving skilled behaviors, such as cooking, grooming, and so on.

Modeling

Modeling refers to the process of learning through observation. Modeling contributes to the learning of both physical and verbal behaviors. Thus, modeling can be a useful strategy for teaching a variety of adaptive life skills ranging from self-care routines to verbal strategies for effective communication with others. In practice, modeling and hands-on instruction will be closely connected because the teacher will often demonstrate a behavioral skill for students (and provide commentary) before giving students the opportunity to practice what they have been observing.

Group Work

A variety of instructional activities can be implemented within the context of **group work,** in which groups of two or more students work together in their efforts to achieve a common goal. Because group work requires individual initiative, collaborative interactions among group members, and progress toward a shared goal, any group work activity will provide students with the opportunity to practice social and occupational skills. Thus, group work activities will help students develop adaptive life skills such as conflict resolution, cooperation, and so on.

Role Play

In **role play** activities, students each assume the identity of a character other than themselves in order to act out a narrative, or they pretend to be themselves as they respond to others in a fictional setting. Role play benefits adaptive life skills involving communication and social functioning, because cooperation is required in order to carry out the role play, perspective-taking and empathy are fostered by assuming the identity of another individual, and imagining oneself responding to others in a fictional setting promotes thinking about social interactions and social relationships.

Authentic Activities

Authentic activities are tasks that are identical or highly similar to meaningful real-life tasks. A distinctive characteristic of authentic activities is that they reflect the ultimate purpose of instruction. The purpose of learning how to add and subtract, for example, is not merely to solve addition and subtraction problems on a test, but to use these mathematical operations to solve real-world problems such as balancing a budget. Instructional approaches that incorporate authentic activities are inevitable when teaching adaptive life skills because practice with these skills constitutes an authentic activity.

Community-Based Instruction

As the name suggests, **community-based instruction** consists of instructional activities that take place in community settings. Instructional activities are grounded in meaningful, everyday tasks—in effect, they are authentic activities carried out in the community. However, community-based instruction is not the same as a field trip. A field trip consists of a visit to a community setting for the purpose of extending instruction. Community-based instruction consists of repeated visits to a community setting in which instruction takes place and is cumulative over time. Community-based instruction is an especially effective means of teaching adaptive life skills, as students can be given the opportunity to practice the skills in these actual settings in which they will some-day be applied.

The Role of Explicit, Systematic Instruction

Although some adaptive life skills consist of learned physical behaviors, others depend in part on the application of basic academic skills such as literacy and numeracy. For this reason, explicit, systematic instruction in these skills contributes to the development of adaptive life skills. To take just one example, the ability to read the following kinds of information will contribute to an individual's functioning in a variety of settings:

- signs
- instructions
- labels
- application forms
- contracts
- policies
- informational resources

The Role of Differentiation

Teachers differentiate instructional methods and strategies for individual students depending on each student's strengths and needs, as well as on the types of skills being supported. For example, with respect to adaptive life skills that require complex physical behaviors, the teacher will need to consider whether the student has any physical limitations that would prevent him or her from performing the behavior. Limitations in the student's attention, memory, understanding, or impulse control may need to be considered when selecting the instructional approach. The teacher will need to decide on the amount of scaffolding initially needed, and student progress will then help determine the tempo of instruction and the rate at which fading occurs (see Chapter 3 for definition).

Chapter 6 Practice Quiz

1. According to the requirements of IDEA, which of the following would be an acceptable post-secondary goal for student John?
    A. With support from his parents, John will develop a considerably more positive outlook on life.
    B. John will be able to get around town successfully, with very little assistance from friends and family.
    C. John will join one organization that promotes cycling, one of his favorite leisure activities.
    D. Before graduation, John will identify a community college to which he may be eligible to apply.

2. Laura is a blind elementary school student who has begun thinking about the kinds of careers that would suit her. Which of the following actions would best promote Laura's growing self-determination?
    A. encouraging Laura's teacher to use authentic activities when teaching Laura
    B. asking Laura's parents to discuss careers and career choices with her
    C. helping Laura develop academic skills that will support her choice of careers
    D. inviting Laura to join the IEP team and participate in planning discussions

3. Which of the following resources would most benefit a high school junior who has entered the career preparation stage and has been learning about the postsecondary training needed to become an auto mechanic?
    A. the autobiography of an automobile executive who began his or her career as a mechanic
    B. a field trip to a local garage in order to observe mechanics at work
    C. a documentary about careers in auto mechanics and related fields
    D. the opportunity to shadow an actual mechanic in his or her place of work

4. Marla is a ninth grader who is paralyzed from the waist down as the result of a childhood injury. Marla's academic performance in middle school and ninth grade is average in all subjects except for mathematics. Marla has made straight A's in every math class she has taken, and her achievement test scores in mathematics are exemplary. In Marla's first discussions with her IEP team about her postsecondary plans, which of the following is among the points that should be raised by the team?

    A. Marla should be discouraged from applying to college, in spite of her excellent academic performance in the subject of math, because her overall grade point average is only average.

    B. Marla should be asked about her interest in practical applications of mathematics, in order to determine whether a career that relies at least to some extent on mathematical skills might appeal to her.

    C. Marla should be made aware of the fact that relatively few women choose careers in mathematics, and that those who do must be courageous in order to overcome gender discrimination in the field.

    D. Marla should be complimented on her mathematical performance, and encouraged to take more advanced mathematics classes in anticipation of college work in some mathematical field.

5. Which of the following students seems to need the most support for self-determination skills?

    A. a student who prefers to be alone and devises strategies for working in isolation from peers and otherwise avoiding social interaction

    B. a student who is experiencing anxiety because she has no preferences as to what career she might pursue following graduation

    C. a student who is unsure which peer to ask for help with a math problem because he cannot tell which one has stronger math skills

    D. a student who is quite rigid in her decision-making process and rarely revisits her decisions once they have been made

6. Lina is a high school senior with a mild emotional disturbance. An IEP team determines that one of Lina's postsecondary goals should be to establish a relationship with an experienced individual in order to obtain regular, on-the-job support concerning non-technical matters (e.g., getting along with co-workers). In particular, Lina needs to find someone she can call for guidance when she becomes frustrated or angry. The IEP team decides that the most suitable individual for this role would be Lina's guidance counselor at school because all agree that Lina has an excellent relationship with the counselor. What is likely to be the main limitation of the IEP team's choice?

   A. The guidance counselor is unlikely to know much about issues that Lina will face in the workplace.

   B. The guidance counselor will probably be unwilling to help Lina further once she graduates.

   C. The guidance counselor may not have time to help Lina at the times when she needs immediate support.

   D. The guidance counselor may provide the wrong kinds of advice to Lina in critical situations.

7. Which of the following agencies would provide the most career-related counseling to an individual with a disability?

   A. independent living center

   B. disability rights organization

   C. assistive career service

   D. vocational rehabilitation agency

Explanatory Answers

1. C

Option C is correct, because it identifies one clear, measurable, postsecondary goal. Options A and B are incorrect because they are too vague to be readily measurable; it is unclear what exactly it means to have a "more positive outlook" or to be able to "get around town" successfully. Although Option D is a measurable goal, it is not a postsecondary goal, and thus this option is incorrect as well.

2. D

Option D is correct, because participation in IEP planning with the IEP team would allow Laura to exercise choices about issues of direct personal relevance. Although authentic activities can promote self-determination, they do not automatically do so, and thus Option A is incorrect. Likewise, discussions with parents may, but do not necessarily, promote self-determination, and thus Option B is incorrect. Option C is incorrect because the teacher will promote academic skills anyway, and doing so will not automatically foster self-determination.

3. D

Option D is correct, because it would allow the student to have significant experience observing and interacting with a mechanic during an ordinary work day. Options A, B, and C each consist of resources that would be useful to the student, but none of them would be likely to provide as much specific, career-related information as the shadowing opportunity provided by Option D. Moreover, Options A, B, and C would not allow the same extent of interaction as the opportunity to shadow a working mechanic.

4. B

Option B is correct, because the IEP team's first conversations with a student about postsecondary plans should include, among other things, an attempt to learn more about the student's interests. Although Marla's mathematics achievement suggests that a career relying to at least some extent on mathematical skills would be a good fit with her particular academic strengths, it does not follow that Marla particularly enjoys mathematics or would desire such a career. Option A is incorrect because it is excessively negative and based on questionable assumptions about the likelihood of Marla attending college. Option C is also incorrect owing to the negativity of its theme. Like Options A and C, Option D is incorrect because it presupposes a particular postsecondary interest on Marla's part, when the purpose of the IEP team's conversation with her should be to learn more about her interests.

5. B

Although anxiety about future careers is commonplace among students, Option B is correct because the student is not even able to articulate her preferences for her future career. Option A is incorrect, even though the student's behavior is problematic, because the student seems to have no difficulty formulating a goal (being alone) and implementing strategies for achieving that goal. Option C is incorrect, because even though the student is experiencing difficulty making a choice, there is a good reason for uncertainty. Option D is incorrect because the student appears to have no difficulty making decisions.

6. C

Option C is correct, because Lina needs someone she can call upon during regular business hours without prior notice, and the guidance counselor is likely to be busy on many of the occasions that Lina calls. Option A is incorrect because Lina needs non-technical support, particularly concerning issues that upset her, and the guidance counselor most probably understands the workplace well enough to appreciate the context for those issues. Option B is incorrect because there is no reason to suppose that the guidance counselor, with whom Lina has an excellent relationship, is completely unwilling to provide extra support. Option D is incorrect because anyone, regardless of background, could conceivably provide less-than-ideal advice in a critical situation. There is no reason to suppose that the guidance counselor is more likely than any other experienced individual to provide bad advice.

7. D

Option D is correct, because career-related counseling is among the many services provided by a vocational rehabilitation agency. Although an independent living center might assist with career counseling, such centers provide non-vocational services as well, and thus Option A is incorrect. Although a disability rights organization might direct an individual to a career counseling service, Option B is incorrect because such services are not part of the mission of such organizations. Option C is incorrect because there are no agencies that are routinely identified as "assistive career services."

PRACTICE TEST 1

FTCE Exceptional Student Education K–12

Also available at the REA Study Center (*www.rea.com/studycenter*)

This practice test is also offered online at the REA Study Center. Since all FTCE exams are computer-based, we recommend that you take the online version of the test to simulate test-day conditions and to receive these added benefits:

- **Timed testing conditions**—help you gauge how much time you can spend on each question
- **Automatic scoring**—find out how you did on the test, instantly
- **On-screen detailed explanations of answers**—gives you the correct answer and explains why the other answer choices are wrong
- **Diagnostic score reports**—pinpoint where you're strongest and where you need to focus your study

Answer Sheet

1. Ⓐ Ⓑ Ⓒ Ⓓ
2. Ⓐ Ⓑ Ⓒ Ⓓ
3. Ⓐ Ⓑ Ⓒ Ⓓ
4. Ⓐ Ⓑ Ⓒ Ⓓ
5. Ⓐ Ⓑ Ⓒ Ⓓ
6. Ⓐ Ⓑ Ⓒ Ⓓ
7. Ⓐ Ⓑ Ⓒ Ⓓ
8. Ⓐ Ⓑ Ⓒ Ⓓ
9. Ⓐ Ⓑ Ⓒ Ⓓ
10. Ⓐ Ⓑ Ⓒ Ⓓ
11. Ⓐ Ⓑ Ⓒ Ⓓ
12. Ⓐ Ⓑ Ⓒ Ⓓ
13. Ⓐ Ⓑ Ⓒ Ⓓ
14. Ⓐ Ⓑ Ⓒ Ⓓ
15. Ⓐ Ⓑ Ⓒ Ⓓ
16. Ⓐ Ⓑ Ⓒ Ⓓ
17. Ⓐ Ⓑ Ⓒ Ⓓ
18. Ⓐ Ⓑ Ⓒ Ⓓ
19. Ⓐ Ⓑ Ⓒ Ⓓ
20. Ⓐ Ⓑ Ⓒ Ⓓ
21. Ⓐ Ⓑ Ⓒ Ⓓ
22. Ⓐ Ⓑ Ⓒ Ⓓ
23. Ⓐ Ⓑ Ⓒ Ⓓ
24. Ⓐ Ⓑ Ⓒ Ⓓ
25. Ⓐ Ⓑ Ⓒ Ⓓ
26. Ⓐ Ⓑ Ⓒ Ⓓ
27. Ⓐ Ⓑ Ⓒ Ⓓ
28. Ⓐ Ⓑ Ⓒ Ⓓ
29. Ⓐ Ⓑ Ⓒ Ⓓ
30. Ⓐ Ⓑ Ⓒ Ⓓ

31. Ⓐ Ⓑ Ⓒ Ⓓ
32. Ⓐ Ⓑ Ⓒ Ⓓ
33. Ⓐ Ⓑ Ⓒ Ⓓ
34. Ⓐ Ⓑ Ⓒ Ⓓ
35. Ⓐ Ⓑ Ⓒ Ⓓ
36. Ⓐ Ⓑ Ⓒ Ⓓ
37. Ⓐ Ⓑ Ⓒ Ⓓ
38. Ⓐ Ⓑ Ⓒ Ⓓ
39. Ⓐ Ⓑ Ⓒ Ⓓ
40. Ⓐ Ⓑ Ⓒ Ⓓ
41. Ⓐ Ⓑ Ⓒ Ⓓ
42. Ⓐ Ⓑ Ⓒ Ⓓ
43. Ⓐ Ⓑ Ⓒ Ⓓ
44. Ⓐ Ⓑ Ⓒ Ⓓ
45. Ⓐ Ⓑ Ⓒ Ⓓ
46. Ⓐ Ⓑ Ⓒ Ⓓ
47. Ⓐ Ⓑ Ⓒ Ⓓ
48. Ⓐ Ⓑ Ⓒ Ⓓ
49. Ⓐ Ⓑ Ⓒ Ⓓ
50. Ⓐ Ⓑ Ⓒ Ⓓ
51. Ⓐ Ⓑ Ⓒ Ⓓ
52. Ⓐ Ⓑ Ⓒ Ⓓ
53. Ⓐ Ⓑ Ⓒ Ⓓ
54. Ⓐ Ⓑ Ⓒ Ⓓ
55. Ⓐ Ⓑ Ⓒ Ⓓ
56. Ⓐ Ⓑ Ⓒ Ⓓ
57. Ⓐ Ⓑ Ⓒ Ⓓ
58. Ⓐ Ⓑ Ⓒ Ⓓ
59. Ⓐ Ⓑ Ⓒ Ⓓ
60. Ⓐ Ⓑ Ⓒ Ⓓ

61. Ⓐ Ⓑ Ⓒ Ⓓ
62. Ⓐ Ⓑ Ⓒ Ⓓ
63. Ⓐ Ⓑ Ⓒ Ⓓ
64. Ⓐ Ⓑ Ⓒ Ⓓ
65. Ⓐ Ⓑ Ⓒ Ⓓ
66. Ⓐ Ⓑ Ⓒ Ⓓ
67. Ⓐ Ⓑ Ⓒ Ⓓ
68. Ⓐ Ⓑ Ⓒ Ⓓ
69. Ⓐ Ⓑ Ⓒ Ⓓ
70. Ⓐ Ⓑ Ⓒ Ⓓ
71. Ⓐ Ⓑ Ⓒ Ⓓ
72. Ⓐ Ⓑ Ⓒ Ⓓ
73. Ⓐ Ⓑ Ⓒ Ⓓ
74. Ⓐ Ⓑ Ⓒ Ⓓ
75. Ⓐ Ⓑ Ⓒ Ⓓ
76. Ⓐ Ⓑ Ⓒ Ⓓ
77. Ⓐ Ⓑ Ⓒ Ⓓ
78. Ⓐ Ⓑ Ⓒ Ⓓ
79. Ⓐ Ⓑ Ⓒ Ⓓ
80. Ⓐ Ⓑ Ⓒ Ⓓ
81. Ⓐ Ⓑ Ⓒ Ⓓ
82. Ⓐ Ⓑ Ⓒ Ⓓ
83. Ⓐ Ⓑ Ⓒ Ⓓ
84. Ⓐ Ⓑ Ⓒ Ⓓ
85. Ⓐ Ⓑ Ⓒ Ⓓ
86. Ⓐ Ⓑ Ⓒ Ⓓ
87. Ⓐ Ⓑ Ⓒ Ⓓ
88. Ⓐ Ⓑ Ⓒ Ⓓ
89. Ⓐ Ⓑ Ⓒ Ⓓ
90. Ⓐ Ⓑ Ⓒ Ⓓ

91. Ⓐ Ⓑ Ⓒ Ⓓ
92. Ⓐ Ⓑ Ⓒ Ⓓ
93. Ⓐ Ⓑ Ⓒ Ⓓ
94. Ⓐ Ⓑ Ⓒ Ⓓ
95. Ⓐ Ⓑ Ⓒ Ⓓ
96. Ⓐ Ⓑ Ⓒ Ⓓ
97. Ⓐ Ⓑ Ⓒ Ⓓ
98. Ⓐ Ⓑ Ⓒ Ⓓ
99. Ⓐ Ⓑ Ⓒ Ⓓ
100. Ⓐ Ⓑ Ⓒ Ⓓ
101. Ⓐ Ⓑ Ⓒ Ⓓ
102. Ⓐ Ⓑ Ⓒ Ⓓ
103. Ⓐ Ⓑ Ⓒ Ⓓ
104. Ⓐ Ⓑ Ⓒ Ⓓ
105. Ⓐ Ⓑ Ⓒ Ⓓ
106. Ⓐ Ⓑ Ⓒ Ⓓ
107. Ⓐ Ⓑ Ⓒ Ⓓ
108. Ⓐ Ⓑ Ⓒ Ⓓ
109. Ⓐ Ⓑ Ⓒ Ⓓ
110. Ⓐ Ⓑ Ⓒ Ⓓ
111. Ⓐ Ⓑ Ⓒ Ⓓ
112. Ⓐ Ⓑ Ⓒ Ⓓ
113. Ⓐ Ⓑ Ⓒ Ⓓ
114. Ⓐ Ⓑ Ⓒ Ⓓ
115. Ⓐ Ⓑ Ⓒ Ⓓ
116. Ⓐ Ⓑ Ⓒ Ⓓ
117. Ⓐ Ⓑ Ⓒ Ⓓ
118. Ⓐ Ⓑ Ⓒ Ⓓ
119. Ⓐ Ⓑ Ⓒ Ⓓ
120. Ⓐ Ⓑ Ⓒ Ⓓ

PRACTICE TEST 1

Time: 2 hours and 30 minutes
  120 questions

Read each question and select the option that best answers the question.

1. Which of the following best describes least restrictive environment (LRE)?

    A. specially designed instruction provided in exceptional student education classrooms

    B. services offered in the public school by support staff

    C. all students taught core academic subjects by teachers who are highly qualified in content areas

    D. a setting as similar as possible to that of students without disabilities in which a student with a disability can be educated with appropriate supports provided

2. Brandon enters the third-grade classroom and begins to stare ahead blankly. He rocks back and forth and makes sounds that are high pitched. When approached by peers he screams and retreats into a corner of the classroom. Brandon has autism. What models of support in accessing the general education curriculum are available for students like Brandon?

    A. No models of support are available for Brandon to access the general education curriculum.

    B. Support staff, such as a behavior specialist, ASD specialist, and paraprofessionals, provide collaborative services as well as social and communication skills.

    C. Brandon can access the general education classroom in all special areas, during lunch, and during social events.

    D. Brandon is placed in a general education classroom and a paraprofessional is provided to assist him daily.

3. An IEP team concludes that an individual may be functioning in the range of an intellectual disability. In order to see how a student is performing in comparison to other students his age, the team members decide which of the following should be included on his assessment plan?

    A. criterion-referenced test

    B. error analysis

    C. standard error of measurement

    D. norm-referenced test

4. IDEA 2004 places more emphasis on assessing *all* students in attaining the standards, leading to more students being included in a(n)

    A. resource room.

    B. general education class.

    C. ESOL room.

    D. assessment resource classroom.

5. Kristin is a third grade student with an intellectual disability. She has just been placed in Mrs. Smith's third grade class. Students in her class are learning their multiplication facts. Kristin is eager to participate in class but instead of allowing Kristin to do the same activity as the other students, Mrs. Smith gives her a worksheet that she obtained from a colleague who teaches kindergarten. Which of the disadvantages of labeling is exemplified by her actions?

    A. The label is causing Mrs. Smith to lower her expectations of Kristin's performance.

    B. The label is being used to address her behavior.

    C. The label is being used to explain her lack of interaction with peers.

    D. The label is being used to limit her resources.

6. Rob is a student with a disability who belongs to a neighborhood gang. He is involved in an argument with another student in math class. Later that night, Rob attends a school-sponsored basketball game. Other students report that Rob has a knife and is threatening to stab a student he argued with earlier. Rob is removed from the basketball game. Members of the IEP team decide to place Rob at an alternative school for 45 days. Were Rob's rights violated?

    A. No, the IEP team made the decision to remove Rob, so multiple perspectives were considered.

    B. No, schools have the right to remove students who bring weapons to school without a hearing.

    C. Yes, a student with a disability cannot be removed from school for more than 10 days.

    D. Yes, a manifestation determination hearing must be conducted before Rob can be removed.

7. Mrs. Abraham is a member of the Down Syndrome Association and is attending an IEP meeting for John, at the request of his parents. As a member of the IEP team and teacher of exceptional students, Mrs. Andrews is nervous about sharing her evaluations of John in front of the advocate as she is uncertain of Mrs. Abraham's role in the IEP meeting. What type of information can Mrs. Abraham provide at the request of the parents?

    A. additional resources and services provided by the Down Syndrome Organization

    B. a decision that this placement is inadequate

    C. a change in setting for John

    D. a paraprofessional for John

8. Maria has a daughter who has developmental delays and has completed the Early Steps program. What type of paperwork is completed after the transition conference?

   A. Individualized Education Plan

   B. Transition Plan (Form I of the IFSP-Individualized Family Support Plan)

   C. Voluntary Pre-Kindergarten Education Program

   D. Children's Medical Service Plan

9. In 1997, a revised funding model for Exceptional Student Education was established and is known as

   A. mental health treatment and services.

   B. School Medicaid Match.

   C. Matrix of Services.

   D. School Readiness Program.

10. The program enacted in 2004, which is designed to prepare four-year-old children for kindergarten and lay the foundation for their success is known as which of the following?

    A. School Readiness Program

    B. Child Care Services Program

    C. VPK Education Program

    D. Family resource specialists

11. John pulled the fire alarm during lunch at school last week. John is identified as having EBD (Emotional Behavior Disorder). The IEP team is conducting a Manifestation Determination Review. Why is this meeting being held?

    A. to determine if a student's misbehavior is a result of his disability

    B. to discuss academic concerns

    C. to help a student with visual impairments

    D. to determine a setting in which the student will receive needed services

12. A group of people from the school or school district that may attend an eligibility staffing include all of the following EXCEPT

    A. school psychologist.

    B. regular classroom teacher.

    C. ESE teacher.

    D. siblings' medical professional.

13. Jane has placed her daughter, Abigail, in the Early Steps program for the past year. Now that her daughter is turning three, she needs to change her current placement. Under IDEA 2004, Part C, what services may be available for Abigail in the school district?

    A. VPK Education Programs

    B. Individual Education Services

    C. Hospital Homebound Services

    D. Vocational Services

14. Federal law (IDEA) requires that all students be included in statewide testing. An exception to this law includes

    A. accommodations in the administration of the statewide assessment.

    B. a small number of students with significant cognitive disabilities who take the Florida Standards Alternate Assessment.

    C. some students who work and are not required to perform assessments.

    D. the end-of-course exams.

15. Professionals who are itinerant teachers

    A. travel between two or more school sites to provide services to students.

    B. offer knowledge about the entire school community.

    C. complete work under the direction of teachers.

    D. help prepare students to leave school for vocational training.

16. Select the statement that does NOT apply to a well-designed learning center.

    A. Students are more actively engaged in learning.

    B. Students increase proficiency in skills acquired.

    C. Students apply knowledge and skills to novel situations.

    D. Students must have assistance from the classroom teacher.

17. Scaffolding is a support process during which students eventually apply new skills independently. Which of the following statements regarding scaffolding would be most descriptive of students with disabilities?

    A. Begin with what the students can do.

    B. Help students achieve success quickly.

    C. Help students "to be" like everyone else.

    D. Help students to be independent when they have command of the activity.

18. Students with disabilities will have detailed planning of their education and related services in a document known as an IEP. Monitoring of these special services must take place

    A. at an annual review.

    B. at a three-year reevaluation.

    C. quarterly.

    D. No review is necessary.

19. Which statement does NOT apply to curriculum-based assessment (CBA)?

    A. It measures students' level of achievement in terms of what they are taught in the classroom.

    B. Results are used to guide instruction.

    C. The performance of the student is compared to the average performance of students who are the same age or grade level.

    D. It is an accurate indicator of student access to the general education curriculum.

20. John has entered first grade at Oakwood Elementary. Mrs. Jones, his teacher, notices that he omits verbs, puts the wrong ending on a word, and has incomplete vocabulary development for his age. She is concerned that he may have a(n)

    A. attention deficit hyperactivity disorder.

    B. emotional disorder.

    C. intellectual disability

    D. language impairment.

21. Jan, a third grader, has difficulty sitting still, never waits for her turn, and is constantly interrupting others. She is displaying characteristics of

    A. impulsivity.

    B. inattention.

    C. hyperactivity.

    D. hyperactive-impulsive.

22. Which organization is responsible for publishing a definition and classification manual that emphasizes systems of support for individuals with intellectual disabilities?

    A. Autism Society of America

    B. The Arc of the United States

    C. The American Association on Intellectual and Developmental Disabilities

    D. National Down Syndrome Congress

23. Tasks presented within real-world contexts that lead to real-world outcomes are known as

    A.   daily activity logs.

    B.   psychological tests.

    C.   authentic learning tasks.

    D.   portfolio assessments.

24. Paraeducators should share information about a student only when

    A.   the school administrator says it is permissible.

    B.   the intended receiver is working with the student and has direct need of it.

    C.   the student does not mind if it is shared.

    D.   the parent asks that the information be shared.

25. The mechanism used to ensure that students have met state standards is

    A.   effective instruction.

    B.   instructional supervision.

    C.   effective leadership.

    D.   standardized testing.

26. Mr. Repp could have asked his students to compute the mileage between several cities using a mileage key. Instead, he has them create their own maps within a real context because he wants to see how well they can apply what they have learned to an actual problem. This would be an example of

    A.   criterion-referenced assessment.

    B.   norm-referenced assessment.

    C.   performance-based assessment.

    D.   portfolio assessment.

27. Assessments that give us some idea of what students need to know to achieve grade-level performance are referred to as

    A.   diagnostic assessments.

    B.   curriculum-based measurement.

    C.   progress monitoring.

    D.   norm-based assessments.

28. A collection of approaches that promote nondiscriminatory assessment practices is known as

    A. culturally responsive assessment.

    B. language variation.

    C. sheltered English.

    D. standard English language learners.

29. The term that describes children having been wrongly placed in exceptional student education programs that deny them appropriate educational interventions is

    A. cultural bias.

    B. disproportionate representation.

    C. curriculum alignment.

    D. incongruity between teachers and diverse students and families.

30. Crystal was referred for a comprehensive evaluation due to classroom performance. It was determined at the eligibility meeting that she was not eligible for exceptional student education services but needed alternative planning in order to be successful in the general education classroom. What document will the team need to write for Crystal?

    A. Individualized Education Plan

    B. 504 Plan of Accommodations

    C. Transition Plan

    D. No documentation is needed.

31. A second-grade student recently enrolled in your school. The student is a recent immigrant from Mexico. Your school determines that the child had not previously been enrolled in school in Mexico due to his parents' lack of funds and due to a lack of transportation to school. The student's mother has recently obtained citizenship. Once the child began to attend your school, it was determined that the child could not read in English or Spanish. What documentation needs to be written based on this information?

    A. Individualized Education Plan

    B. 504 Plan of Accommodations

    C. Alternative Instructional Plan

    D. No documentation should be written.

32. The process of requiring students to demonstrate that they have met specified state standards and holding teachers responsible for students' performance is best described as

    A. standardization.

    B. proficiency.

    C. accountability.

    D. adoption.

33. Parental signature, which grants permission to proceed through the eligibility, classification, and placement process and indicates that parents have been made aware of their due process rights, is referred to as

    A. mediation.

    B. notice.

    C. pre-referral intervention.

    D. informed consent.

34. Parents being fully notified in their native language of all educational activities to be conducted during a nondiscriminatory evaluation of their child is called

    A. procedural safeguard.

    B. parental consent.

    C. informed consent.

    D. eligibility determination.

35. A classroom teacher, along with a team of other educational professionals, determined that John, who has multiple disabilities, is not able to participate in the statewide assessment. The team develops which of the following to assess John's attainment of educational goals?

    A. Individualized Education Plan

    B. Transition Plan

    C. Alternative Assessment

    D. Authentic Assessment

36. The Teacher Assistance Team of a middle school receives a referral regarding a student who seems to have behavioral difficulty in only one of his classes during the day. In order to determine what is happening in this one classroom, the team decides that a(n) ___ should be conducted.

    A. observation
    B. assessment
    C. intervention
    D. meeting

37. Elisabeth's teacher gives a spelling test at the end of each week to determine student mastery of the words. This type of assessment is considered a

    A. criterion-related assessment.
    B. criterion-referenced assessment.
    C. curriculum-based assessment.
    D. curriculum-based measurement.

38. Kevin is a third grader who continues to sound out many words when he reads and reads very slowly. He uses so much effort in identifying the words that he frequently misses the main points of the story. He concentrates his effort on unlocking the word rather than on reading the word automatically. Kevin's main barrier to comprehension is his

    A. background knowledge.
    B. fluency.
    C. self-monitoring skills.
    D. vocabulary knowledge.

39. Students with disabilities who are unable to participate in statewide assessments are tested using

    A. portfolio assessment.
    B. alternative assessment.
    C. cognitive assessment.
    D. summative assessment.

40. Ms. Cooper is preparing a lesson on how to find the area of a rectangle. Before beginning the lesson, she gave her students a multiplication probe and discovered that almost half the class was still having problems with multiplication facts. What is Ms. Cooper's next step?

    A. Introduce finding the area of a rectangle as scheduled.

    B. Set up a tutoring program in which students who knew their facts are paired with students who do not; pairs practice facts for 10 minutes a day for a week.

    C. Use a calculator.

    D. Complain to her colleague that her class does not know multiplication facts.

41. An elementary school student with severe physical disabilities requires adult assistance with feedings. Which of the following information would be most important for the student's exceptional student education teacher to know in this situation?

    A. whether the student can partially hold eating utensils or cups

    B. how much food and liquid the student commonly consumes at home

    C. whether the student has demonstrated preferences for certain foods

    D. what type of consistency the student's foods and liquids should be

42. If a story reads, "Charlie went to the store, and bought a box of cookies. On his way home he stopped by his friend's house and shared the cookies with his friend, Tom. Tom was happy, and gave Charlie a ball. Charlie went home to show his ball to his brother." The chronological order would be:

    A. Charlie shared cookies with Tom, Charlie went to the store, bought a box of cookies, Tom gave Charlie a ball, and Charlie went home to show his ball to his brother.

    B. Charlie went to the store, bought a box of cookies, went home to show his ball to his brother, Tom gave Charlie a ball, and Charlie shared cookies with Tom.

    C. Charlie went to the store, bought a box of cookies, shared cookies with Tom, got a ball from Tom, and went home to show the ball to his brother.

    D. Charlie went home to show the ball to his brother, Charlie went to the store, bought a box of cookies, shared cookies with Tom, and got a ball from Tom.

43. Professional organizations attempt to influence public policy by each of the following means EXCEPT

    A. filing amicus briefs with the courts.

    B. testifying before Congress.

    C. running for public office.

    D. lobbying state and federal legislators.

44. When focusing on comprehension, if students pay close attention to whether or not the text is making sense to them, they are using the comprehension strategy known as

    A. question generating.

    B. clarifying.

    C. scaffolding.

    D. modeling.

45. What approach to instruction is extending the concept of language experience throughout the grades by immersing students in reading, writing, talking, listening and viewing activities?

    A. language-experience approach

    B. basal reading approach

    C. integrated language arts approach

    D. literature-based approach

46. It is important that you, as a classroom teacher, provide effective reading instruction and support to all your students, including those who struggle with reading. Which is NOT a feature of effective reading instruction?

    A. using appropriate and ongoing screening, assessment, and progress monitoring

    B. providing intensive instruction

    C. collaborating with the reading specialist/special education teacher

    D. obtaining early intervention when needed

47. Strategic competence is an aspect of mathematical proficiency. Of the following, choose the phrase that best describes strategic competence:

    A. understanding mathematic concepts and operations

    B. being able to accurately and efficiently conduct operations and mathematics practices

    C. ability to formulate and conduct mathematical problems

    D. thinking about, explaining, and justifying mathematical work

48. An essential characteristic of effective instructional practices is that of differentiated instruction. Which of the following does NOT apply to differentiated instruction?

    A. providing materials and tasks at varied levels of difficulty

    B. using whole-class direct instruction

    C. varying levels of instructional support

    D. varying evaluation strategies

49. Following the teaching practice as it was provided in the research is called

    A. instructional accommodations.
    B. differentiated instruction.
    C. treatment fidelity.
    D. instructional modifications.

50. In 1990, what two disability categories did IDEA add?

    A. Autism and pervasive developmental disorder
    B. Pervasive developmental disorder and down syndrome
    C. Autism and traumatic brain injury
    D. Down syndrome and traumatic brain injury

51. When you begin teaching, you will be required to work with standards in the content areas you teach. When working with standards, what will be your *first task*?

    A. Interpreting the meaning of the state standard
    B. Designing learning activities to help your students meet the mandates of the state standard
    C. Designing assessments to help determine whether your students have met the state standard
    D. Deciding how to integrate the state standard with other content areas

52. Mr. Jones explains to the students how they should work in pairs. First, he models what he would like them to do and then explains four different activities in a row. Throughout his 30-minute explanation, he provides several examples. He prompts them to listen by saying, "Settle down, and pay attention please. We have a lot to get through today." He becomes frustrated when his students fidget and lose attention. He could improve his instruction by

    A. providing scaffolding and further modeling.
    B. limiting teacher talk and increasing opportunities for student response.
    C. writing the instructions on the board as he talks.
    D. prompting students to listen before each example.

53. When a target behavior transfers across settings, persons, and materials, which stage of learning has been completed?

    A. maintenance
    B. entry
    C. acquisition
    D. generalization

54. Bruce has ADD and follows a schedule that lists all of the tasks that he needs to do during class time. If he completes the tasks, he gets five extra minutes on the computer at the end of the day. Using the computer is his favorite activity. Which of the following is being used to increase Bruce's on-task behavior?

    A. negative reinforcement

    B. shaping

    C. extinction

    D. positive reinforcement

55. What is the purpose of using independent learning as a grouping format?

    A. to allow students to practice a skill that they have already learned

    B. to allow students to learn new skills independently

    C. to allow students of different levels to assist each other

    D. to allow students to work collaboratively

56. A benefit of consultation and collaboration includes

    A. increased time for lesson planning.

    B. a streamlined approach to teaching.

    C. reduced caseload management for special education teachers.

    D. reduced mislabeling of kids as disabled.

57. Mrs. Robbins is a fourth-grade teacher who has several students in her class who struggle with reading. The exceptional student education teacher gives her some ideas on how to modify their assignments and homework. Mrs. Robbins is resistant to make these accommodations because she believes that all students should receive the same assignments and everyone should be expected to do the same work. After all, when these students finish school, they will not get accommodations, so why should they now? What dilemma is illustrated by Mrs. Robbins's situation?

    A. individual versus class focus

    B. content versus accommodation

    C. real world versus the student's world

    D. new roles for exceptional student education teachers

58. All of the following are true about family and school collaboration EXCEPT

    A. family involvement and collaboration is fundamental to students' success.

    B. the focus of any discussion should be on the needs and wants of the family and student and not on their values.

    C. most family members try to provide poor parenting.

    D. family and school collaboration can increase if you accept the family and student as they are.

59. Mr. Halpern is about to start a unit on the American Civil War. He has several students with learning disabilities in his class and some students who are English language learners. What is his first step in getting ready to teach the chapter?

    A. Have the students make predictions about what will happen in the chapter.

    B. Instruct the students to make graphic organizers of the framework of the chapter.

    C. Select the major concepts and related vocabulary to be taught.

    D. Have the students preview the chapter.

60. Students who have auditory discrimination difficulties may benefit from

    A. electronic books.

    B. direct instruction.

    C. the whole-language approach.

    D. speech to text programs.

61. Mr. Jones will begin a unit on the American Civil War. He introduces supplemental print reading materials. These supplemental materials are known as

    A. basal readers.

    B. textbooks.

    C. trade books.

    D. software.

62. Data from progress monitoring should be reviewed systematically to make necessary adjustments in intervention. One process that works hand-in-hand with progress monitoring is

    A. functional behavior assessment.

    B. initial identification.

    C. universal screening.

    D. initial screening.

63. An exceptional student education teacher provides reading instruction to a small group of second-grade students. Each student has Individualized Education Program (IEP) goals related to increasing their sight word vocabulary and fluency. Which of the following assessment procedures should the teacher use to monitor the students' progress toward these goals?

   A. administering an informal reading inventory to each student monthly

   B. developing individual portfolios in which each student collects a list of mastered sight words weekly

   C. conducting an error analysis of each student's oral reading monthly

   D. reviewing data on each student's reading accuracy and speed on a graph weekly

64. When a teacher keeps written notes of a student's actions or words, gathered while they happen or shortly after, the teacher is completing a(n)

   A. permanent product recording.

   B. duration recording.

   C. anecdotal recording.

   D. event recording.

65. A curriculum-based assessment provides information primarily about a student's

   A. eligibility for special education services.

   B. progress in acquiring specific academic skills.

   C. aptitude for future academic success.

   D. ability to use assistive technology to perform academically.

66. When students are taught to monitor their own behavior, make judgments about its appropriateness, and change it as needed, they are implementing

   A. positive reinforcement.

   B. extinction.

   C. a behavior contract.

   D. cognitive behavior management strategies.

67. A continuum of policies and procedures implemented throughout the school for all students is called

   A. response to intervention.

   B. positive behavior support.

   C. culturally responsive teaching.

   D. positive reinforcement.

68. A student is taught to observe and record a peer's behavior and provide the peer with feedback. This describes which of the following?

   A. peer tutoring

   B. peer support and confrontation

   C. positive peer reporting

   D. peer monitoring

69. When students are suspended for more than 10 days, the school must

   A. provide a free public education for the student.

   B. arrange a formal hearing (with advance notice of time, place, and procedure).

   C. give an oral or written notice of charges and an opportunity to respond to charges.

   D. take no action as the school has no particular obligations in this situation.

70. It is important to follow the established basal and ceiling levels when administering a standardized achievement test to

   A. develop the student's individualized instructional objectives.

   B. determine the student's grade equivalency.

   C. rank the student's abilities among peers.

   D. focus on the student's specific range of academic skills.

71. The courts recognize the importance of giving teachers and school administration authority over student behavior. This is called

   A. *in loco parentis.*

   B. procedural due process.

   C. manifest determination.

   D. Individualized Education Plan.

72. Which of the following terms best completes this sentence: "Behaviors that are precisely defined are stated in terms that are _____ and _____"?

   A. measurable . . . appropriate

   B. appropriate . . . subjective

   C. observable . . . measurable

   D. clear . . . frequent

73. An exceptional student education teacher works with Doug, a third-grade student with a mild intellectual disability. Doug often hugs peers and adults when he sees them, and some of his classmates have stated that they are not comfortable with hugging. The exceptional student education teacher is planning to work with Doug to reduce this behavior. Which of the following strategies would be most effective in addressing this goal?

   A. using a verbal cue (e.g., "use your words") to remind Doug not to hug others and asking other teachers to do the same

   B. teaching Doug appropriate ways to greet others and having him practice these greetings throughout the school day

   C. talking with Doug about his classmates' reactions to being hugged and encouraging classmates to tell him if he makes them feel uncomfortable

   D. providing Doug with a list of appropriate verbal and physical greetings (e.g., handshake, saying hello) to refer to throughout the day

74. Event recording should be used when the target behavior

   A. is long in duration.
   B. is continuous.
   C. is discrete and uniform in duration.
   D. rarely occurs.

75. A term of measurement that involves the amount of delay before behavior is initiated after a direction is given is

   A. latency.
   B. duration.
   C. frequency.
   D. rate.

76. What is the objective of all behavior change?

   A. increase instructional time in the classroom
   B. all students learning in a safe and peaceful environment
   C. benefit the student's self-discipline or self-control
   D. increase test score and district rating on score cards

77. The first step of the behavior change process is to

   A.   collect baseline behavior.

   B.   select a target behavior.

   C.   identify reinforcers.

   D.   evaluate the effects of intervention.

78. An exceptional student education teacher and a general education teacher will be co-teaching a second-grade class, and they are planning activities for the first day of school. Which of the following strategies would be most effective for the teachers to use in promoting positive interactions between students?

   A.   creating questions for students to use in interviewing each other to find out specific information, then having students share the results of these interviews with the class

   B.   asking each student to bring in a favorite family photograph to post on a classroom bulletin board

   C.   pairing students who are known to be quiet with students who are known to be more outgoing to work together on various tasks and play together at recess

   D.   assigning students to write a paragraph about their likes and dislikes to read aloud to the class

79. Cathy has a class of 12th graders in her Biology II classroom. She notices that one of her students, Louis, is acting silly and being very disruptive. Cathy realizes that Louis is seeking attention and will attempt to engage the class in disruptive behavior. What strategy would best be used by Cathy in this scenario?

   A.   extinction/ignoring disruptive behavior by the teacher and the class

   B.   using a social script to highlight desired behavior

   C.   using differential reinforcement throughout the day

   D.   providing social skills instruction to the entire class

80. A fourth-grade teacher is concerned that an English language learner's academic achievement is significantly below grade level. The pre-referral team decides to try providing the student with an aide to translate assignments. The teacher is also asked to keep anecdotal records regarding the student's informal verbal interactions with classmates. The pre-referral team's actions are likely to be most useful for providing information about

   A. whether the student's academic difficulties are related to language difference.

   B. whether the student is motivated to achieve in school.

   C. whether the student's learning style is compatible with the teacher's instructional style.

   D. whether the student is exhibiting a delay in social-emotional development.

81. The ability to read a restaurant logo is one of the first literacy accomplishments of a preschool child. This happens in which development of word learning?

   A. partial-alphabetic phase

   B. full-alphabetic phase

   C. consolidated-alphabetic phase

   D. pre-alphabetic phase

82. When children can unlock the pronunciation of unknown words they are in the

   A. pre-alphabetic phase.

   B. partial-alphabetic phase.

   C. full-alphabetic phase.

   D. consolidated-alphabetic phase.

83. When the teacher says "I am thinking of words that end with the same sound. Listen to the words: tan, fan, man, ran." The teacher is modeling

   A. rhyming.

   B. segmenting speech sounds.

   C. blending speech sounds.

   D. adding printed letters.

84. The correspondence between letters and sounds is known as

   A. morphemic.

   B. graphophonemic.

   C. syntactic.

   D. semantic.

85. Researchers who have studied children's acquisition of English grammatical morphemes have found that

    A. there is great individual variation across children.

    B. order of acquisition is determined by the frequency with which each morpheme is heard.

    C. all 14 morphemes studied are mastered in the early stages of language development.

    D. most children acquire the morphemes in roughly the same order.

86. Which of the following best practices would be most beneficial for a middle school student struggling with fluency?

    A. Fluency Development Lesson (FDL)

    B. support reading strategy

    C. cross-age reading

    D. oral recitation

87. Which of the following activities would best teach vocabulary acquisition in depth?

    A. defining the word

    B. restating the definition in the student's own words

    C. finding an antonym

    D. fitting the word in a sentence

88. "Apple is to fruit as carrot is to vegetable" is an example of a(n)

    A. synonym.

    B. antonym.

    C. analogy.

    D. multiple-meaning word.

89. Reflecting on what you have learned from a text and how well you understand it is an example of

    A. prediction.

    B. metacognition.

    C. using a graphic organizer.

    D. using a semantic organizer.

90. Lee is a first-grade student with cerebral palsy who uses a communication board with speech output. He will soon begin receiving instruction in a general education classroom for part of each school day. Which of the following steps should Lee's exceptional student education teacher take first to promote his communication skills within the new classroom environment?

    A. assigning the students in the general education class to write questions about Lee's communication board and having him answer the questions on his first day in class

    B. asking the general education teacher to discuss with the class different ways which people communicate, including using communication boards

    C. having Lee introduce himself to the general education class and explain how and when he began using the communication board

    D. ensuring that the general education teacher understands how Lee uses the communication board before his transition into the class

91. If a student decodes words through regular letter patterns such as *dish*, *fish*, *wish*, *swish*, which phonics instruction is the teacher using?

    A. synthetic

    B. linguistic

    C. implicit

    D. analytic

92. Jim is a seven-year-old who often has difficulty communicating about topics that are not in his immediate environment. For example, while trying to describe his weekend trip with his family to an amusement park, he couldn't remember the words for roller coaster or Ferris wheel, so he called them the "fast thing" and the "round thing." Based on this information, with which aspect of language does Jim have difficulty?

    A. syntax

    B. phonology

    C. morphology

    D. semantics

93. Sandra is a third grader who often uses nonspecific words (e.g., thing, stuff) for specific words. Sandra most likely has a

    A. word-finding problem.

    B. phonological deficit.

    C. receptive language delay.

    D. pragmatic deficit.

94. When planning a language program for students with delayed language skills, begin by

    A. adhering closely to a language curriculum.

    B. determining what knowledge and skills a student has already acquired.

    C. focusing on receptive language before expressive language.

    D. focusing on expressive language before receptive language.

95. Which type of intervention is delivered to persons who do not yet show signs of a communication disorder?

    A. compensation

    B. remediation

    C. consultation

    D. prevention

96. Any device that maintains or improves the functioning of individuals with disabilities is known as

    A. decoding.

    B. assistive technology.

    C. intervention methods.

    D. fluency.

97. Conventional word-processing programs, closed captioning, and text telephones for students who are deaf or hearing impaired are considered which of the following?

    A. sign language

    B. speech impairments

    C. communication supports

    D. Braille

98. Which concept is found in the pre-reading stage of reading development?

    A. decoding

    B. concepts of print

    C. alphabet principle

    D. fluency

99. Differentiated small-group reading lessons are characterized by

    A. group memberships that remains consistent throughout the school year.

    B. the use of different text and activity levels for each group.

    C. a focus on oral language activities.

    D. the use of standardized assessments.

100. When students frequently read orally and face criticism for being incorrect, they

    A. pay little attention to meaning.

    B. learn to read the words fluently.

    C. develop automatic recognition of words.

    D. learn to use context as a means of word identification.

101. Recent, widely accepted research on reading instruction indicates that

    A. there is no instructional difference due to method.

    B. the whole-word method has produced somewhat better results.

    C. there is not enough statistical data to arrive at a conclusion.

    D. underlying skills such as phonemic awareness and facility with letter–sound correspondences are crucial.

102. Progress monitoring students with curriculum-based measures allows teachers to

    A. assess students' higher-order thinking skills.

    B. revise the intervention if it is ineffective.

    C. work with smaller groups of students.

    D. effectively utilize all specialists in the classroom.

103. Which form of assessment is designed to identify students' reading strengths and weaknesses?

    A. screening

    B. progress monitoring

    C. diagnostic

    D. outcome

104. An exceptional student education teacher meets twice a week with Carla, a ninth grader who has a learning disability. When reviewing the notes Carla has taken to prepare for a geography report, the teacher sees that they are excessively detailed and do not distinguish between major ideas and minor points. The teacher's best response in this situation, would be to

A. show Carla how to use a more telegraphic style when she takes notes.

B. provide Carla with index cards to limit the amount of space available for taking notes.

C. remind Carla that she can use a photocopier for sections of a source that require extensive note-taking.

D. teach Carla how to use text headings and subheadings to focus her note-taking on key concepts.

105. Cara cannot read very well but has an excellent speaking voice. After her group wrote a report on the 2016 presidential election, Cara was given the task of presenting the report to the whole class. Which statement best identifies this scenario?

A. It gives the student responsibility.

B. It gives the student a chance to show her strengths.

C. It teaches the student to reinforce herself.

D. It sets a reasonable goal for the student.

106. Self-determination is one of the most important skills for students with disabilities who wish to pursue postsecondary education. Which attribute would NOT be a factor in succeeding in higher education?

A. The student increases self-awareness by investigating his or her disability.

B. The student must have realistic goals.

C. The student must have self-advocacy skills.

D. The student must have appropriate academic preparation.

107. If a student is expressing an interest in attending karate class at the local YMCA, what type of instructional procedures could determine successful adaptive life skills at this location for the student?

A. interviews and questionnaires

B. ecological assessment that involves carefully examining the environment in which the activity actually occurs

C. complete a mapping form from the parents

D. curriculum-based assessment

108. A tenth-grade student with posttraumatic stress disorder will soon return to school after receiving six weeks of inpatient psychiatric care. The student is stabilized, but unrelated stressors have the potential to trigger angry outbursts and symptoms of depression. Which of the following strategies should the exceptional student education teacher implement first to prevent the student from experiencing unnecessary anxiety?

    A. meeting with the student and reviewing the school's code of conduct

    B. requesting that the student's parents meet with their son each morning to review his daily schedule

    C. establishing a predictable routine for the student with advanced notice of changes

    D. providing a quiet area in the school where the student can go to calm down

109. An initial evaluation has been completed on a fourth-grade student who has been struggling in mathematics. Based on the student's present level of educational performance, the Individualized Education Program (IEP) team finds the student eligible for exceptional education services. Which of the following components must be included in the students' IEP?

    A. a detailed plan for fully supporting the student's upcoming transition to fifth grade

    B. a description of how the team plans to monitor the student's progress

    C. a statement naming a designated service coordinator to implement the program

    D. a statement reflecting the family's desired academic outcome for the student

110. A sixth-grade student with attention-deficit/hyperactivity disorder (ADHD) is having significant difficulty getting started on a long-term writing assignment given by her English language arts teacher. The student tells her exceptional student education resource room teacher that she feels overwhelmed by the assignment, cannot find any information about the topic, and thinks she might not write the report. Which of the following responses from the exceptional student education teacher would likely be most effective in this situation?

    A. asking the library media specialist to research and locate information for the student on her assigned writing topic

    B. working with the student and the English language arts teacher to break down the assignment into smaller, more manageable parts

    C. scheduling a meeting with the student and her parents to discuss her negative attitude toward the assignment

    D. suggesting that the English language arts teacher provide the student with a different topic for the writing assignment

111. A middle school English language arts (ELA) teacher comes to the exceptional student education teacher for advice about Ana, a student with a learning disability in writing. The ELA teacher says that while Ana writes fluently and has many original ideas, her inattention to punctuation makes her work difficult to read. The exceptional student education teacher has worked with Ana on punctuation and seen significant improvement on exercises and drills in the resource room. The exceptional student education teacher's best response would be to suggest that the ELA teacher

    A. send Ana to the resource room to review final drafts for punctuation errors before submitting her work.

    B. set a short period aside each day for Ana to work on punctuation exercises.

    C. hold Ana accountable for punctuation errors when grading her work, as articulated in the IEP.

    D. have Ana and a classmate exchange final drafts and correct each other's punctuation errors.

112. It is best practice for students to be active members of their IEP team. Select the best statement that describes the self-determination skills needed by students who are actively involved.

    A. Students who are self-determined overcome fears and speak up for themselves regarding what they want in life and what is needed to succeed.

    B. Students who are self-determined do not need to be present during IEP meetings.

    C. Students who are self-determined are always punctual.

    D. Students who are self-determined allow other team members to make decisions for them.

113. Which of the following activities would likely be most difficult for an eight-year-old student with a mild intellectual disability?

    A. recognizing the letters within his or her first name

    B. following basic two-step oral directions

    C. using a previously learned skill in a new setting

    D. matching two similar objects together

114. The ultimate goal for young adults with disabilities is to be competitively employed. Which of the following statements is NOT a key characteristic that will increase the likelihood of successful employment outcomes for the students?

   A.   Curriculum stresses functional skills.

   B.   Opportunities to learn the interpersonal skills necessary to work effectively with colleagues are ample.

   C.   Unpaid and volunteer work experience is valuable for students with disabilities.

   D.   Prepare students with disabilities through career education at the high school level.

115. James is investigating his community recreation center to determine what types of after-work activities he can participate in. He is considering playing team sports. He needs to look at how to sign up for these activities as well as how much it will cost him to participate. James lives in a residential living facility and is assisted by residential personnel. What essential domain of transition planning activity is James involved in?

   A.   person-social

   B.   general community functioning

   C.   employment

   D.   leisure-recreational

116. Which of the following activities would be included in the general community-functioning domain of transition planning?

   A.   shopping, transportation, banking

   B.   assessment, plan, instruct, and evaluate

   C.   assistive technology

   D.   job shadowing, internship

117. Which activity would be included in the employment domain of transition planning?

   A.   attending the career fair at the community college

   B.   speaking to the guidance counselor about vocational education

   C.   developing budgeting skills with the ESE teacher

   D.   receiving training in clothing care

Question 118 is based on the following scenario.

Vong is a 15-year-old sophomore of Hmong descent. He has ADHD and is often impulsive and easily distracted. He is included in most academic classes with peers. He is inquisitive and enjoys math and science. Vong's IEP team learned, from a questionnaire that he and his family completed with the help of an interpreter, that Vong enjoys NASCAR events and building model race cars. His mother thought Vong might also enjoy the high school's cross-county team. As a result of this meeting, the following goals were added to Vong's IEP:

1. Vong will participate in a physical fitness class to prepare him for participation in the cross-county team,
2. Vong will enroll in a six-week summer motorsports course, and,
3. Vong will complete a self-monitoring behavior checklist at the end of each day of participation.

118. What type of transition planning does this describe?

    A. self-determination for leisure and recreational planning for diverse cultural and linguistic backgrounds
    B. self-determination for vocational planning for diverse cultural and linguistic backgrounds
    C. self-determination for socioeconomic planning for diverse cultural and linguistic backgrounds
    D. self-determination for gender planning for diverse cultural and linguistic backgrounds

119. Compared to a young child with normal vision, a young child with a visual impairment is likely to find it significantly more challenging to

    A. develop a sense of identity.
    B. acquire incidental information from the environment.
    C. maintain positive peer relationships.
    D. comprehend concrete concepts through direct instruction.

120. The process of individualized transition planning must encourage students to make many results-oriented decisions as students prepare to leave high school according to the

    A. Individuals with Disabilities Education Act, IDEA 2004.
    B. No Child Left Behind Act, NCLB 2001.
    C. Goals 2000: Educate America Act, 1994.
    D. Vocational Education Act, 1976.

FTCE COMPETENCIES AND SKILLS	Question No.
Competency 1. Knowledge of foundations of exceptional student education	
Skill 1. Identify state and federal legislation that govern the education of students with exceptionalities.	9, 13, 14, 22
Skill 2. Classify the characteristics of students with exceptionalities using the eligibility criteria of categories included in current state and federal laws and regulations governing K–12 education programs.	4, 50
Skill 3. Compare typical and atypical development of physical, cognitive, linguistic, social, and emotional stages of students in the K–12 educational system.	20, 21
Skill 4. Interpret principles and practices in the provision of education for students with exceptionalities based on legal and ethical standards.	1, 10, 11
Skill 5. Apply knowledge of the requirements for developing individualized education plans (IEPs), educational plans (EPs), and transition IEPs.	3, 8, 12, 18
Skill 6. Evaluate the role and function of system-wide models of support for assisting all students, including students with exceptionalities, in accessing the general education curriculum and achieving high expectations.	2, 5, 16, 17, 19
Skill 7. Apply effective methods of communication, consultation, and collaboration with students, parents, caregivers, and all other stakeholders, including those from culturally and linguistically diverse backgrounds, as equal members of educational teams.	43
Skill 8. Use effective methods for coaching and supporting paraprofessionals, tutors, and volunteers to assist students with exceptionalities across settings	24, 56, 57, 58
Skill 9. Determine the purposes and functions of professionals, advocacy organizations, and agencies relevant to educating students with exceptionalities.	6, 7, 15
Skill 10. Determine the factors associated with disproportionality in exceptional student education.	28, 29
Competency 2. Knowledge of assessment and evaluation	
Skill 1. Determine the purposes and characteristics of different types of assessments and the appropriate use.	32, 33, 65, 70

(continued)

FTCE COMPETENCIES AND SKILLS *(continued)*	Question No.
Skill 2. Apply the legal requirements and ethical principles regarding assessment of students with exceptionalities.	31, 34
Skill 3. Identify measurement concepts (e.g., reliability and validity), characteristics, and uses of norm-referenced and criterion-referenced assessments for students with exceptionalities.	23
Skill 4. Determine the purpose and requirements for participation of students with disabilities in the statewide assessment program and available accommodations, waivers, and exemptions.	25, 26, 27
Skill 5. Interpret and apply the results of formal, informal, and performance-based assessments to address specific needs of students with exceptionalities.	30, 35, 36, 39
Skill 6. Analyze assessment data to identify student needs and evaluate student progress in acquiring, generalizing, and maintaining skills across settings.	37
Competency 3. Knowledge of instructional practices in exceptional student education	
Skill 1. Select reliable sources of evidence-based instructional practices and interventions.	48, 49, 51
Skill 2. Apply appropriate instructional approaches, strategies, and materials based on assessments of the student's educational needs (e.g., grade-level standards, academic and functional performance, effect of exceptionality).	46, 47
Skill 3. Choose effective instructional strategies to promote a student's generalization of knowledge and skills across content areas, curriculum, and settings.	53, 55, 78
Skill 4. Identify the characteristics and purposes of the core curriculum, supplemental programs, and intensive interventions as they relate to language arts and mathematics in a multi-tiered system of supports.	40, 42, 113
Skill 5. Apply techniques for differentiating, accommodating, and modifying classroom instruction to meet the educational needs of individual students with exceptionalities.	38, 104
Skill 6. Apply flexible grouping strategies (e.g., academic, behavioral, social) for specific instructional activities.	52, 54

FTCE COMPETENCIES AND SKILLS *(continued)*		Question No.
Skill 7.	Use criteria for selecting and utilizing print and non-print media for instructional use to match student needs and interests.	59, 60, 61
Skill 8.	Analyze characteristics of specialized instructional approaches for students with significant disabilities.	41, 44, 45, 80, 90, 108, 119
Competency 4. Knowledge of positive behavioral support process		
Skill 1.	Identify and choose appropriate prevention and intensive intervention strategies for students who display challenging behaviors.	72, 73, 74, 75
Skill 2.	Distinguish the various concepts and models of positive behavior support.	66, 67, 68
Skill 3.	Analyze the legal and ethical issues pertaining to positive behavior support strategies and disciplinary procedures for students with exceptionalities.	69, 71
Skill 4.	Interpret individual and group data to apply interventions that increase positive behavior.	62, 64
Skill 5.	Interpret the essential elements of a functional behavior assessment and measure the effects of the behavior intervention plan through data collection strategies.	76, 77, 79, 96
Competency 5. Knowledge of multiple literacies and communication skills		
Skill 1.	Identify language development and the components of language structure.	87, 88
Skill 2.	Distinguish characteristics of communication disorders and the impact on academic achievement and functional skills.	93, 94
Skill 3.	Identify appropriate assistive technology and alternative communication systems to facilitate communication across all educational settings.	81, 82, 97
Skill 4.	Determine the sequence of reading development and the critical components of reading proficiency included in the state standards.	84, 85, 86
Skill 5.	Apply specialized instructional methods and techniques to address deficits in phonological processing in students with exceptionalities.	63, 83, 103

(continued)

FTCE COMPETENCIES AND SKILLS *(continued)*	Question No.
Skill 6. Apply evidence-based instructional methods for increasing reading proficiencies in phonics, word recognition, and fluency that meets the specific educational and functional needs of individual students with exceptionalities.	100, 101
Skill 7. Apply evidence-based instructional methods for increasing literacy (e.g., oral language, vocabulary, reading comprehension) in all content areas that meet the specific educational and functional needs of individual students with exceptionalities.	98, 99, 102
Skill 8. Determine and apply strategies for facilitating students' critical-thinking, executive functioning, and metacognition skills.	91, 92, 95
Skill 9. Select and use effective instructional methods and supports for teaching writing foundations, the writing process, and purposes of writing to meet specific educational and functional needs of individual students with exceptionalities across all content areas.	110, 111
Skill 10. Apply evidence-based instructional methods for increasing mathematic skills in all content areas that meet the specific educational and functional needs of individual students with exceptionalities.	89, 109
Competency 6. Knowledge of the transition process	
Skill 1. Determine appropriate programs for career development and career and technical education that meet the needs of individual students with disabilities.	107, 118, 120
Skill 2. Use results of transition assignments to determine appropriate planning strategies to assist the student, parents, caregivers, and stakeholders in developing postsecondary education, career goals, and post-school outcomes.	115, 116, 117
Skill 3. Select instructional approaches to assist students with exceptionalities to engage in self-determination and self-advocacy practices.	105, 106
Skill 4. Identify and compare resources and strategies that can assist individual students with disabilities to function independently in postsecondary education, home and community living, and employment.	112, 114

Answer Explanations

1. D

Least Restrictive Environment (LRE) refers to a setting that is as similar as possible to that for students without disabilities in which a student with a disability can be educated with appropriate supports provided. Answer choice (A), "specially designed instruction in special education classrooms," is more restrictive as this answer choice describes a separate setting. Answer choice (B) describes the services offered, but not the environment. Answer choice (C) is not correct since it describes "the teacher" and not the setting. (Competency 1/Skill 4)

2. B

The ASD specialist, behavior specialist, and paraprofessionals address the needs of students with autism. Answer choice (A) is incorrect since students with autism require a significant amount of specialist support. Brandon can access social settings, such as lunch, special areas, and social events (choice C), but he will need support as students with autism need staff support to develop social skills. Brandon will need paraprofessional support in the general education classroom (choice D), but this response does not address all the necessary support staff for the specific needs of students with autism. (Competency 1/Skill 6)

3. D

Norm-referenced tests compare test scores of students from a certain age group. Criterion-reference testing uses an objective standard or achievement level by performing tasks at various levels of difficulty (choice A). Answer choice (B), error analysis, refers to the individual errors in scores and does not compare scores with other students. Standard error of measurement (choice C) is an estimate of error to use in an individual's test score. (Competency 1/Skill 5)

4. B

IDEA 2004 and ESSA include provisions for increasing inclusion of students with disabilities in general education classrooms. Resource rooms, choice (A), are more restrictive and are not as inclusive as general education classrooms. The ESOL setting, answer choice (C), is also restrictive and is not as inclusive as general education classrooms. Assessment resource classrooms, answer choice (D), are more restrictive and would not provide students with access to all standards. (Competency 1/Skill 2)

5. A

Mrs. Smith is relying heavily on Kristin's label and less on her actual performance. The label Kristin is given does not identify the behaviors she may or may not exhibit (choice B). Kristin's identification or label does not address peer interaction (choice C). Kristin's label may limit her resources (choice D), but the main concern in this scenario is how limiting the teacher's interpretation of the label may affect the types of tasks Kristin is asked to complete in her general education classroom. (Competency 1/Skill 6)

6. B

Schools do have a right to remove students who bring a weapon to school. The IEP team could have met to determine whether Rob should be removed from school (choice A), but Rob is being removed because he came to school with a weapon. Rob's rights were not violated (choice C) since arriving to school with a weapon takes precedence over other determining factors. Manifestation determination (choice D) has to do with the relationship between the child's behavior and disability. (Competency 1/Skill 9)

7. A

As an advocate from the Down Syndrome Association, Mrs. Abraham can provide services and resources for John. As an advocate, Mrs. Abraham cannot decide that John's placement is inadequate, require a change in setting, or a paraprofessional for John (choices B, C, and D). Those decisions are made by the IEP team. (Competency 1/Skill 9)

8. B

The transition plan (Form I of the IFSP-Individualized Family Support Plan) is the paperwork that needs to be completed after the transition conference. The IFSP is needed for any child with developmental delays who attends the Early Steps program. An Individualized Education Plan is to be completed for students older than five years who are identified as having a disability (choice A). Voluntary Pre-Kindergarten Education Programs do not require specific paperwork (choice C). A child's Medical Service Plan is only needed to specify plans for medical issues (choice D). (Competency 1/Skill 5)

9. C

The matrix of services is a funding model that was revised in 1997. The other choices do not refer to the funding model. Mental health treatment and services refers to centers or hospitals that specifically provide services for those with mental illness. The School Medicare Match program includes school districts that are part of the public education system and are eligible to participate in the certified school match program. The School Readiness program offers qualified parents financial assistance for child care through a variety of services. (Competency 1/Skill 1)

10. C

Voluntary Pre-Kindergarten Education Programs were enacted in 2004 and were designed to prepare four-year-old children for kindergarten. The School Readiness program offers financial assistance for childcare through a variety of services (choice A). Child Care Services Program is responsible for the administration of childcare licensing and training throughout Florida (choice B). The Family Resource Specialist is a resource for families served through the local Early Steps and is a community link to support family-centered efforts and activities (choice D). (Competency 1/Skill 4)

11. A

A Manifestation Determination meeting is held to determine whether a student's misbehavior is a result of his or her disability. The meeting is not held to determine academic concerns, visual impairments, or a setting in which the student will receive needed services (choices B, C, and D). (Competency 1/Skill 4)

12. D

The siblings' medical professional should not attend the student's eligibility meeting since this person cannot offer relevant information about the student; he or she does not offer direct care to that student. School psychologists, regular classroom teachers, and exceptional education teachers are connected to the school district and possess more information about the student. (Competency 1/Skill 5)

13. A

Voluntary Pre-Kindergarten (VPK) Education Programs would be the next step in the progression of services provided following the Early Steps program. Individual Education Services (choice B) are provided for school-age children. Hospital Homebound Services (choice C) are provided in the home for students who cannot attend school for medical reasons. Vocational services (choice D) are provided in a secondary education setting. (Competency 1/Skill 1)

14. B

An exception to the IDEA statewide testing requirement includes a small number of students with significant cognitive disabilities who take the Florida Standards Alternate Assessment. Accommodations in the administration of the statewide assessment, some students who work and are not required to take assessments, and the end-of-course exams are not exceptions to test-taking requirements (choices A, C, and D). (Competency 1/Skill 1)

15. A

Itinerant teachers travel between two or more school sites to provide services to students. An administrator would offer knowledge about the entire school community (choice B), a paraprofessional completes tasks/work under the direction of teachers (choice C), and a transition specialist helps prepare students to leave school for vocational training (choice D). (Competency 1/Skill 9)

16. D

A well-designed learning center should be designed for students to work either alone or in groups as they engage in activities without the assistance of the classroom teacher. Students are more actively engaged in learning, students increase proficiency in skills acquired, and students apply knowledge and skills to novel situations are all effective uses of learning centers. (Competency 1/Skill 6)

17. C

All four statements of scaffolding into instruction are valuable, however, from the viewpoint of the student who has a disability, he or she expresses a need to be similar to and accepted by his or her peers. If given the opportunity and support, students will most likely work harder at tasks in order to appear more like their peers. (Competency 1/Skill 6)

18. A

At least once a year, annual goals must be reviewed and the IEP revised or updated. A three-year evaluation is performed when students are reassessed to determine if needs have changed (choice B). Quarterly evaluations (choice C) are a formal communication of student learning progress (quarterly report). "No review is necessary" (choice D) is incorrect since any plan must have a review to demonstrate evidence of progress. (Competency 1/Skill 5)

19. C

Curriculum-based assessment (CBA) measures students' level of achievement as it relates to what is taught in the classroom, results are used to guide instruction, and it is an accurate indicator of student access to the general education curriculum. A norm-referenced test indicates the performance of the student as compared to the average performance of students who are the same age or grade level (choice C). (Competency 1/Skill 6)

20. D

An uncharacteristic pattern of language development signals the present of a language disorder. An attention deficit hyperactivity disorder is present in someone who exhibits inattention, excessive activity or impulsivity (choice A). Emotional disorder includes social, behavioral, and academic challenges (choice B). Intellectual disability (choice C) is a significant limitation in intellectual functioning. (Competency 1/Skill 3)

21. D

Jan has both hyperactivity (having a difficult time remaining seated) as well as impulsivity (difficulty waiting for her turn and interrupts others). Impulsivity, inattention, and hyperactivity are not correct individually (choices A, B, and C). (Competency 1/Skill 3)

22. C

The American Association on Intellectual and Developmental Disabilities is the correct answer as this association is responsible for classification and identification of individuals with intellectual disabilities. Council for exceptional children is not responsible for classification and identification of intellectual disabilities but reports on all exceptionalities through its publications. Autism Society of America reports on autism, and the National Down Syndrome Congress reports only on Down Syndrome and not all forms of intellectual disabilities. (Competency 1/Skill 1)

23. C

Authentic learning tasks match as nearly as possible the real-world tasks of professional in practice, rather than decontextualized or classroom-based tasks. Daily activity logs (choice A) provide ongoing information of activities and achievement for students and their parents. Psychological tests (choice B) measure abilities that affect how efficiently students learn in an instructional situation. Portfolio assessment (choice D) is a collection of student work that determines effort, progress, and achievement in one or more areas. (Competency 2/Skill 3)

24. B

Information is very restrictive and must only be shared with professionals directly working with that student in a professional capacity. Obtaining school administration, parent, or student permission for sharing may be given but this is usually obtained prior to any information being shared. The paraprofessional should be directed by the exceptional education teacher to only share necessary information with professionals working directly with the student either in general or exceptional student education classes. (Competency 1/Skill 8)

25. D

Standardized testing is the tool used by school districts to ensure students have met state standards. Standardized testing is in the same format for all who take it. It often relies on multiple-choice questions and the testing conditions — including instructions, time limits, and scoring rubrics — are the same for all students, though sometimes accommodations on time limits and instructions are made for disabled students. Effective instruction is important but it does not show accountability for mastered standards. Instructional supervision and effective leadership are very valuable to standards implementation but these two areas do not contain an accountability tool for measurement of acquired standards. (Competency 2/Skill 4)

26. C

A performance-based assessment measures learning processes. A criterion-referenced assessment (choice A) measures student performance as it relates to a "benchmark." Norm-referenced assessment (choice B) compares one student to the average performance of other students who are the same age or grade level. A portfolio assessment (choice D) gauges different kinds of work over a period of time. (Competency 2/Skill 4)

27. D

Norm-based assessments determine how the student's performance compares with other students of the same age or in the same grade. Diagnostic assessments (choice A) provide specific information about how a student is performing and what she or he needs to know. Curriculum-based measurement and progress monitoring measure student progress and highlight the close association between curriculum and student performance (choices B and C). (Competency 2/Skill 4)

28. A

Culturally responsive assessment is effective for ELLs. Language variation (choice B) refers to the fact that language varies from place to place and from group to group. Sheltered English (choice C) refers to a type of English-as-a-second-language instruction in which the goal is to teach English language skills at the same time that students are gathering content-area knowledge. Standard English language learners (choice D) approach learning through differences in language, not deficits. (Competency 1/Skill 10)

29. B

Disproportionate representation refers to children who have been incorrectly or wrongly placed in special education programs. Cultural bias, curriculum, alignment, and incongruity between teachers and diverse students and their families are factors that influence disproportionate representation (choices A, C, and D). (Competency 1/Skill 10)

30. B

The 504 Plan of Accommodations requires that students who have disabilities or needs, but who are not eligible to receive services under IDEA, must have accommodations for their disabilities or needs in the regular classroom setting. A 504 accommodation plan is designed to implement needed accommodations. An Individualized Education Plan (choice A) provides for students who have been previously identified as students with disabilities; a transition plan (choice C) is provided to identified students with disabilities during adolescence. "No documentation is needed" is not the appropriate response to the scenario. (Competency 2/Skill 5)

31. D

No documentation should be written because adequate information was not provided. Individualized Education Plan, 504 Plan of Accommodations, and Alternative Instructional Plan (choices A, B, and C) are not correct as the information provided is based on socioeconomic status and lack of transportation; there is not enough academic detail to determine academic goals. (Competency 2/Skill 2)

32. C

Accountability is the notion that people (e.g., students or teachers) or an organization (e.g., a school, school district, or state department of education) should be held responsible for improving student achievement and should be rewarded or sanctioned for their success or lack of success in doing so. Standardization is in the same format for all who take it. It often relies on multiple-choice questions and the testing conditions — including instructions, time limits, and scoring rubrics — are the same for all students, though sometimes accommodations on time limits and instructions are made for disabled students. Proficiency is the mastery or ability to do something at grade level. Adoption refers to the chosen curriculum of a particular school or district. (Competency 2/Skill 1)

33. D

Informed consent is the term used to define parental consent for the eligibility process. Medication, notice, and pre-referral intervention (choices A, B, and C) are terms used in an IEP conference, but these terms do not describe the eligibility process for parental consent. (Competency 2/Skill 1)

34. C

Informed consent requires that a parent be fully informed of all educational activities to be conducted and that information is provided in the native language or necessary mode of communication. Procedural safeguards (choice A) are given to parents during an IEP meeting, parental consent (choice B) is indicated by having a parent give permission for testing, and eligibility determination (choice D) is based on testing results and classroom performance. (Competency 2/Skill 2)

35. C

Alternative Assessment refers to the type of testing used to assess the students who do not participate in standardized statewide assessment. Individualized education plan, transition plan, and authentic assessments (choices A, B, and D) are incorrect as these responses are related to an overall education plan or are not alternatives to standardized testing procedures. (Competency 2/Skill 5)

36. A

Conducting an observation can determine what is occurring from an additional viewpoint. Assessments (choice B) are unnecessary at this point, interventions (choice C) cannot be determined as the behavior is not identified, and it is too early to conduct a meeting (choice D). (Competency 2/Skill 5)

37. C

Curriculum-based assessments, such as chapter tests, are used to determine how a student is performing in or mastering the actual curriculum. Criterion-related (based) assessments, criterion-referenced assessments, and curriculum-based measurements (choices A, B, and D) are incorrect as these tests and measurements are either not specific to the curriculum or are measurements, not assessments. (Competency 2/Skill 6)

38. B

Fluency is the correct response as Kevin's inability to sound out words at a reasonable rate has hindered his ability to comprehend words. Background knowledge is incorrect as there is no reference to Kevin's lack of background knowledge in the scenario. Self-monitoring skills are not identified in the scenario and this skill would not impede his word output. His vocabulary knowledge would affect his comprehension but because Kevin is having difficulty with unlocking the words, fluency is the correct answer. (Competency 3/Skill 5)

39. B

Alternative Assessment is used to assess students who are unable to participate in statewide assessment. Portfolio assessment is a collection of work, systematically collected by a teacher to determine learning gains and current performance levels. Cognitive assessment is an individually administered test of cognitive functioning. Summative assessment is a test given at the end of a course or semester to determine proficiency levels. (Competency 2/Skill 5)

40. B

Setting up a tutoring program in which students who knew their facts were paired with students who did not and instructing the pairs to practice the facts for 10 minutes a day for a week will provide practice on *preskill* before the students perform a more complex skill. Introduce "finding the area of a rectangle" as scheduled (choice A) is not correct as students will struggle because they do not know the multiplication facts. Use a calculator (choice C) would be an effective tool for students who have mastered the multiplication facts. Complain to her colleague that her class does not know multiplication facts (choice D) is unprofessional. (Competency 3/Skill 4)

41. D

The consistency of the food and liquids is important for the exceptional student education teacher to know as the type of food and liquids can determine whether or not the student can safely consume the items without threat to choking or other safety hazards. The other items, holding a cup and food preferences, can be determined by observation. Home food preferences can be determined from a conversation with home-care givers. (Competency 3, Skill 8)

42. C

Charlie went to the store, bought a box of cookies, shared cookies with Tom, got a ball from Tom, and went home to show the ball to his brother are the events and the order in which they occurred. The remaining answer choices (A, B, and D) present the correct events, but not in the correct sequence. (Competency 3/Skill 4)

43. C

Professional organization members are not in the habit of running for political office. The purpose of a professional organization is to serve by filing amicus briefs with the courts, testifying before Congress, and lobbying state and federal legislators. (Competency 1/Skill 7)

44. B

When clarifying, students look for words and concepts they do not understand. Question generating (choice A) refers to students generating questions about text content. Scaffolding (choice C) is an approach that helps students bridge the gap between their current abilities and the intended goal. Modeling refers to providing a sample (or example) of what is expected. (Competency 3/Skill 8)

45. C

Integrated language arts approach is the correct answer. A language-experience approach (choice A) uses language to communicate thoughts, ideas, and meaning. A basal reading approach (choice B) uses the reading lesson or story with a small group of students during a specified time and location. Literature-based approach (choice D) focuses on meaning, interest, and enjoyment as well as individual student differences in reading abilities. (Competency 3/Skill 8)

46. C

Collaborating with the reading specialist/special education teacher is not a feature of effective reading instruction. Although collaborating is important, using appropriate and ongoing screening, assessment, and progress monitoring; providing intensive instruction; and obtaining early intervention when needed are directly connected to effective reading instruction (choices A, B, and D). (Competency 3/Skill 2)

47. C

The ability to formulate and conduct mathematical problems is the correct answer. The other choices are also aspects of mathematical proficiency—understanding mathematical concepts and operations (choice A) is *conceptual understanding*; the ability to accurately and efficiently conduct operations and mathematics practices (choice B) is *procedural fluency*; thinking about, explaining, and justifying mathematical work (choice D) is *adaptive reasoning*. (Competency 3/Skill 2)

48. B

Whole class direct instruction would not be applicable to differentiated instruction. Providing materials and tasks at varied levels of difficulty, varying levels of instructional support, and varying evaluations strategies are also applicable to differentiated instruction (choices A, C, and D). (Competency 3/Skill 1)

49. C

Treatment fidelity is the correct answer. Instructional accommodations are supports provided to help students gain full access to class content and instruction (choice A). Differentiated instruction (choice B) and instructional modifications (choice D) include using a variety of strategies to meet the range of needs. (Competency 3/Skill 1)

50. C

Autism and traumatic brain injury was added under IDEA in 1990. The other combinations: autism and pervasive developmental disorder (A), pervasive developmental disorder and down syndrome (B), down syndrome and traumatic brain injury (D) include one disability that was not accurately added under IDEA in 1990. (Competency 1/Skill 2)

51. A

The most important first task for including state standards is interpreting the meaning of the standard. Designing lesson activities, assessment, and integration are important but first a thorough understanding of the standard must be the initial task. (Competency 3/Skill 1)

52. B

Limiting teacher talk and increasing opportunities for student response is the correct answer. When a teacher spends too much time providing directions, the students lose interest and become distracted. Providing scaffolding and further modeling (choice A), writing the instructions on the board as he talks (choice C), and prompting students to listen before each example (choice D) are all examples of increased teacher talking and less student response time. (Competency 3/Skill 6)

53. D

Generalization is the correct response. The student is able to transfer information across settings and can use the information learned. Maintenance, acquisition, and entry are incorrect as the behavior is not at the initial stage—acquisition has already occurred and is being maintained. (Competency 3/Skill 3)

54. D

The teacher is using positive reinforcement in order to increase Bruce's on-task behavior. Negative reinforcement (choice A), shaping (choice B), and extinction (choice C) are not correct as the strategies the teacher uses are positive. Reinforcers (choice D) were discussed prior to implementation to ensure that Bruce had input. (Competency 3/Skill 6)

55. A

The teacher is allowing students to practice an already-learned skill. To allow students to learn new skills independently (choice B), to allow students of different levels to assist each other (choice C), and to allow students to work collaboratively (choice D) do not allow for practice of the specific skill. (Competency 3/Skill 3)

56. D

If there is communication with personnel in the building, there is less likelihood that students will be mislabeled. Increased time for lesson planning (choice A), a streamlined approach to teaching (choice B), and reduced caseload management for special education teachers (choice C) are not goals or reasons for collaboration or consultation. (Competency 1/Skill 8)

57. D

New roles for special education teachers is the correct response. The special education teacher must inform the general education teacher of how she will be included into the general education classroom and be a collaborative source for Mrs. Robbins. Answer choices A, B, and C are not as comprehensive as they relate to the overall concept of the scenario. (Competency 1/Skill 8)

58. C

Parenting poorly is not intentional and may just require some additional suggestions for collaboration in the home. Family involvement and collaboration is fundamental to students' success. The focus of any discussion should include the needs and wants of the family and the student and not their values. Family and school collaboration can increase if you accept the family and student as they are. (choices A, B, and D). (Competency 1/Skill 8)

59. C

The students with learning disabilities and English language learners do best when vocabulary and main ideas are discussed prior to the lesson. Have the students make predictions about what will happen in the chapter (choice A), instruct the students to make graphic organizers of the framework of the chapter (choice B), and have the students preview the chapter (choice D) are incorrect as these responses do not provide enough insight into the chapter and primarily reflect that the students are doing the pre-work, rather than the teacher. (Competency 3/Skill 7)

60. A

Electronic books reflect text that is read to the student. Direct instruction, the whole-language approach, and speech-to-text programs do not offer individualized instruction for students who require auditory discrimination. (choices B, C, and D). (Competency 3/Skill 7)

61. C

Trade books are examples of supplemental reading materials. Basal readers and textbooks (choices A and B) refer to the class text and software (choice D) is a technological supplement. (Competency 3/Skill 7)

62. A

Functional behavior assessment is the correct answer. Initial identification, universal screening, and initial screening (choices B, C, and D) are all processes that take place before process monitoring is in place. (Competency 4/Skill 4)

63. D

The focus is on the sight word vocabulary and fluency. The reading components would be best assessed weekly and data recorded and graphed. There is no need to perform an error analysis (choice C) as there is no indication that a specific test question requires monitoring for validity and reliability. Monitoring a reading inventory (choice A) monthly is too infrequent to note progress and development. Mastered sight words can more efficiently be indicated through weekly progress monitoring rather than in portfolio form (choice B). (Competency 5/Skill 5)

64. C

Anecdotal recording is the correct answer. Permanent product recording (choice A) involves keeping samples of work as a means of measuring behavior. Duration recording (choice B) is the length of time the behavior occurs. Event recording (choice D) refers to how many times a behavior occurs in each period of time. (Competency 4/Skill 4)

65. B

A curriculum-based assessment tests a student's knowledge of a specific content. A curriculum-based assessment does not indicate a measurement for exceptional student education referral (choice A), nor is it indicative of how a student will perform in future academics (choice C) as the content of the measurement is very specific. Curriculum-based assessment also does not measure assistive technology use for academic progress (choice D) as it only covers content specific information. (Competency 2/Skill 1)

66. D

A cognitive behavior management strategy enables students to manage their own classroom conduct and social behavior. Positive reinforcement (choice A) is responding to a behavior with a consequence. Extinction (choice B) is decreasing a negative behavior by stopping reinforcement. A behavior contract (choice C) is an agreement between the teacher and student that clearly specifies expectations for the student, the rewards for meeting those expectations, and the consequences for not meeting them, as well as the timeframe for which the agreement is valid. (Competency 4/Skill 2)

67. B

Positive behavior support is a problem-solving model involving all stakeholders. Response to intervention (choice A) is a model for screening students and using their response to intervention as a data source to identify students who need special education services. Culturally responsive teaching (choice C) is incorporating students' language and culture into the curriculum. Positive reinforcement (choice D) maintains or increases the target behavior. (Competency 4/Skill 2)

68. D

Peer monitoring is the correct answer. In peer tutoring (choice A), students serve as academic or social-skills tutors for each other. In peer support and confrontation (choice B), peers are trained to acknowledge one another's positive behaviors, and when inappropriate behavior occurs, peers are trained to explain why the behavior is inappropriate and suggest or model an appropriate response. In positive peer reporting (choice C), students are taught, encouraged, and reinforced for reporting each other's positive behaviors. (Competency 4/Skill 2)

69. C

Give an oral or written notice of charges and an opportunity to respond to charges is the correct answer. Provide a free public education for the student (choice A), arrange a formal hearing (with advance notice of time, place, and procedure) (choice B), and the school has no particular obligations in this situation (choice D) are all incorrect. (Competency 4/Skill 3)

70. B

A curriculum-based assessment tests a students' knowledge of a specific content. A curriculum based assessment does not indicate a measurement for exceptional student education referral (choice A), nor is it indicative of how a student will perform in future academics (choice C) as the content of the measurement is very specific. Curriculum-based assessment also does not measure assistive technology use for academic progress (choice D) as it only covers content specific information. (Competency 2/Skill 1)

71. A

The correct answer is *in loco parentis*. According to this concept, parents grant school personnel a measure of control over their children. Procedural due process, manifest determination, and the Individualized Education Plan (IEP) (choices B, C, and D) refer to different legal aspects of the exceptional education student. (Competency 4/Skill 3)

72. C

Behavior needs to be observable and measurable in order to be shaped and changed. Answer choices A, B, and D do not address the specifications of behavior measurement. (Competency 4/Skill 1)

73. B

Continued practice will replace the inappropriate behavior and allow Doug to realize appropriate interactions with teachers and peers. Using verbal cues (choice A) may be a good reminder but may lack consistency and reinforcement of appropriate behaviors. Doug may not have substantially developed communication skills (choice C) and may find it difficult to understand peer relationships. Giving Doug a list may be helpful (choice D) but difficult for Doug to grasp and transfer to a variety of settings. (Competency 4/Skill 1)

74. C

Event recording is used when behavior is discrete and uniform in duration. Long in duration (choice A), continuous (choice B), and rarely occurs (choice D) describe other behaviors that could not be measured by event or frequency recording. (Competency 4/Skill 1)

75. A

Latency is the correct answer. Duration, frequency, and rate refer to different descriptions of behavior measurement. (Competency 4/Skill 1)

76. C

Benefit the student's self-discipline or self-control is the correct answer. The objective of behavior change is directly related to the student obtaining control of his or her behavior. Increase instructional time in the classroom (choice A), provide a safe and peaceful environment for learning for all other students (choice B), and increase test score and district rating on score cards (choice D) involve the performance off all students in the classroom rather than on individual behavior goals. (Competency 4/Skill 5)

77. A

Collecting baseline behavior is the first step in initiating behavior change. Select a target behavior, identify reinforcers, and evaluate the effects of intervention (choices B, C, and D) are steps that follow the initial step of the behavior change process. (Competency 4/Skill 5)

78. A

Creating interview questions ahead of time allows the students to have a degree of comfort with a known quantity with students they are unfamiliar with and allows for teachers to work together and plan for their students. Having students post a picture may be fun and interesting but it also may be a source of embarrassment for students who come from different socioeconomic backgrounds (choice B). Discussing likes and dislikes may prove to be too open and overly inviting for students to share. Discussing likes and dislikes may also limit students with poor vocabulary and writing skills (choice D). Pairing students at the beginning of the school year will be difficult as the teachers are still learning about their students and who may or may not be a good match. (Competency 3/Skill 3)

79. A

Ignoring disruptive behavior (extinction) is the correct answer. Using a social script to highlight desired behavior (choice B), using differential reinforcement throughout the day (choice C), and providing social skills instruction to the entire class (choice D) are incorrect as these responses do not provide for the necessary behavior strategies. (Competency 4/Skill 5)

80. A

The major concern of the pre-referral team should be the language skills as they relate to academic performance as this may be causing the other behaviors exhibited in the classroom: motivation, social emotional development and learning style compatibility might be studied if it is discovered that language is not the problem. (Competency 3/Skill 8)

81. D

Pre-alphabetic phase is the correct answer. In partial-alphabetic phase (choice A), children develop some knowledge about letters and can detect letter-sound relationships. In full-alphabetic phase (choice B), readers identify (choice B) words by matching all of the letters and sounds. In consolidated-alphabetic phase (choice C), readers can segment the words and analyze multisyllabic words. (Competency 5/Skill 3)

82. C

Full-alphabetic phase refers to readers' ability to identify words by matching all of the letters and sounds. Pre-alphabetic phase (choice A) involves recognizing words at sight due to visual or contextual cues. Partial-alphabetic phase (choice B) involves the ability to develop some knowledge about letters and detect letter-sound relationships. In consolidated-alphabetic phase (choice D), readers can segment the words and analyze multisyllabic words. (Competency 5/Skill 3)

83. A

Rhyming is the correct answer. Segmenting speech sounds (choice B) would involve separating each sound in the word. Blending speech sounds (choice C) involves taking each sound and blending them to create a word. Adding printed letters (choice D) involves adding the "visual" of printed letters with the sound. (Competency 5/Skill 5)

84. B

Graphophonemic is the correct answer. Letters are graphemes and sounds are phonemes. Their connectedness is graphophonemic. Morphemic is a combination of sounds that have meaning. Syntactic refers to the study of the rules that dictate how the parts of sentences combine. Semantic refers to the study of the meaning of words in a language. (Competency 5/Skill 4)

85. D

Research indicates that children learning English master the grammatical morphemes in a particular order, predictable not on the basis of frequency of exposure, but on linguistic complexity. Individual variation among children is incorrect as research indicates that children do acquire morphemes in a given order not with individual variations. Order of acquisition is incorrect as frequency is not a determining factor of hearing the morpheme. Mastery of morphemes is incorrect as all 14 morphemes are not always mastered at an early stage of language development. (Competency 5/Skill 4)

86. C

Cross-age reading provides readers with a lesson cycle that includes modeling by the teacher, discussing the text, supplying opportunities for practicing reading the text, and reading the text to younger children. Fluency Development Lesson (FDL), support reading strategy, and oral recitation (choices A, B, and D) are excellent practices in primary grades. (Competency 5/Skill 4)

87. B

Restating the definition in his or her own words is "applying the knowledge." Defining the word, finding the antonym, and fitting the word into a sentence (choices A, C, and D), although good activities, are nevertheless, lower-level thinking activities. (Competency 5/Skill 1)

88. C.

An analogy explains the relationship that exists between two words. Synonym refers to a word that is similar in meaning to another word. An antonym is a word that is opposite in meaning to another word. Multiple-meaning word refers to one word operating in different contexts. (Competency 5/Skill 1)

89. B

Metacognition is the correct answer. Metacognition refers to thinking of one's own knowledge, mental capacities, and thought processes. Prediction (choice A) refers to thinking ahead and anticipating information and events in a text. Using a graphic organizer and using a semantic organizer (choices C and D) are visual representations of concepts and facts. (Competency 5/Skill 10)

90. D

The general education teacher needs to invest time in acquainting herself or himself with the devices and equipment used by Lee in his general education environment. If the teacher cannot use the communication board, it is unlikely that the other students in the classroom will try and communicate with Lee in the general education classroom environment. It will be important soon to do the other activities (Lee's introduction to the class, having the students write on Lee's communication board and have students discuss multiple means of communication) but for now the key to future communication is to have the general education teacher learn how to use Lee's communication board. (Competency 3/Skill 8)

91. B

Linguistic is the correct answer. It refers to learning to decode words through regular letter patterns. Synthetic is a part-to-whole phonics approach. Implicit and analytic (choices C and D) refer to whole-to-part approaches to word study. (Competency 5/Skill 8)

92. D

Semantics is the correct answer. Jim is having trouble finding the exact word that is associated with "Ferris Wheel." He is not having trouble sounding out the word (choices B and C) or describing the Ferris Wheel (choice A). (Competency 5/Skill 8)

93. A

Sandra is having difficulty finding the specific words. Phonological deficit, receptive language delay, and pragmatic deficit (choice B, C, and D) are incorrect as Sandra does not have difficulty producing sounds or understanding word meaning. (Competency 5/Skill 2)

94. B

Determining what knowledge and skills a student has already acquired is the correct answer. It is best to begin with a baseline and then expand with additional necessary skills. Adhering closely to a language curriculum, focusing on receptive language before expressive language, and focusing on expressive language before receptive language occur well into language development. (Competency 5/Skill 2)

95. D

Prevention is the correct answer as the intervention provided is an attempt at avoiding a disorder from developing or an attempt to identify the disorder at an early age. Compensation, remediation, and consultation are incorrect as these steps are performed once a disorder is identified. (Competency 5/Skill 8)

96. B

Assistive technology is the correct answer. Assistive technology refers to devices that are available to individuals with disabilities. Decoding, intervention methods, and fluency skill instruction (choices A, C, and D) are not always appropriate devices for instruction. (Competency 4/Skill 5)

97. C

Communication supports include conventional word programs, closed captioning, and text telephones. Sign language and Braille are supports for vision impaired students. Speech impairment is a disability. (Competency 5/Skill 3)

98. B

Concepts of print is the correct answer. Decoding, alphabet principle, and fluency (choices A, C, and D) are concepts of the "learning to read" stage of reading development. (Competency 5/Skill 7)

99. B

A different text and activity level for each group is the correct answer. Group membership that remains consistent throughout the school year (choice A) is incorrect as group membership can change at any time during the year. A focus on oral language activities is incorrect as the focus should not be limited to oral language. Standardized assessments (choice D) is incorrect as grouping for differentiated instruction based on standardized testing should not be a determining factor. (Competency 5/Skill 7)

100. A

Pay little attention to meaning is the correct answer. With ongoing criticism, the student will focus on how to pronounce words rather than focus on the content. Learning to read the words fluently, develop automatic recognition of words, and learn to use context as a means of word identification are incorrect as these choices would be the preferred outcomes of reading fluency. (Competency 5/Skill 6)

101. D

Underlying skills such as phonemic awareness and facility with letter-sound correspondences are crucial factors in effective reading instruction. There is no instructional difference due to method (choice A), the whole-word method has produced somewhat better results (choice B), and there is not enough statistical data to arrive at a conclusion (choice C) do not address current successful (proven) choices in reading instruction. (Competency 5/Skill 6)

102. B

Revise the intervention if it is ineffective. Progress monitoring is a teaching tool used for accurately defining where interventions should be conducted. Assess students' higher-order thinking skills (choice A), work with smaller groups of students (choice C), and effectively utilize all specialists in the classroom (choice D) are incorrect as these responses do not directly include progress monitoring in measuring instruction and interventions. (Competency 5/Skill 7)

103. C

Diagnostic testing identifies a student's strengths and weaknesses. Screening is the initial stage of assessment, progress monitoring refers to the monitoring of student skills, and outcome (choices A, B, and D) are incorrect as these refer to assessment and monitoring results. (Competency 5/Skill 5)

104. D

The exceptional education teacher needs to have Carla focus on the difference between major and minor content. Teaching Carla about headings is the best way to organize content and large amounts of information. The ESE teacher does not need to work on improving Carla's note taking strategy, nor should Carla rely on the copier to provide her with notes as this would prove to be a large amount of information to organize, and finally the index cards are a good strategy for limiting information but do not provide enough instruction for organizing the information. (Competency 3/Skill 5)

105. B

The classroom scenario gives the student a chance to show her strengths. Student responsibility, student reinforcement, and setting reasonable goals (choices A, C, and D) are strategies that enhance student self-image. (Competency 6/Skill 3)

106. A

The student increases self-awareness by investigating his or her disability is the beginning stage of career development and should begin in elementary school. Realistic goals, self-advocacy skills, and academic preparation (choices B, C, and D) are all necessary attributes as one graduates from high school. (Competency 6/Skill 3)

107. B

Ecological assessment that involves carefully examining the environment in which the activity actually occurs is the correct answer since the student is expressing an interest in a specific location. Interviews and questionnaires (choice A) is incorrect as the student is not completing a questionnaire or interview. The student is specifically identifying a location and an interest. Mapping form from the parents (choice C) is not correct because at the moment, parental involvement is not being sought. Curriculum-based assessment is incorrect because the student has expressed an interest—it is not a curriculum-based issue. (Competency 6/Skill 1)

108. C

For a student who has just returned to school from post-traumatic disorder, the best strategy is to provide the student with a reliable schedule and establish a routine. The student needs to have a schedule that she can rely on to maintain focus and carry on through her day. Parents (Choice B) should not be included in the schedule as the student of this age needs to maintain a daily schedule. The other two choices D and A (quiet place and reviewing the code of conduct) will be important as strategies to continue progress across the curriculum but not as initial strategies. (Competency 3/Skill 8)

109. B

For a fourth-grade student, the initial IEP must include a plan for monitoring a student's progress. It is important that the teacher and student can share and identify areas of math that the student may struggle in and see outcomes toward his goals. A transition plan (Choice A) is not required on an IEP until the student is 14 and a more established transition plan when the student reaches 16 years old. The primary responsibility for IEP implementation will be the exceptional education teacher (Choice C). A statement from the parents (Choice D) indicating their plan for their student's academic future may be included but is not required. (Competency 5/Skill 10)

110. B

The most effective strategy of assisting a student who is overwhelmed with an assignment is to break the assignment down into smaller more manageable parts. It is not a good idea for either the librarian (Choice A) or the English teacher (Choice D) to do the work for the student. In this case the student can perform the assignment as it is presented, she just is overwhelmed with the writing process. In this case, it is unnecessary to meet with the parents to discuss the student's attitude as the student has identified the issues she is having and just need assistance in carrying out the assignment to completion. (Competency 5/Skill 9)

111. C

Ana can identify errors in the resource room and now needs to transfer the tools learned to her ELA classroom. Going to the resource room (Choice A) for corrections would not be the appropriate choice as Ana can already perform the corrections when in the resource room. Ana can already locate errors in her work so pairing her with another student (Choice D) or setting aside time to go over punctuation errors (Choice B) would not be an effective strategy of support. (Competency 5/Skill 9)

112. A

Students who are self-determined overcome fears and speak up for themselves regarding what they want in life and what is needed to succeed. Students who are self-determined do not need to be present during IEP meetings is not correct since it contradicts best practices. Students who are self-determined are not always punctual. Although punctuality is a desired quality trait, it is not a self-determined trait. Students who are self-determined do not allow other team members to make decisions for them. (Competency 6/Skill 4)

113. C

Students with mild intellectual disabilities have difficulty transferring information from one setting to another. Students with mild intellectual disabilities have less difficulty with recognizing letters in their name (Choice A), following two step directions (Choice B), and matching two similar objects together (Choice D). (Competency 3/Skill 4)

114. D

Prepare students with disabilities through career education at the high school level is not a key characteristic. Preparation of students through career education should be implemented during elementary, middle, and high school years. (Competency 6/Skill 4)

115. D

Leisure-recreational describes the leisure time domain presented in the scenario. Person-social, general community functioning, and employment are not included in the leisure time domain. (Competency 6/Skill 2)

116. A

Shopping, transportation, and banking relate to activities in the community. Assessment, planning, instruction, and evaluation, assistive technology, job shadowing, and internship (choices B, C, and D) relate to technology and actual employment. (Competency 6/Skill 2)

117. A

Attending the career fair at the community college is the correct answer as it involves knowledge of jobs available in the community. Speaking to the guidance counselor about vocational education, developing budgeting skills with the ESE teacher, and receiving training in clothing care (choices B, C, and D) are activities presented in the remaining domains of transition planning. (Competency 6/Skill 2)

118. A

Self-determination for leisure and recreational planning for diverse cultural and linguistic backgrounds is the correct answer. Both cultural background and leisure planning are addressed in the paragraph. Self-determination for vocational planning for diverse cultural and linguistic backgrounds (choice B), self-determination for socioeconomic planning for diverse cultural and linguistic backgrounds (choice C), and self-determination for gender planning for diverse cultural and linguistic backgrounds (choice D) are incorrect as the other areas (employment, vocational planning, and socioeconomic planning) are not specifically addressed. (Competency 6/Skill 1)

119. B

Students with visual impairment have difficulty in finding information from their environment due to limitations in their visual ability. Students with autism (Choice C) have a difficult time with positive peer relationships. Students with Emotional Behavior Disorders (Choice A) have a difficulty developing a sense of identity. Students with Intellectual Disabilities (Choice D) comprehend objects through direct instruction. (Competency 3/Skill 8)

120. A

Individuals with Disabilities Education Act, IDEA 2004 is the correct answer. IDEA specifically addressed post-school outcomes. No Child Left Behind Act, NCLB 2001, Goals 2000: Education America Act, 1994; and Vocational Education Act, 1976 are not correct as these involved funding, accountability, parental involvement, and math and science goals, but they do not specifically state that transition planning and post-school outcomes are needed. (Competency 6/Skill 1)

PRACTICE TEST 2

FTCE Exceptional Student Education K–12

Also available at the REA Study Center (*www.rea.com/studycenter*)

This practice test is also offered online at the REA Study Center. Since all FTCE exams are computer-based, we recommend that you take the online version of the test to simulate test-day conditions and to receive these added benefits:

- **Timed testing conditions**—help you gauge how much time you can spend on each question
- **Automatic scoring**—find out how you did on the test, instantly
- **On-screen detailed explanations of answers**—gives you the correct answer and explains why the other answer choices are wrong
- **Diagnostic score reports**—pinpoint where you're strongest and where you need to focus your study

Answer Sheet

1. Ⓐ Ⓑ Ⓒ Ⓓ	31. Ⓐ Ⓑ Ⓒ Ⓓ	61. Ⓐ Ⓑ Ⓒ Ⓓ	91. Ⓐ Ⓑ Ⓒ Ⓓ
2. Ⓐ Ⓑ Ⓒ Ⓓ	32. Ⓐ Ⓑ Ⓒ Ⓓ	62. Ⓐ Ⓑ Ⓒ Ⓓ	92. Ⓐ Ⓑ Ⓒ Ⓓ
3. Ⓐ Ⓑ Ⓒ Ⓓ	33. Ⓐ Ⓑ Ⓒ Ⓓ	63. Ⓐ Ⓑ Ⓒ Ⓓ	93. Ⓐ Ⓑ Ⓒ Ⓓ
4. Ⓐ Ⓑ Ⓒ Ⓓ	34. Ⓐ Ⓑ Ⓒ Ⓓ	64. Ⓐ Ⓑ Ⓒ Ⓓ	94. Ⓐ Ⓑ Ⓒ Ⓓ
5. Ⓐ Ⓑ Ⓒ Ⓓ	35. Ⓐ Ⓑ Ⓒ Ⓓ	65. Ⓐ Ⓑ Ⓒ Ⓓ	95. Ⓐ Ⓑ Ⓒ Ⓓ
6. Ⓐ Ⓑ Ⓒ Ⓓ	36. Ⓐ Ⓑ Ⓒ Ⓓ	66. Ⓐ Ⓑ Ⓒ Ⓓ	96. Ⓐ Ⓑ Ⓒ Ⓓ
7. Ⓐ Ⓑ Ⓒ Ⓓ	37. Ⓐ Ⓑ Ⓒ Ⓓ	67. Ⓐ Ⓑ Ⓒ Ⓓ	97. Ⓐ Ⓑ Ⓒ Ⓓ
8. Ⓐ Ⓑ Ⓒ Ⓓ	38. Ⓐ Ⓑ Ⓒ Ⓓ	68. Ⓐ Ⓑ Ⓒ Ⓓ	98. Ⓐ Ⓑ Ⓒ Ⓓ
9. Ⓐ Ⓑ Ⓒ Ⓓ	39. Ⓐ Ⓑ Ⓒ Ⓓ	69. Ⓐ Ⓑ Ⓒ Ⓓ	99. Ⓐ Ⓑ Ⓒ Ⓓ
10. Ⓐ Ⓑ Ⓒ Ⓓ	40. Ⓐ Ⓑ Ⓒ Ⓓ	70. Ⓐ Ⓑ Ⓒ Ⓓ	100. Ⓐ Ⓑ Ⓒ Ⓓ
11. Ⓐ Ⓑ Ⓒ Ⓓ	41. Ⓐ Ⓑ Ⓒ Ⓓ	71. Ⓐ Ⓑ Ⓒ Ⓓ	101. Ⓐ Ⓑ Ⓒ Ⓓ
12. Ⓐ Ⓑ Ⓒ Ⓓ	42. Ⓐ Ⓑ Ⓒ Ⓓ	72. Ⓐ Ⓑ Ⓒ Ⓓ	102. Ⓐ Ⓑ Ⓒ Ⓓ
13. Ⓐ Ⓑ Ⓒ Ⓓ	43. Ⓐ Ⓑ Ⓒ Ⓓ	73. Ⓐ Ⓑ Ⓒ Ⓓ	103. Ⓐ Ⓑ Ⓒ Ⓓ
14. Ⓐ Ⓑ Ⓒ Ⓓ	44. Ⓐ Ⓑ Ⓒ Ⓓ	74. Ⓐ Ⓑ Ⓒ Ⓓ	104. Ⓐ Ⓑ Ⓒ Ⓓ
15. Ⓐ Ⓑ Ⓒ Ⓓ	45. Ⓐ Ⓑ Ⓒ Ⓓ	75. Ⓐ Ⓑ Ⓒ Ⓓ	105. Ⓐ Ⓑ Ⓒ Ⓓ
16. Ⓐ Ⓑ Ⓒ Ⓓ	46. Ⓐ Ⓑ Ⓒ Ⓓ	76. Ⓐ Ⓑ Ⓒ Ⓓ	106. Ⓐ Ⓑ Ⓒ Ⓓ
17. Ⓐ Ⓑ Ⓒ Ⓓ	47. Ⓐ Ⓑ Ⓒ Ⓓ	77. Ⓐ Ⓑ Ⓒ Ⓓ	107. Ⓐ Ⓑ Ⓒ Ⓓ
18. Ⓐ Ⓑ Ⓒ Ⓓ	48. Ⓐ Ⓑ Ⓒ Ⓓ	78. Ⓐ Ⓑ Ⓒ Ⓓ	108. Ⓐ Ⓑ Ⓒ Ⓓ
19. Ⓐ Ⓑ Ⓒ Ⓓ	49. Ⓐ Ⓑ Ⓒ Ⓓ	79. Ⓐ Ⓑ Ⓒ Ⓓ	109. Ⓐ Ⓑ Ⓒ Ⓓ
20. Ⓐ Ⓑ Ⓒ Ⓓ	50. Ⓐ Ⓑ Ⓒ Ⓓ	80. Ⓐ Ⓑ Ⓒ Ⓓ	110. Ⓐ Ⓑ Ⓒ Ⓓ
21. Ⓐ Ⓑ Ⓒ Ⓓ	51. Ⓐ Ⓑ Ⓒ Ⓓ	81. Ⓐ Ⓑ Ⓒ Ⓓ	111. Ⓐ Ⓑ Ⓒ Ⓓ
22. Ⓐ Ⓑ Ⓒ Ⓓ	52. Ⓐ Ⓑ Ⓒ Ⓓ	82. Ⓐ Ⓑ Ⓒ Ⓓ	112. Ⓐ Ⓑ Ⓒ Ⓓ
23. Ⓐ Ⓑ Ⓒ Ⓓ	53. Ⓐ Ⓑ Ⓒ Ⓓ	83. Ⓐ Ⓑ Ⓒ Ⓓ	113. Ⓐ Ⓑ Ⓒ Ⓓ
24. Ⓐ Ⓑ Ⓒ Ⓓ	54. Ⓐ Ⓑ Ⓒ Ⓓ	84. Ⓐ Ⓑ Ⓒ Ⓓ	114. Ⓐ Ⓑ Ⓒ Ⓓ
25. Ⓐ Ⓑ Ⓒ Ⓓ	55. Ⓐ Ⓑ Ⓒ Ⓓ	85. Ⓐ Ⓑ Ⓒ Ⓓ	115. Ⓐ Ⓑ Ⓒ Ⓓ
26. Ⓐ Ⓑ Ⓒ Ⓓ	56. Ⓐ Ⓑ Ⓒ Ⓓ	86. Ⓐ Ⓑ Ⓒ Ⓓ	116. Ⓐ Ⓑ Ⓒ Ⓓ
27. Ⓐ Ⓑ Ⓒ Ⓓ	57. Ⓐ Ⓑ Ⓒ Ⓓ	87. Ⓐ Ⓑ Ⓒ Ⓓ	117. Ⓐ Ⓑ Ⓒ Ⓓ
28. Ⓐ Ⓑ Ⓒ Ⓓ	58. Ⓐ Ⓑ Ⓒ Ⓓ	88. Ⓐ Ⓑ Ⓒ Ⓓ	118. Ⓐ Ⓑ Ⓒ Ⓓ
29. Ⓐ Ⓑ Ⓒ Ⓓ	59. Ⓐ Ⓑ Ⓒ Ⓓ	89. Ⓐ Ⓑ Ⓒ Ⓓ	119. Ⓐ Ⓑ Ⓒ Ⓓ
30. Ⓐ Ⓑ Ⓒ Ⓓ	60. Ⓐ Ⓑ Ⓒ Ⓓ	90. Ⓐ Ⓑ Ⓒ Ⓓ	120. Ⓐ Ⓑ Ⓒ Ⓓ

PRACTICE TEST 2

Time: 2 hours and 30 minutes
   120 questions

Read each question and select the option that best answers the question.

1. As a result of P.L. 94-142, what changes occurred in education for students with disabilities?

   A. Exceptional education programs were required for children ages 3 to 5.

   B. Education is to be provided to all children (6–18) who meet age eligibility requirements.

   C. Students may not be denied education or exclusion from school when their misbehavior is related to their handicap.

   D. "Separate but equal" facilities on the basis of race must be provided.

2. What important refinement in special education was a result of the Individuals with Disabilities Education Improvement Act (IDEA, 2004)?

   A. Established that special education teachers become highly qualified if they teach core academic content to students with disabilities.

   B. Confirmed that a free public education must be provided for all students.

   C. Recognized that most students with disabilities spend all or most of their school time in general education settings.

   D. Decreed that students with disabilities should be addressed in the same manner as other students, using either the same assessment instrument employed with typical learners or some type of alternative assessment.

3. Rule 6A-6.03011, Florida Administrative Code (FAC), stated that the term "mental retardation" be changed to

   A. intelligence scale.

   B. intellectual disability.

   C. disordered reading.

   D. functional disability.

4. The 2004 Amendments to IDEA emphasize that more than 30 years of research indicate that the education of children with disabilities can be made more effective by

    A. separating all exceptional education students into their own classrooms.

    B. sending all students with disabilities to a separate school.

    C. providing each child born with disabilities with a paraprofessional.

    D. providing incentives for whole school approaches and pre-referral intervention to reduce the need to label children as disabled in order to address their learning needs.

5. P. L. 99–457 extended the services provided to school-aged children with disabilities. Select the correct range of ages addressed by this law.

    A. 4–7 years

    B. 0–3 years

    C. 3–5 years

    D. 7–10 years

6. Maria and her family came to the United States mainland from Puerto Rico last year. Maria speaks only Spanish and seems unable to learn English despite extended help from an ESL teacher. Maria is failing all subjects. The school psychologist administered an intelligence test in Spanish. Maria is performing in a mentally deficient range for her age level. Based on these findings, the IEP team is recommending that Maria receive special education services as a student with an intellectual disability. Did Maria receive a nondiscriminatory evaluation as required by IDEA?

    A. Yes, the test was administered in Spanish.

    B. Yes, the IEP team was in agreement with the test results.

    C. No, there was only one test administered.

    D. No, the test giver was not Hispanic.

7. Courtney is a student with an autism spectrum disorder. She does not speak. She types what she wants to say into a device that converts the text to speech. The device helps Courtney to express her desires and needs. This is an example of

    A. corrective reading.

    B. assistive technology.

    C. speech and language therapy.

    D. universal design for learning.

8. According to federal law IDEA 2004, Part C, at what age is a child no longer eligible for the Early Steps program?

    A.   36 months

    B.   12 months

    C.   24 months

    D.   48 months

9. The amendment to the Federal Higher Education Opportunity Act of 2008

    A.   provided federal funding to expand three existing transition programs.

    B.   created programs to cover diagnostic screening.

    C.   negotiated a compact for insurance coverage and access for services for persons with developmental disabilities.

    D.   created a new program to expand the number of postsecondary programs for students with intellectual disabilities.

10. Max was having difficulty in the second grade classroom. His teacher brought her concerns to the IEP team after conducting problem solving strategies in a multi-tiered system of supports. Mr. and Mrs. Jones gave written permission for an initial evaluation to occur. The IEP team now wishes to conduct an eligibility staffing to discuss Max's initial evaluation. Which of the following does NOT meet the requirement for informing parents that the IEP team is conducting an eligibility staffing?

    A.   The team plans and implements the evaluation findings without informing the parents.

    B.   Parents attend the staffing at the suggested date and time.

    C.   Parents ask to reschedule the meeting and suggest other dates and times they can meet.

    D.   Parents decide that it is impossible to attend the staffing and tell the school to go ahead with the meeting and discuss the results with them afterward.

11. Requirements outlined in IDEA that give parents the rights to participate, receive notice, and give permission (consent) are known as

    A.   self-advocacy.

    B.   reevaluation.

    C.   eligibility criteria.

    D.   procedural safeguards.

12. According to IDEA, what term describes the right of students with a disability to special services that will meet their individual learning needs, at no cost to the parents?

    A. independent educational evaluation

    B. functional behavior assessment

    C. free and appropriate public education

    D. due process hearing

13. Michelle and her son have moved from a county in North Florida to a county in Central Florida. Michelle's son has been identified as developmentally delayed and is four years old. When Michelle enrolls her son in school in Central Florida what can she expect?

    A. Children who qualify for ESE services in one Florida school district qualify for ESE services everywhere in Florida.

    B. Michelle will need to go through the eligibility criteria testing for her son again.

    C. Michelle needs to enroll her son in a private school.

    D. Michelle will need to have her son repeat prekindergarten.

14. A paraeducator is assigned to a general education classroom that includes several students with learning disabilities. Which of the following best describes a responsibility of the paraeducator in this setting?

    A. assisting the students with learning disabilities during small-group instruction

    B. scheduling related support services for the students with learning disabilities

    C. planning weekly lessons and activities for the entire class

    D. administering formal classroom assessments to the entire class

15. The professional who has the most detailed knowledge of the day-to-day needs of students with disabilities is the

    A. exceptional student education teacher.

    B. general education teacher.

    C. counselor.

    D. administrator.

16. A person who serves as an advisor and sometimes represents parents at meetings related to their children with disabilities is a(n)

    A. mobility specialist.

    B. resource teacher.

    C. advocate.

    D. teaching assistant.

17. A key to success for students with disabilities is to make the learning visible. Select the most appropriate strategy that will help make content more understandable.

    A. study guides

    B. graphic organizers

    C. anticipation guides

    D. self-monitoring

18. Select the statement that applies to instructional modifications.

    A. School expectations that students meet learning standards remain unchanged.

    B. Content expectations are altered and the performance outcomes expected of students change.

    C. Students are expected to learn everything their classmates without disabilities are supposed to learn.

    D. Highlighted text, extended time on assignments, and preferential seating are provided.

19. The most meaningful information about student progress is determined by

    A. observation.

    B. a checklist.

    C. a standardized achievement test.

    D. direct and frequent measures of student performance.

20. Select the statement that best describes curriculum information explained in an IEP.

    A. It considers the strengths of the child.

    B. Each area of functioning that is adversely affected by the student's disability must be represented by an annual goal on the IEP.

    C. The entire scope and sequence of what a student is to learn is included.

    D. The concerns of parents for enhancing education of their child are considered.

21. Signals for learning disabilities are characteristics of students with learning disabilities. Select the signal that would NOT apply to a student with a learning disability.

   A.   has trouble understanding and following directions

   B.   is learning English as a second language

   C.   is not efficient or effective in using learning strategies

   D.   has difficulty allocating time and organizing work

22. Federal law (IDEA) requires that all students be included in statewide testing. An exception to this law includes

   A.   accommodations in the administration of the statewide assessment.

   B.   a small number of students with significant cognitive disabilities take the Florida Standards Alternate Assessment.

   C.   a statement that some students work and are not required to perform assessments.

   D.   the end-of-course exams.

23. High stakes tests are assessments designed to measure whether students have attained learning standards. These tests are a type of assessment referred to as

   A.   norm-referenced.

   B.   criterion-referenced.

   C.   performance-based.

   D.   standardized achievement tests.

24. Select the test that summarizes student performance using grade equivalents and/or percentile ranks.

   A.   norm-referenced

   B.   criterion-referenced

   C.   portfolio assessment

   D.   psychological test

25. Alternate assessments can be collected in the following ways EXCEPT by

   A.   portfolio.

   B.   performance assessment.

   C.   checklist of skills.

   D.   norm-referenced test.

26. Addie, a student with a reading disability, attained benchmark levels in reading fluency and comprehension for her grade level. She was integrated into general education for the entire reading block, and her progress was carefully monitored to ensure that her gains were maintained. This scenario describes which decision-making area?

    A. program evaluation

    B. screening

    C. instructional evaluation

    D. program placement

27. A frequent and ongoing measurement of student knowledge and skills and the examination of student data to evaluate instruction is

    A. response to intervention.

    B. progress monitoring.

    C. regular education initiative.

    D. inclusion.

28. Choose the phrase that is NOT a consideration when assessing student progress, designing interventions, and interpreting English language learners' (ELLs') responses to interventions.

    A. second language acquisition

    B. best practices for English language learners

    C. cultural variations

    D. high responders

29. Which is NOT a quality of a universally designed assessment?

    A. nonbiased items

    B. simple, clear instructions and procedures

    C. frequent breaks during testing

    D. precise definition of what is being measured

30. Bill comes from a single-parent home in the city. When he read a story on a standardized achievement test about an affluent two-parent family in the suburbs, he had difficulty predicting the outcome. This scenario exemplifies

    A. curriculum alignment.

    B. cultural bias.

    C. incongruity between teachers and diverse students.

    D. disproportionate representation.

31. Florida's adoption of the Florida Standards has led to the development of a new assessment system that aligns with the Florida Standards. This system is known as which of the following?

    A. Florida Standards Assessments

    B. Smarter Balanced assessments

    C. End-of-Course assessments

    D. FTCE tests

32. One of the primary purposes of early intervention services is to

    A. decide the classification category.

    B. classify students with learning and/or behavior disorders.

    C. recommend interventions and document attempts for academic and/or behavior problems.

    D. provide a rationale for retention in a grade.

33. During the evaluation plan when the type of testing is determined, it is decided that the referred student should have her fine motor skills assessed. The specialist who performs this type of assessment is the

    A. physical therapist.

    B. occupational therapist.

    C. guidance counselor.

    D. behavior specialist.

34. After the passage of a law, legal guidelines for implementing the law are written. These guidelines are called

    A. regulations.

    B. due process.

    C. compliance.

    D. litigation.

35. Which of the following sections is typically presented first in psychoeducational reports?

    A. background and referral information

    B. identifying data

    C. test results

    D. test interpretations

36. Marlon is not progressing as the teacher believes he should for his age expectancy. The teacher uses teacher-made tests, observation, and criterion-referenced tests to gather information about the student. What method is his teacher using to discover why the student is not making progress?

    A. goals

    B. strategies

    C. behavior management

    D. assessment

37. Mr. Crown collects student products over the course of the year to demonstrate the progress his students make. Mr. Crown is utilizing what type of assessment?

    A. dynamic assessment

    B. portfolio assessment

    C. informal assessment

    D. performance-based assessment

38. Informal assessments that can be tailored for individual students, used to identify mastery of a skill, and/or used to determine a curriculum include

    A. standardized testing.

    B. norm-referenced testing.

    C. curriculum-based assessment.

    D. checklists, rating scales, and observations.

39. Thomas was born with cerebral palsy and requires the use of a wheelchair. He is able to use a computer for word processing and completes all of his assignments using either his laptop or his computer at home. Thomas's most recent statewide assessments indicate that he is at or above the level expected in all academic areas. Thomas can be served with a(n)

    A. Individualized Education Plan.

    B. 504 Plan with Accommodations.

    C. Transition Plan.

    D. Behavior Intervention Plan.

40. Tamika is in Mr. Hernandez's Algebra 1 class. She is having difficulty solving basic equations with one unknown because she has yet to master basic math computational skills. What would be Mr. Hernandez's most effective strategy in helping Tamika?

   A. Do nothing; she will catch on eventually.

   B. Give practice work for her to do at home.

   C. Assess Tamika on the relevant preskills and, if necessary, teach these skills.

   D. Pair her with another student who is also struggling.

41. Which is NOT a correct guideline when using manipulatives?

   A. use of verbal explanation accompany object manipulation

   B. selection of materials that suit the concept and developmental stage of the students

   C. use of a variety of materials

   D. teacher demonstration with manipulatives as students observe

42. Focusing on text structure helps students set up a framework to organize the information that students will be reading. One very effective way to focus on text structure is to use

   A. incremental rehearsal.

   B. pre-teaching of sight vocabulary.

   C. word walls.

   D. graphic organizers.

43. A text strategy used to compare and contrast characters, events, and/or settings is a

   A. Venn diagram.

   B. story map.

   C. concept map.

   D. prediction/reflection chart.

44. Which statement is NOT a step for explicitly pre-teaching vocabulary words?

   A. Bring students' attention to the word by pronouncing the word, showing it to them in the text selection, and reading the sentence that contains the word aloud to the students.

   B. Provide a quick meaningful explanation and an example or two of the word's meaning.

   C. Vocabulary words are displayed on word cards or on a vocabulary chart.

   D. Invite students to use the word in a meaningful sentence.

45. Mrs. Jones blocks out 20 minutes for word study every day. She models skills and strategies that children need to decipher unknown words, explains why it is important to learn the skill or strategy, and guides students in their acquisition of the skill or strategy. What instructional method is she implementing?

    A. explicit instruction

    B. implicit instruction

    C. direct teaching

    D. logical instructional sequence

46. The Common Core State Standards which provided the foundation for the Florida Standards were built on international benchmarks and enable our students

    A. to improve End-of-Course assessment performance.

    B. to compete with peers on both national and international levels.

    C. to decrease the need for remediation.

    D. to improve higher order thinking skills.

47. Jane Saunders, a second-grade teacher, has a room filled with print that interests students and is readily available to them. She plans times when students can engage in recreational reading. She models by reading aloud to students daily. She is implementing effective reading instruction by

    A. using appropriate and ongoing screening.

    B. providing intensive instruction.

    C. establishing an environment to promote reading.

    D. obtaining early intervention when needed.

48. The process of focusing on predetermined goals or benchmarks that identify the content students should understand and the skills they should have after completing an area of study is best described as

    A. an explicit curriculum.

    B. an implicit curriculum.

    C. content-driven education.

    D. standards-based education.

49. All of the following apply to evidence-based practices EXCEPT

    A. practices based on personal experience, opinion, and preference.

    B. sources that evaluate research objectively.

    C. sources that evaluate research according to the highest scientific standards.

    D. quality of research that shows that the practice leads to increased student achievement.

50. Sarah exhibits social skills difficulties in her first-grade classroom. She often displays defiant behavior toward other students and lashes out verbally or physically when she becomes frustrated. Her language skills are delayed for her age. She sees a speech-language therapist twice a week in a small group for assistance with language and social skills. The type of support she receives from the speech-language therapist is considered

    A. specialized instruction.

    B. curriculum-based instruction.

    C. least restrictive instruction.

    D. independent instruction.

51. One of the major obstacles in evaluating student progress is

    A. too much paperwork.

    B. the assessments are too lengthy.

    C. the lack of inservices for teachers.

    D. not planning and organizing an evaluation system.

52. Which of the following refers to the use of a variety of grouping practices that change depending on the goals and objectives for the lesson?

    A. scaffolding

    B. individualizing instruction

    C. curriculum-based measurement

    D. flexible grouping

53. Patrick is a first grader who struggles with math. When he gets frustrated, he provokes other children in class by hitting and biting. Before each in-class math assignment, the teacher calls Patrick up to her desk and reminds him of how well he did on the previous assignment and shows him a graph of his improved grades. She provides him with a modified assignment and then has him sit with a math buddy. Patrick's teacher reduces his undesired behavior by

    A. providing positive reinforcement.

    B. manipulating antecedents.

    C. providing negative reinforcement.

    D. using cognitive strategy instruction.

54. Documents published by the states that typically include standards, learning activities, and expectations for students are best described as

    A. curriculum guidelines.

    B. lesson plans.

    C. target curricula.

    D. implicit curricula.

55. Silvia frequently laughs out loud at inappropriate times during class discussion. She likes the reaction of her classmates and her teacher when they look at her and scold her to be quiet. Her teacher ignores these outbursts and also advises the students to ignore those who interrupt discussion. To eliminate Silvia's behavior, her teacher is using

    A. extinction.

    B. peer confrontation.

    C. peer interaction.

    D. punishment.

56. The Florida Standards, while focusing on the essential knowledge and skills for success in life, address which major issues in the U.S.?

    A. Teacher pay and compensation

    B. Success of all students entering either college or career tracks

    C. Graduation and workforce decline

    D. Government and policy involvement

57. Mr. Rhodes is a tenth-grade social studies teacher. His state requires that all tenth-grade students take a social studies achievement test at the end of the year. The scores of students at his school have been poor in the past, and Mr. Rhodes is under pressure from the principal to raise the scores. He covers a large amount of material each day to prepare his students for this test and some of his struggling students are falling behind. What barrier to successful inclusion is Mr. Rhodes experiencing?

    A.   student ownership
    B.   content versus accommodation
    C.   individual versus class focus
    D.   lack of preparation time

58. If student assessment shows that co-teaching for a particular group of students is not effective, what is the next best course of action?

    A.   Spend more time co-planning.
    B.   Increase the intensity of instruction by decreasing the teacher-student ratio (e.g., more small-group support).
    C.   Increase the total instructional time.
    D.   Discontinue co-teaching and resume a pull-out model.

59. A tenth-grade student with intellectual disabilities attends the district's vocational training program. The student is initially placed at a workstation that measures the speed and accuracy of sorting and classifying skills. What activity is this an example of?

    A.   criterion-referenced test
    B.   adaptive behavior checklist
    C.   personal interest inventory
    D.   performance-based assessment

60. What level of text should be used for repeated reading?

    A.   The level at which the student has 50 percent word recognition
    B.   Any level as long as it engages the student
    C.   Instructional level
    D.   A level that is slightly higher than the student's level

61. What is the primary reason to use the Internet for educational purposes?

    A. Students spend less time in the classroom completing coursework at their convenience.

    B. It is structured and leveled.

    C. It provides discussion, chat rooms, and other group activities.

    D. It provides virtual learning experiences.

62. Which commonality does NOT describe someone as having emotional disorders/behavioral disorders?

    A. behavior falls considerably outside the norm

    B. behavior falls at the lower range of the norm

    C. chronic in nature

    D. socially or culturally unacceptable

63. A functional behavior assessment (FBA)

    A. identifies the needs of students with emotional or behavioral disorders.

    B. addresses the needs of students with emotional or behavioral disorders.

    C. identifies and addresses the needs of students with emotional or behavioral disorders.

    D. is not mandated by IDEIA.

64. Assessment procedures are typically administered in a certain order. Identify the answer choice that lists these procedures in the correct order.

    A. general interviews, use of rating scales, problem identification/problem analysis interview, observation

    B. observation, general interviews, use of rating scales, problem identification/problem analysis interview

    C. problem identification/problem analysis interview, general interviews, use of rating scales, observation

    D. use of rating scales, general interviews, problem identification/problem analysis interview, observation

65. Making a positive phone call to a parent is an example of a(n)

    A. activity reinforcer.

    B. tangible reinforcer.

    C. primary reinforcer.

    D. social reinforcer.

66. Services that are coordinated through school, home, and community settings are described as

    A. wraparound processes.

    B. social learning.

    C. social skills training.

    D. self-monitoring.

67. Which is NOT considered a step in teaching cognitive behavior management strategies?

    A. clearly specifying the expectations for the student

    B. discussing the strategy with the student and presenting a rationale for its use

    C. modeling for the student what is expected

    D. providing practice and feedback

68. Which would NOT be an effective strategy when working with students with emotional and behavioral disorders?

    A. Be consistent with clear procedures and expectations.

    B. Be in control in stressful situations.

    C. Be stern and never laugh.

    D. Spend time with students in nonacademic situations.

69. A manifestation determination is a review of

    A. possible interim alternative educational settings for a student.

    B. a legal term related to a student's Individualized Education Plan.

    C. the relationship between a student's disability and misconduct.

    D. the danger posed by a given child to the school community.

70. According to Section 504 of the Rehabilitation Act of 1973 (Public Law 93-112), which of the following is true?

    A. Students do not need to be enrolled in special education to receive related services.

    B. A learner's education may be composed of only special education.

    C. A weapon is defined as guns, bombs, grenades, rockets, and missiles.

    D. Schools must demonstrate adequate yearly progress in reading, math, and science.

71. What laws require school-based teams to use positive behavior interventions and supports, and to move away from reliance on punishment when addressing problem behavior?

    A.   Public Law 94-142
    B.   IDEA 1997 and IDEA 2004
    C.   manifestation determination
    D.   *Brown vs. Board of Education*

72. If Jonas arrives to school with a weapon and is suspended, what is the length of time Jonas can be placed in an appropriate interim alternative education setting?

    A.   15 days
    B.   30 days
    C.   25 days
    D.   45 days

73. The behavioral criteria of an objective should be based mainly on

    A.   the ultimate or long-term goal.
    B.   past performance.
    C.   the student's home behavior.
    D.   baseline data.

74. During a momentary time sample, the observer records

    A.   the absence or presence of a behavior during each interval.
    B.   everything observed about the individual's behavior.
    C.   the behavior every time it occurs in a specific time period.
    D.   whether behavior occurred at a particular moment.

75. A graph that displays the data over time by adding each day to previous ones is called a

    A.   bar graph.
    B.   line graph.
    C.   cumulative graph.
    D.   frequency graph.

76. Functional behavioral assessment provides the information needed to increase the likelihood that an intervention will be successful. Which of the following best describes the functional assessment?

    A. the behavior of concern, where the behaviors can occur, consequences that maintain the behaviors, and data that support the hypotheses

    B. the home life of the student, the history of grades, teaching styles of the student's instructors, and how many times the student has moved in the past 10 years

    C. the management system in all the classrooms that the student is present in, the intelligence quotient results, and standardized test results

    D. medical conditions that exist in the family, the overall behavioral patterns of peers and how the school generally handles discipline problems, and a clearly defined zero tolerance policy

77. When discussing positive behavior support and functional behavioral assessment, teachers view the student in which of the following ways?

    A. in relationship to the factors that influence the behavior

    B. in isolation so that the behavior is not confused with the environment

    C. with expectations and roles that are established patterns and proven

    D. in terms of eliminating the inappropriate behavior

78. Which of the following behaviors warrant a behavior change program?

    A. annual two-minute tantrum

    B. occasional reading reversal

    C. bimonthly bus-missing behavior

    D. lack of attention to tasks

79. Carmen, a student in Mr. Tanaka's class, is constantly asking, "What time is it?" She does this about fifteen times a day. Mr. Tanaka considers this to be attention-getting behavior and wishes to eliminate it. He usually responds to Carmen's request by telling her the time. Using the example of Carmen which of the interventions do you think will be the most effective?

    A. differential reinforcement

    B. reprimand

    C. extinction

    D. time-out

80. Teaching for automaticity means

   A. breaking down words into their component sounds.

   B. reading instruction should take place in groups of four or fewer.

   C. giving enough practice so that students are able to read both accurately and fluently.

   D. teaching the alphabet code directly and systematically.

81. Instruction for children who have difficulties learning to read must be

   A. explicit, comprehensive, intensive, supportive.

   B. implicit, comprehensive, intensive, supportive.

   C. explicit, selective, intensive, supportive.

   D. explicit, comprehensive, moderate, supportive.

82. When children use their knowledge of familiar and predictable letter patterns to speed up the process of reading words, they are in the

   A. pre-alphabetic phase.

   B. partial-alphabetic phase.

   C. full-alphabetic phase.

   D. consolidated-alphabetic phase.

83. Choose the statement that is NOT a guideline for teaching phonemic awareness.

   A. Keep it simple and explicit.

   B. Teach students to segment and blend phonemes.

   C. Teach phonemic awareness as whole-class instruction.

   D. Keep it short.

84. The understanding that individual spoken words can be broken down into individual syllables (wonderful:won-der-ful) is known as

   A. rhyming.

   B. phonics.

   C. phonological awareness.

   D. phonemes.

85. Which of the following is a strategy that revolves around vocabulary learning by providing a visual display of how words are related to other words?

    A. a word sort

    B. a synonym

    C. a semantic map

    D. an antonym

86. High-frequency words are taught as sight words early in children's reading instruction. Which strategy is NOT effective in teaching sight words?

    A. word walls

    B. environmental print

    C. word games

    D. repeated readings

87. Which of the following techniques assists students when considering ways to get across the author's meaning using prosodic cues such as pitch, loudness, stress, and pauses?

    A. timed reading

    B. reader's theater

    C. repeated reading

    D. choral reading

88. Contextual analysis is using surrounding context and student prior knowledge of syntax and content for increasing vocabulary acquisition. What strategy would be effective in contextual analysis?

    A. cloze

    B. vocabulary notebook

    C. vocabulary field trip

    D. definitional knowledge

89. Which of the following graphic organizers is a visual that consists of at least two overlapping circles, in which the common area represents similarities and the outer areas represent differences?

    A. story map

    B. concept map

    C. flow chart

    D. Venn diagram

90. Strategies used during the reciprocal teaching approach framework are

    A. prediction, as well as visualization of key concepts, events, and individuals.

    B. prediction, clarification, summarization.

    C. prediction, questioning, clarification, summarization.

    D. inferencing, clarification, summarization.

91. The following represents the sequence of instruction:

    a. Observe a list of known words with a common letter-sound relationship.
    b. Begin questioning about how the words look alike and sound the same and how they are different.
    c. Elicit the common letter-sound relationship and discuss.
    d. Have the learners phrase a generalization about the letter-sound relationship.

    In this case, the teacher is using which type of phonics instruction?

    A. synthetic

    B. implicit

    C. explicit

    D. linguistic

92. A person's ability to understand language is referred to as

    A. expressive language.

    B. receptive language.

    C. syntax.

    D. semantics.

93. Which of the following systems of language govern the structure of words and word forms?

    A. morphology

    B. syntax

    C. phonology

    D. pragmatics

94. Ms. Leonard is working with a second grader who is an ELL and has difficulty forming complex sentences and causal structures. The second grader said, "I didn't arrive school on time. The bus was late." Ms. Leonard says, "Oh, you didn't arrive to school on time because the bus was late." What technique is she using to assist this second grader?

    A. self-talk

    B. expansion

    C. chunk information

    D. slow pacing

95. For the majority of people around the world, communication abilities develop

    A. in the same order but not at all the same ages.

    B. in different orders depending on the language of the geographical area.

    C. in the same order and at roughly the same ages.

    D. in the same order until the child actually uses language, and then at different paces around the world.

96. Which of the following statements about communication intervention for school-age children compared to younger children is true?

    A. Intervention goals for school-age children shift from secondary to primary.

    B. Intervention moves at a much faster pace with school-age children.

    C. Intervention must link directly to academic curriculum for school-age children.

    D. Because intervention for school-age children is federally mandated, the commitment of the child is no longer critical.

97. Visually impaired students are being increasingly supported by special computer programs. Examples of these special computer programs include all of the following EXCEPT

    A. screen magnification software.

    B. digital book readers.

    C. personal amplification devices.

    D. screen readers.

98. Identify the sequence of reading development.

    A. pre-reading, learning to read, transitional reading, reading to learn

    B. reading to learn, pre-reading, learning to read, traditional reading

    C. pre-reading, transitional reading, reading to learn, learning to read

    D. Pre-reading, reading to learn, learning to read, transitional reading

99. During the reading to learn stage of reading development, what abilities continue to develop and progress?

    A. Read critically.

    B. Develop fluency.

    C. Develop alphabetic principles.

    D. Manipulate language sounds.

100. When planning a year-long strategy instruction curriculum

    A. plan to teach all nine comprehension strategies in the school year.

    B. teach exactly what your core reading program suggests.

    C. choose a few key strategies to teach in-depth.

    D. start the year with teaching inferencing.

101. Choice in student learning is considered

    A. an option for enrichment for certain students.

    B. a powerful motivating tool.

    C. appropriate within basal programs only.

    D. detrimental to classroom management.

102. For students who find school difficult, teachers should

    A. not encourage them to take risks.

    B. give them challenges appropriate for their skills.

    C. give them extra literacy homework.

    D. let them work on their own.

103. One way to reduce isolation of weaker readers is to

    A.   make all instruction whole-class.

    B.   have all students reading the same text.

    C.   ask stronger readers to read the texts to weaker readers.

    D.   have all students reading texts on a common theme.

104. When confronted with difficult situations, if the student says, "What's the use? I never do anything right anyway," she is displaying

    A.   learned helplessness.

    B.   social skills problems.

    C.   self-control training.

    D.   a need for a behavior contract.

105. Conducting an environmental inventory will

    A.   enable a student to learn to solve problems and complete tasks independently.

    B.   teach students to reinforce themselves.

    C.   give students a chance to show their strengths.

    D.   define what modifications are needed to increase the participation of students in the classroom as well as in community environments.

106. Which statement would NOT apply to effective student self-advocacy training?

    A.   Students learn their strengths and weaknesses.

    B.   Students learn the support they need to succeed.

    C.   Students learn the skills required to communicate their needs positively and assertively.

    D.   Students learn pre-skills as basic skills necessary for performing more complex skills.

107. Identify an effective family involvement strategy for successful adaptive life skills attainment.

    A.   Develop high school skills for graduation.

    B.   Involve the student in household chores and allow the student to take responsibility in as many age-appropriate life activities as possible.

    C.   Provide assistive technology devices.

    D.   Complete all necessary paperwork for transition.

108. Direct observation or situational assessment is usually conducted by an expert in the environment or community setting. Who would be most qualified to make an observation in a community setting?

    A. job coach or vocational educator

    B. classroom teacher

    C. principal

    D. physical education teacher

109. Which answer choice identifies the four stages of career development in the correct sequential order.

    A. exploration, awareness, preparation, placement

    B. awareness, exploration, preparation, placement

    C. preparation, awareness, exploration, placement

    D. placement, preparation, exploration, awareness

110. Choose an activity related to career awareness.

    A. on-campus jobs

    B. service learning projects

    C. studying community service workers

    D. community-based shadowing

111. Which category of transition activities prepares a student for a future career?

    A. instruction

    B. related services

    C. community experiences

    D. employment

112. For each student who is 16 years of age or older, part of the IEP is an outcomes-oriented description of strategies and services for ensuring that the student will be prepared to leave school for adult life. This part of the IEP is called a

    A. behavior intervention plan.

    B. due process.

    C. transition plan.

    D. mediation.

113. Effective family involvement includes all of the following strategies EXCEPT:

A. Allow the child to take responsibility for as many age-appropriate life activities as possible.

B. Attend all meetings related to transition, and ensure that family members have input in determining who is invited and the content of the agenda.

C. Verbally assure the child that he or she is supported in decisions regarding life after graduation.

D. Develop a career portfolio in which students accumulate information related to career interests.

114. Community-based training consists of experiences where students can develop actual career-related skills. Opportunities where students work alongside employees of area businesses for a few hours are known as

A. internships.

B. job shadowing.

C. apprenticeships.

D. volunteerism.

115. Identify the essential domains of transition planning.

A. parent involvement, supported living, community presence

B. personal-social, general community functioning, employment, leisure-recreational

C. assess, plan, instruct, evaluate

D. person-centered planning, self-advocacy, problem-solving skills

116. Debbie has severe physical disabilities and is attempting to secure a paid community-based employment preparation position. The IEP team met to discuss Debbie's options. Debbie's grandmother was in attendance at her IEP meeting. Some of the barriers to Debbie's situation were transportation and monetary concerns. Debbie's grandmother was willing to provide transportation to Debbie's work site but was concerned that Debbie's working would result in a loss of her Social Security benefits. How can the IEP team support Debbie's transition planning and keep aware of family concerns for her economic status?

A. Refer Debbie's grandmother and Debbie to a Social Security work incentive consultant for clarification of the Social Security benefits Debbie receives.

B. Promise the benefits will be available for Debbie regardless of her paid position.

C. Dismiss the concerns of Debbie's grandmother and avoid the situation entirely.

D. Talk about the transportation options for Debbie.

117. Which activity would be included in the leisure-recreational domain of transition planning?

    A.   Complete a career portfolio.

    B.   Receive tutoring in science.

    C.   Participate in job shadowing experiences.

    D.   Participate in guitar lessons at the YMCA.

118. Identify the activity that would be included in the personal–social domain of transition planning.

    A.   Set up a savings account for expenses related to purchasing a car.

    B.   Obtain a part-time job at Lowe's.

    C.   Complete a career portfolio.

    D.   Participate in scheduling dance classes after school.

119. Which individuals experience poorer outcomes because they tend not to have access to the full array of transition services while in high school?

    A.   young men with disabilities

    B.   young women with disabilities

    C.   all children with autism

    D.   middle school boys with ADHD

120. Glen attended both general education and exceptional education classes in high school. During his IEP meetings, Glen shared his desires of owning his own home one day. Glen's teachers provided him with opportunities to visit local affordable housing programs and write a term paper on his experiences. After several years of employment, Glen decided to pursue his dream of owning his own home. Glen knew that his low income would present some challenges of being a homeowner. Glen's case manager and some of his family members began meeting with him once a month to help him achieve his goal. What aspect of transition planning is presented in this scenario that involves development of positive post-school outcomes?

    A.   gender

    B.   cultural and linguistic

    C.   career planning

    D.   socioeconomic status

FTCE COMPETENCIES AND SKILLS	Question No.
Competency 1. Knowledge of foundations of exceptional student education	
Skill 1. Identify state and federal legislation that govern the education of students with exceptionalities.	1, 3, 5, 9, 22
Skill 2. Classify the characteristics of students with exceptionalities using the eligibility criteria of categories included in current state and federal laws and regulations governing K–12 education programs.	2, 4, 8, 13
Skill 3. Compare typical and atypical development of physical, cognitive, linguistic, social, and emotional stages of students in the K–12 educational system.	21
Skill 4. Interpret principles and practices in the provision of education for students with exceptionalities based on legal and ethical standards.	11, 12
Skill 5. Apply knowledge of the requirements for developing individualized educational plans (IEPs), educational plans (EPs), and transition IEPs.	19, 20
Skill 6. Evaluate the role and function of system wide models of support for assisting all students, including students with exceptionalities, in accessing the general education curriculum and achieving high expectations.	7, 17
Skill 7. Apply effective methods of communication, consultation, and collaboration with students, parents, caregivers, and all other stake holders, including those from culturally and linguistically diverse backgrounds, as equal members of educational teams.	6, 10
Skill 8. Use effective methods for coaching and supporting paraprofessionals, tutors, and volunteers to assist students with exceptionalities across settings.	14
Skill 9. Determine the purposes and functions of professionals, advocacy organizations, and agencies relevant to educating students with exceptionalities.	15, 16
Skill 10. Determine the factors associated with disproportionality in exceptional student education.	28, 29, 30
Competency 2. Knowledge of assessment and evaluation	
Skill 1. Determine the purposes and characteristics of different types of assessments and the appropriate use.	31, 32, 33
Skill 2. Apply the legal requirements and ethical principles regarding assessment of students with exceptionalities.	34, 35, 39

FTCE COMPETENCIES AND SKILLS *(continued)*	Question No.
Skill 3. Identify measurement concepts (e.g., reliability and validity), characteristics, and uses of norm-referenced and criterion-referenced assessments for students with exceptionalities.	23, 24, 25
Skill 4. Determine the purpose and requirements for participation of students with disabilities in the statewide assessment program and available accommodations, waivers, and exemptions..	18
Skill 5. Interpret and apply the results of formal, informal, and performance-based assessments to address specific needs of students with exceptionalities.	26, 27
Skill 6. Analyze assessment data to identify student needs and evaluate student progress in acquiring, generalizing, and maintaining skills across settings.	36, 37, 38
Competency 3. Knowledge of instructional practices in exceptional student education	
Skill 1. Select reliable sources of evidence-based instructional practices and interventions.	48, 49
Skill 2. Apply appropriate instructional approaches, strategies, and materials based on assessments of the student's educational needs (e.g., grade-level standards, academic and functional performance, effect of exceptionality).	51, 58
Skill 3. Choose effective instructional strategies to promote a student's generalization of knowledge and skills across content areas, curriculum, and settings.	46, 47, 56, 59
Skill 4. Identify the characteristics and purposes of the core curriculum, supplemental programs, and intensive interventions as they relate to language arts and mathematics in a multi-tiered system of supports.	54
Skill 5. Apply techniques for differentiating, accommodating, and modifying classroom instruction to meet the educational needs of individual students with exceptionalities.	53, 57
Skill 6. Apply flexible grouping strategies (e.g., academic, behavioral, social) for specific instructional activities.	52, 55
Skill 7. Use criteria for selecting and utilizing print and non-print media for instructional use to match student needs and interests..	60, 61
Skill 8. Analyze characteristics of specialized instructional approaches for students with significant disabilities.	102, 103

(continued)

FTCE COMPETENCIES AND SKILLS *(continued)*	Question No.
Competency 4. Knowledge of positive behavioral support process	
Skill 1. Identify and choose appropriate prevention and intensive intervention strategies for students who display challenging behaviors.	62, 63, 64, 65
Skill 2. Distinguish the various concepts and models of positive behavior support.	66, 67, 68, 74
Skill 3. Analyze the legal and ethical issues pertaining to positive behavior support strategies and disciplinary procedures for students with exceptionalities.	69, 70, 71, 72
Skill 4. Interpret individual and group data to apply interventions that increase positive behavior.	73, 75
Skill 5. Interpret the essential elements of a functional behavior assessment and measure the effects of the behavior intervention plan through data collection strategies.	76, 77, 78, 79
Competency 5. Knowledge of multiple literacies and communication skills	
Skill 1. Identify language development and the components of language structure.	92, 93
Skill 2. Distinguish characteristics of communication disorders and the impact on academic achievement and functional skills.	94
Skill 3. Identify appropriate assistive technology and alternative communication systems to facilitate communication across all educational settings.	97
Skill 4. Determine the sequence of reading development and the critical components of reading proficiency included in the state standards.	95, 96
Skill 5. Apply specialized instructional methods and techniques to address deficits in phonological processing in students with exceptionalities.	83, 84, 98, 99
Skill 6. Apply evidence-based instructional methods for increasing reading proficiencies in phonics, word recognition, and fluency that meets the specific educational and functional needs of individual students with exceptionalities	81, 82, 85, 86, 87, 91, 100, 101
Skill 7. Apply evidence-based instructional methods for increasing literacy (e.g., oral language, vocabulary, reading comprehension) in all content areas that meet the specific educational and functional needs of individual students with exceptionalities.	42, 80, 88, 104

FTCE COMPETENCIES AND SKILLS *(continued)*	Question No.
Skill 8. Determine and apply strategies for facilitating students' critical-thinking, executive functioning, and metacognition skills.	89, 90
Skill 9. Select and use effective instructional methods and supports for teaching writing foundations, the writing process, and purposes of writing to meet specific educational and functional needs of individual students with exceptionalities across all content areas.	43, 44, 45
Skill 10. Apply evidence-based instructional methods for increasing mathematic skills in all content areas that meet the specific educational and functional needs of individual students with exceptionalities.	40, 41
Competency 6. Knowledge of the transition process	
Skill 1. Determine appropriate programs for career development and career and technical education that meet the needs of individual students with disabilities.	109, 110, 111
Skill 2. Use results of transition assignments to determine appropriate planning strategies to assist the student, parents, caregivers, and stake holders in developing postsecondary education, career goals, and post-school outcomes.	105, 115, 117, 118
Skill 3. Select instructional approaches to assist students with exceptionalities to engage in self-determination and self-advocacy practices.	50, 106, 119, 120
Skill 4. Identify and compare resources and strategies that can assist individual students with disabilities to function independently in postsecondary education, home and community living, and employment.	107, 108, 112, 113, 114, 116

Answer Explanations

1. B

Education is to be provided to all children (6–18 years old) who meet age eligibility requirements. "Exceptional education programs were required for children ages 3 to 5" (choice A) was included in P.S. 99-457. "Students may not be denied education or exclusion from school when their misbehavior is related to their handicap" (choice C) was decided in *Honig v. Doe* (1986)." "Separate but equal" facilities on the basis of race must be provided" (choice D) was decided in *Brown v. Board of Education of Topeka* (1954). (Competency 1/Skill 1)

2. A

The Individuals with Disabilities Education Improvement Act (IDEA, 2004) established that special education teachers become highly qualified if they teach core academic content to students with disabilities. A free public education must be provided for all students (choice B) is the result of *PARC v. Commonwealth of Pennsylvania* (1972). Recognizing that most students with disabilities spend all or most of their school time in general education settings (choice C) and that students with disabilities should be addressed like other students, using either the same assessment instrument employed with typical learners or some type of alternative assessment (choice D) are provisions of IDEA (1997). (Competency 1/Skill 2)

3. B

The term "Mental Retardation" was changed to "Intellectual Disability." "Intelligence Scale," "Disordered Reading," and "Functional Disability" (choices A, C, and D) are not the terms indicated in this particular legislation. (Competency 1/Skill 1)

4. D

The purpose of IDEA (2004) in regard to "response to intervention" is to provide incentives for whole school approaches and pre-referral intervention to reduce the need to label children as disabled in order to address their learning needs. Separating all exceptional students into their own classrooms (choice A), sending all students with disabilities to a separate school (choice B), and providing each child born with disabilities with a paraprofessional (choice C) are reflective of former attitudes toward exceptional education students. (Competency 1/Skill 2)

5. C

Three to five years of age is the correct response. Four to seven years of age (choice A), zero to three years of age (choice B), and seven to ten years of age (choice D) are not the age ranges indicated in P.L. 99-457. (Competency 1/Skill 1)

6. C

No, there was only one test administered. Spanish test administration, IEP team agreement, and non-Hispanic test giver do address the evaluation, according to IDEA. (Competency 1/Skill 7)

7. B

Assistive technology is the correct answer. Corrective reading, speech and language therapy, and universal design for learning (choices A, C, and D) do not address the main instrument, which is the assistive technology device. (Competency 1/Skill 6)

8. A

Thirty-six months is the correct answer. Twelve, twenty-four, and forty-eight months (choices B, C, and D) are incorrect, according to the specification IDEA, Part C. (Competency 1/Skill 2)

9. D

The amendment to the Federal Opportunity Act of 2008 created a new program to expand the number of postsecondary programs for students with intellectual disabilities. Provided federal funding to expand three existing transition programs (choice A), created programs to cover diagnostic screening (choice B), and negotiated a compact for insurance coverage and access for services for persons with developmental disabilities (choice C) refer to other legislation. (Competency 1/Skill 1)

10. A

Planing and implementing the evaluation findings without informing the parents does not meet the requirement. Parents attend the staffing at the suggested date and time (choice B), parents ask to reschedule the meeting and suggest other dates and times they can meet (choice C), and parents decide that it is impossible to attend the staffing and tell the school to go ahead with the meeting and discuss the results with them afterward (choice D) are incorrect as answers since they do meet the requirements for informing parents about Eligibility Staffing. (Competency 1/Skill 7)

11. D

The requirements mentioned are a procedural safeguard. Self-advocacy, reevaluation, and eligibility criteria (choices A, B, and C) do not meet the definition requirements. (Competency 1/Skill 4)

12. C

The term that describes the right of a student with a disability to special services that will meet their individual learning needs, at no cost to the parents is free and appropriate public education. Independent educational evaluation, functional behavior assessment, and due process hearing (choices A, B, and D) are not compliant with the definition. (Competency 1/Skill 4)

13. A

When Michelle enrolls her son in school in central Florida she can expect that her son qualifies for ESE services. Children who qualify for ESE services in one Florida school district qualify for ESE services everywhere in Florida. The statements: Michelle will need to go through the eligibility criteria testing for her son again (choice B), Michelle needs to enroll her son in a private school (choice C), and Michelle will need to have her son repeat pre-kindergarten (choice D) do not follow policy for moving within Florida. (Competency 1/Skill 2)

14. A

A paraprofessional's primarily assignment is to assist the students who are included in the general education classroom. Therefore, the best response is that the paraprofessional should assist with the student with a learning disability in a small group setting. The paraprofessional is there for support and not to conduct whole group lessons. The paraprofessional should not plan lessons, schedule support services, or conduct formal assessments. These activities should be performed by the general education teacher.(Competency 1/Skill 8)

15. B

The general education teacher is the person most likely to bring to the attention of other professionals a student whom he or she suspects has a disability. Special education teacher, the counselor, and the administrator (choices A, C, and D) are professionals who offer services/support and with whom the general education teacher will have much interaction. (Competency 1/Skill 9)

16. C

An advocate helps parents who are not knowledgeable enough about the legal and educational requirements of special education. A mobility specialist (choice A) helps students with visual impairments to travel from place to place safely. A resource teacher (choice B) works with students and teachers and a teaching assistant (choice D) works with teachers. (Competency 1/Skill 9)

17. B

Graphic organizers are visual maps that give students a good idea of where they are going. The other three strategies, although very effective, are not as helpful for making content more understandable quickly. A study guide (choice A) is a helpful tool in improving comprehension for students with special needs. Anticipation guides (choice C) help activate student knowledge about a particular topic. Self-monitoring (choice D) allows students to watch and check themselves to make sure they performed targeting tasks. (Competency 1/Skill 6)

18. B

Content expectations are altered and the performance outcomes expected of students change. Students who receive modifications have disabilities that are so significant that the curricular expectations in general education are inappropriate. School expectations that students meet learning standards remain unchanged (choice A), students are expected to learn everything their classmates without disabilities are supposed to learn (choice C), and highlighted text, extended time on assignments, and preferential seating (choice D) are terms used for instructional accommodations. (Competency 2/Skill 4)

19. D

A direct and frequent measure of student performance is correct since use of multiple assessment sources provides a clear picture of student progress. An observation (choice A) is what is seen and noted. A checklist (choice B) is a list of observable behaviors or performance criteria expected from students. A standardized achievement test (choice C) would be only one source. (Competency 1/Skill 5)

20. B

Each area of functioning that is adversely affected by the student's disability must be represented by an annual goal on the IEP. This information will lead to instruction being specially designed. Strengths of the child and concerns of parents (choices A and D) are general factors considered in an IEP. The entire scope and sequence of what a student is to learn (choice C) makes reference to the curriculum. (Competency 1/Skill 5)

21. B

Learning English as a second language is the correct answer since the student may be struggling because the home language is other than English, which is not by itself an indication of a learning disability. Understanding directions, effective learning strategies, and time and organization (choices A, C, and D) are signals for possible learning disabilities. (Competency 1/Skill 3)

22. B

A small number of students with significant disabilities take the Florida Alternate Assessment. Accommodations, students working, and end-of-course exams (choices A, C, and D) are not exceptions to test-taking requirements. (Competency 1/Skill 1)

23. B

Criterion- referenced assessments involves comparing student performance to a specific level of performance or benchmark. Norm-referenced (choice A) and standardized achievement tests (choice D) compare performance to a norm or average. Performance-based (choice C) measures learning processes, rather than focusing only on learning products. (Competency 2/Skill 3)

24. A

Norm-referenced is the correct answer since the performance of one student is compared to the average performance of other students in the country who are the same age and grade level. Criterion-referenced (choice B) involves comparing student performance to a benchmark. Portfolio assessment (choice C) is a collection of student work. Psychological testing (choice D) measures abilities that affect how efficiently students learn in an instructional situation. (Competency 2/Skill 3)

25. D

A norm-referenced test is administered to all students in class of the same age and level. A portfolio, a performance assessment, and a checklist of skills (choices A, B, and C) are various ways of collecting alternate assessment information. (Competency 2/Skill 3)

26. A

Program evaluation is the correct answer as there was a change in program. Screening (choice B) is the initial area for determining the presence of a disability. Instructional evaluation (choice C) involves instructional procedures, and program placement (choice D) is the setting during which services are provided. (Competency 2/Skill 5)

27. B

Progress monitoring designs instruction to meet individual student needs. Response to intervention is a model for screening students and using their response to intervention as a data source to facilitate identifying students who need special education services. Regular education initiative and inclusion (choices C and D) promote the placement of students with disabilities in the general education classroom for most of the school day. (Competency 2/Skill 5)

28. D

"High responders" refers to students who respond well to intervention and are able to maintain grade-level performance. Second language acquisition, best practices for English language learners, and cultural variations (choices A, B, and C) refer to ELLs. (Competency 1/Skill 10)

29. C

Frequent breaks during testing is not a quality of a universally designed assessment. It is timing testing accommodation, non-biased items, clear instructions and procedures, and precise definitions of measurement that are qualities of a universally designed assessment. (Competency 1/Skill 10)

30. B

Cultural bias is an example of bias in the assessment process. Curriculum alignment and incongruity between teachers and diverse students are factors that influence disproportionate representation. (Competency 1/Skill 10)

31. A

Florida adopted a Florida Standards test series dubbed the Florida Standards Assessments. Smarter Balanced assessments (choice B) are used in other states for Common Core testing. End-of-Course assessments (choice C) do not specifically align with all benchmarks and standards in a grade level. FTCE tests (choice D) do not apply because they are a series of Florida teacher-certification tests. (Competency 2/Skill 1)

32. C

Recommend interventions and document attempts for academic and/or behavior problems is the correct answer as the other responses refer to the identification of students at upper grade levels. Classification category (choice A) refers to the classification of a child during the kindergarten year, classifying learning or behavior disorders (choice B) is incorrect as the classification of these students occurs in upper grades, and rationale for grade retention (choice D) is incorrect as students are usually not retained until they are in kindergarten or upper grades. (Competency 2/Skill 1)

33. B

The occupational therapist is the person responsible for fine motor testing. Physical therapists (choice A) evaluate gross motor skills, guidance counselors (choice C) may evaluate environmental concerns, and behavior specialists (choice D) evaluate behavior and social skills. (Competency 2/Skill 1)

34. A

After each reauthorization, regulations, which are the legal guidelines for implementing the law, are written. Due process, compliance, and litigation (choices B, C, and D) are different terminology involving the legal process. (Competency 2/Skill 2)

35. B

Identifying data is typically the information presented in a psychoeducational evaluation report. Background and referral information (choice A), test results (choice C) and test interpretations (choice D) are included in the report but not presented first. (Competency 2/Skill 2)

36. D

The assessments given can help the teacher narrow down the areas of need. Goals, strategies, and behavior management (choices A, B, and C) are not accurate descriptions of teacher-made tests, observations, and criterion-referenced tests. (Competency 2/Skill 6)

37. B

Portfolio assessment is the collection of progression based on a cumulative body of work. The other assessments in dynamic, informal, and performance-based assessment (choices A, C, and D) are not collected over time and do not constitute a year's worth of work. (Competency 2/Skill 6)

38. D

Checklists, rating scales, and observations are all informal assessments that can be used for individual students to determine mastery of a skill and/or placement in a curriculum. Standardized, norm-referenced, and curriculum-based assessment (choices A, B, and C) must adhere to a strict outline and content. (Competency 2/Skill 6)

39. B

Because Thomas is performing at an acceptable level in all academic areas, he would not be eligible for special education services under IDEA. Thomas should be on a Section 504 plan to ensure that the technology he requires is available and used without prejudice. Individualized education plan, transition plan, and behavior intervention plan (choices A, C, and D) do not address Thomas's specific needs. (Competency 2/Skill 2)

40. C

Pre-skills are basic skills necessary for performing more complex skills. Tamika needs additional instruction on her computational skills. Doing nothing (choice A) is not correct as she needs additional instruction. Practice work (choice B) would be correct after additional instruction is given. Pairing Tamika with a struggling student (choice D) would not be effective since both students would need additional instruction. (Competency 5/Skill 10)

41. D

Teacher demonstrates with manipulatives as students observe is the correct answer because students need to interact actively with manipulatives. Verbal explanation, materials for developmental stages, and using variety (choices A, B, and C) are correct guidelines when using manipulatives. (Competency 5/Skill 10)

42. D

Graphic organizers are visuals used to fill in information from the text. Incremental rehearsal, pre-teaching sight vocabulary, and word walls (choices A, B, and C) are activities used for directly teaching high-frequency words. (Competency 5/Skill 7)

43. A

Venn diagrams are overlapping circles in which comparison of elements be presented in overlapping sections and contrast would be presented in outer area of circles. A story map (choice B) is a graphic organizer that defines the beginning, middle, and end of a story. A concept map (choice C) is used to organize facts and knowledge and the relationship between them visually. A prediction/reflection chart (choice D) is a chart in which the left side, "prediction," presents writing what you predict will happen by looking at cover, pictures and so on. After reading the story, you write what actually took place under "reflection." (Competency 5/Skill 9)

44. C

Vocabulary words are displayed on word cards or on a vocabulary chart is the correct answer as this would help students to review the words on a regular basis to ensure the words remain familiar to the students after they have been taught. Reading the word aloud, quick meaningful explanation, and inviting students to use the word in a sentence (choices A, B, and D) are the steps for explicitly pre-teaching vocabulary words. (Competency 5/Skill 9)

45. A

Explicit instruction is the correct answer. Direct teaching and logical instructional sequence are included in implicit instruction (choices B, C, and D). (Competency 5/Skill 9)

46. B

The purpose of including international benchmarks was to specifically compete with peers on both national and international levels. End-of-Course assessment improvement, decreasing the need for remediation, and improving higher order thinking skills do not address the international component. (Competency 3/Skill 3)

47. C

Establishing an environment to promote reading is the correct answer. Using appropriate and ongoing screening (choice A) determines how students perform. Providing intensive instruction (choice B) refers to finding ways to provide instruction that meets individual students' needs and are intensive enough for progress to occur. Obtaining early intervention when needed (choice D) is addressing students' reading difficulties as soon as they become apparent. (Competency 3/Skill 3)

48. D

Standards-based education describes what students should know or be able to do at the end of a prescribed period of study, and accountability is the process of requiring students to demonstrate that they have met specified standards and making teachers responsible for students' performance. Explicit curriculum is written as part of formal instruction of the schooling experience. It may refer to a curriculum document, texts, and supportive materials that are overtly chosen to support the intentional instructional agenda of a school. An implicit curriculum is one that is crafted within the thinking processes of individual teachers but not written down or published, and therefore not able to be replicated by others. Content-based education is commonly used to describe approaches to integrating language and content instruction. Although these types of education and curriculum are important, the focus of common core relies on standards-based education and benchmarks. (Competency 3/Skill 1)

49. A

Practices based on personal experience, opinion, and preference is the correct answer as this is referred to as best practices. Sources evaluate resources objectively (choice B), sources evaluate research according to high standards (choice C), and quality of research shows that the practice leads to increased student achievement (choice D) apply to evidence-based practices. (Competency 3/Skill 1)

50. A

Specialized instruction is the correct response. Sarah receives two sessions of speech and language per week. Her speech therapist does need to work on language and behavior concerns. Independent instruction, curriculum-based instruction, and least-restrictive instruction responses (choices B, C, and D) do not supply the type of intense services Sarah needs in order to be successful. (Competency 6/Skill 3)

51. D

Not planning and organizing an evaluation system is the correct response. The main obstacle for teachers is to carve out time to set up and organize a method or system for evaluating their student progress. Too much paperwork, assessments are too lengthy, lack of inservices for teachers (choices A, B, and C) are subjective reasons for not including evaluation in the classroom. (Competency 3/Skill 2)

52. D

Flexible grouping is the correct answer. Scaffolding, individualizing instruction, and curriculum-based measurements (choices A, B, and C) have to do with assessment, instruction, or measurement. (Competency 3/Skill 6)

53. B

Manipulating antecedents is the correct response. The teacher is controlling what precedes Patrick's math class and therefore manipulates antecedents or those activities preceding the math class activity. Providing positive reinforcement, providing negative reinforcement, and using cognitive strategy instruction (choices A, C, and D) do not adequately identify what is happening at this particular time during these math activities. (Competency 3/Skill 5)

54. A

Curriculum guidelines is the correct answer. Guides do include documents about standards, learning activities, and performance expectations. Lesson plans, target curricula, and implicit curricula do not include the necessary documents for Florida State Standards. (Competency 3/Skill 4)

55. A

Extinction is the correct answer. The teacher is trying to eliminate the behavior through ignoring it. Peer confrontation, peer interaction, and punishment (choices B, C, and D) would serve to increase the behavior rather than decrease it. (Competency 3/Skill 6)

56. B

The main purpose for developing the Florida Standards was to focus on the success of all students who enter either college or career tracks. Although the other areas addressed are important: Teacher pay and compensation, graduation and workforce decline, and government and policy involvement, they do not address the essential question points of knowledge and skills for success in life. (Competency 3/Skill 3)

57. B

Content versus accommodation is the correct response. Mr. Rhodes is overwhelmed with the amount of content he is covering and feels he needs to include all of this information in working with his struggling students. More emphasis needs to be placed in the accommodations portion of his planning. Student ownership, individual versus class focus, and lack of preparation time (choices A, C, and D) refer to student responsibility or teacher planning. (Competency 3/Skill 5)

58. B

Increase the intensity of instruction by decreasing the teacher-student ratio (e.g., more small-group support) is the correct response. The setting and services should be examined first. Spending more time co-planning, increase total instructional time, and discontinue co-teaching and resume a pull-out model (choices A, C, and D) are incorrect as the teachers are limited in their planning time and instruction time; discontinuing co-teaching altogether is not preferred. (Competency 3/Skill 2)

59. D

Performance-based assessment directly provides performance practice for classification and sorting. Criterion-referenced tests (choice A) are associated with academics, adaptive behavior checklists (choice B) are associated with behavior in work setting, and personal interest inventories (choice C) have to do with student interests and preferences. (Competency 3/Skill 3)

60. C

Instructional level is the correct answer as the student needs to practice and perform repeated reading at his or her instructional level. The level at which the student has 50 percent word recognition (choice A), any level as long as it engages the student (choice B), and a level that is slightly higher than the student's level (choice D) are responses that are either too vague or too accelerated to meet the individual needs of the student. (Competency 3/Skill 7)

61. A

Students spend less time in the classroom completing coursework at their convenience. Students who participate in distance education that is Internet-based spend less time in the classroom and can complete coursework at their convenience within settings of their own choice. That it is structured and leveled, it provides discussion, chat rooms, and other group activities, and it provides virtual learning experiences (choices B, C, and D) are not the primary educational reasons for using the Internet. Students generally choose to use the internet for educational progression as it is more convenient for course completion. (Competency 3/Skill 7)

62. B

Behavior falls at the lower range of the norm is the correct answer because behavior falls considerably outside the norm, is chronic in nature, and socially or culturally unacceptable. (Choices A, C, and D) are commonalities describing someone with emotional/behavioral disorders. The behavior must fall considerably outside the norm. (Competency 4/Skill 1)

63. C

Identifies and addresses the needs of students with emotional or behavioral disorders is the correct answer as this is the purpose of a functional behavior assessment. Identifies the needs of the student and addresses the needs of the student are incomplete responses (choices A and B). FBA (choice D) is mandated by IDEIA. (Competency 4/Skill 1)

64. A

General interviews, use of rating scales, problem identification/problem analysis interview, observation is the correct answer. First there are general interviews, followed by use of rating scales. Then the problem identification/problem analysis interview takes place followed by observations. (Competency 4/Skill 1)

65. D

Social reinforcer is the correct answer. An example of activity reinforcer (choice A) is having extra recess. An example of tangible reinforcer (choice B) is earning a prize. An example of a primary reinforcer (choice C) is a food that a student finds rewarding. (Competency 4/Skill 1)

66. A

Wraparound processes provide coordinated services to parents and students. Social learning (choice B) involves observing and modeling the behavior of others. Social skills training (choice C) provides students with specific instruction about acquisition, performance, and fluency of social skills. Self-monitoring (choice D) helps students become aware of their own behaviors. (Competency 4/Skill 2)

67. A

Clearly specifying the expectations for the student applies to a behavior contract. Discussing the strategy with the student and presenting a rationale for its use, modeling for the student what is expected, and providing practice and feedback (choices B, C, and D) are the steps for teaching cognitive behavior management strategies. (Competency 4/Skill 2)

68. C

Be stern and never laugh is the correct answer as laughter is very important and students need to see the teacher enjoying him- or herself. Be consistent with clear procedures and expectations, be in control in stressful situations, and spend time with students in nonacademic situations (choices A, B, and D) are all effective strategies when working with students with emotional and behavioral disorders. (Competency 4/Skill 2)

69. C

The relationship between a student's disability and misconduct is the correct answer as a student's behavior needs to be analyzed to see if his disability is the reason that the student acted in the manner that he did. Possible interim alternative educational settings for a student (choice A), a legal term related to a student's Individualized Education Plan (choice B), and the danger posed by a given child to the school community (choice D) relate to various aspects of behavior and not to manifestation determination. (Competency 4/Skill 3)

70. A

Students do not need to be enrolled in special education to receive related services. Students can receive 504 Accommodations and not be in ESE-related services. A learner's education may be composed of only special education (choice B), a weapon is defined as guns, bombs, grenades, rockets, and missiles (choice C), and schools must demonstrate adequate yearly progress in reading, math, and science (choice D) are not related to the 504 Accommodations. (Competency 4/Skill 3)

71. B

IDEA 1997 and IDEA 2004 is the correct answer. Public Law 94-142, manifestation determination, and *Brown v. Board of Education of Topeka* (choices A, C, and D) refer to other aspects of Exceptional Student Education or civil rights. (Competency 4/Skill 3)

72. D

Forty-five days is the correct answer. Fifteen, thirty, and twenty-five days (choices A, B, and C) are the incorrect number of days for alternative setting for weapon possession. (Competency 4/Skill 3)

73. D

Baseline data is representative of a starting point. The ultimate or long-term goal, past performance, and student's home behavior (choices A, B, and C) are not necessarily starting points even though they are overall aspects of a student's behavior. (Competency 4/Skill 4)

74. C

The observer records the behavior every time it occurs in a specific time period as the documentation for a given time sample. The absence or presence of a behavior during each interval (choice A), everything observed about the individual's behavior (choice B), and whether behavior occurred at a particular moment or not (choice D) are incorrect as these options describe a different type of recording. (Competency 4/Skill 2)

75. C

A cumulative graph builds on information presented over time. Bar graphs, line graphs, and frequency graphs (choices A, B, and D) cannot present progressive data. (Competency 4/Skill 4)

76. A

The behavior of concern, where the behaviors can occur, consequences that maintain the behaviors, and data that support the hypotheses is the correct response as it involves the behavior specifically. The home life of the student, the history of grades, teaching styles of the student's instructors, and how many times the student has moved in the past 10 years (choice B); the management system in all the classrooms that the student is present in, the intelligence quotient results, and standardized test results (choice C); and medical conditions that exist in the family, the overall behavioral patterns of peers and how the school generally handles discipline problems, a clearly defined zero tolerance policy (choice D) involve viewpoints of social work, entire school management, and medical history. (Competency 4/Skill 5)

77. A

In relationship to the factors that influence the behavior is the correct response. Behavior support and functional analysis are in direct relationship with the factors of behavior. In isolation so that the behavior is not confused with the environment (choice B), with expectations and roles that are established patterns and proven (choice C), and in terms of eliminating the inappropriate behavior (choice D) correspond to behaviors in isolation, expectations, and extinction. (Competency 4/Skill 5)

78. D

Lack of attention to tasks is the correct answer as this behavior is ongoing and can cause serious regression in the students' educational processes. Annual two-minute tantrum, occasional reading reversal, and bimonthly bus-missing behavior (choices A, B, and C) are behaviors that do not occur on a regular basis or that can be responsive to instructional interventions. (Competency 4/Skill 5)

79. A

The behavior is attention-seeking. Differential reinforcement may be applied to behaviors that are habits, do not need to be reduced rapidly, and do not need to be reduced to zero. Reprimand, extinction, and time-out choices (B, C, and D) are types of interventions for different behavior types. (Competency 4/Skill 5)

80. C

Giving enough practice so that students are able to read both accurately and fluently is the correct answer. Breaking down words into their component sounds (choice A) is direct instruction in language analysis. Reading instruction should take place in groups of four or fewer (choice B) is intensive instruction. Teaching the alphabet code directly and systematically (choice D) is having a highly structured phonics program. (Competency 5/Skill 7)

81. A

Explicit, comprehensive, intensive, supportive is the correct answer. *Implicit* is the opposite of *explicit*. *Selective* is the opposite of *comprehensive*. *Moderate* is the opposite of *intensive*. (Competency 5/Skill 6)

82. D

Consolidated-alphabetic phase is the correct answer. Pre-alphabetic phase (choice A) is recognizing words at sight due to visual or contextual cues. Partial-alphabetic phase (choice B) is being able to develop some knowledge about letters and detect letter-sound relationships. In full-alphabetic phase (choice C), readers identify words by matching all of the letters and sounds. (Competency 5/Skill 6)

83. C

Teach phonemic awareness as whole class instruction is the correct answer as the guideline is to teach to students in small groups. Keep it simple and explicit, teach students to segment and blend phonemes, and keep it short (choices A, B, and D) are guidelines for teaching phonemic awareness. (Competency 5/Skill 5)

84. C

Phonological awareness is the correct answer. Rhyming (choice A) refers to words with the same sound. Phonics (choice B) refers to blending printed letter sounds to identify words. Phoneme (choice D) is the individual speech sound. (Competency 5/Skill 5)

85. C

A semantic map is the correct answer. A word sort (choice A) refers to grouping words into different categories by looking for shared features among their meanings. A synonym (choice B) is a word that is similar in meaning to other words. An antonym (choice D) is a word that is opposite in meaning. (Competency 5/Skill 6)

86. D

Repeated reading is a strategy to develop rapid, fluent, oral reading. Word walls, environmental print, and word games (choices A, B, and C) take place at the initial stages of reading instruction. (Competency 5/Skill 6)

87. D

Choral reading is the correct answer. Timed reading (choice A) refers to reading a passage within a certain amount of time. Reader's theater (choice B) refers to the oral presentation of drama, prose, or poetry by two or more readers. Repeated reading (choice C) is a strategy to develop rapid, fluent, oral reading. (Competency 5/Skill 6)

88. A

A cloze passage involves supplying a likely word replacement based on content in passage. Vocabulary notebook (choice B) is a method to practice unfamiliar terms. Vocabulary field trip (choice C) involves brainstorming sessions on a particular concept. Definitional knowledge (choice D) is the ability to relate new words to known words through synonyms, antonyms, and multiple-meaning words. (Competency 5/Skill 7)

89. D

Venn diagram is the correct answer. A story map (choice A) helps students identify key elements that make up a story: character, setting, problem, and solution. A concept map (choice B) is a special form of a web diagram for exploring knowledge. A flow chart (choice C) uses arrows in its diagram and can be used to illustrate cause and effect. (Competency 5/Skill 8)

90. C

The grouping of prediction, questioning, clarification, and summarization is the correct answer. Prediction, as well as visualization of key concepts, events, and individuals (choice A) is another strategy used to support reading comprehension. Prediction, clarification, summarization (choice B) is missing the topic questioning. In inferencing, clarification, summarization (choice D), inferencing is another strategy used to support reading comprehension. (Competency 5/Skill 8)

91. B

Implicit is the correct answer as it is a whole-to-part approach to word study. Synthetic and explicit (choices A and C) are part-to-whole phonics approaches. Linguistic (choice D) is learning to decode words through regular letter patterns. (Competency 5/Skill 6)

92. B

Receptive language is the correct answer. Expressive language, syntax, and semantics are incorrect as they refer to other language acquisition components and do not refer to understanding language. (Competency 5/Skill 1)

93. A

Morphology is the correct answer as it is the definition of language regarding structure of words and word formations. Syntax, phonology, and pragmatics (choices B, C, and D) do not refer to word formations. (Competency 5/Skill 1)

94. B

Mrs. Leonard expanded on the information the child was stating by adding words the child had missed. Self-talk, chunk information, and slow-pacing (choices A, C, and D) are incorrect as these strategies did not include adding words to what the child already had said. (Competency 5/Skill 2)

95. C

"In the same order and at roughly the same ages" is a general statement about communication. In the same order but not at all the same ages (choice A), in different orders depending on the language of the geographical area (choice B), and in the same order until the child actually uses language, and then at different paces around the world (choice D) are incorrect. The generalized statement regarding communication is most reflective of the response in answer choice C. (Competency 5/Skill 4)

96. C

Intervention must link directly to academic curriculum for school-age children, as interventions are related to the academic curriculum once the child reaches school age. Intervention goals for school-age children shift from secondary to primary (choice A), intervention moves at a much faster pace with school-age children (choice B), and because intervention for school-age children is federally mandated, the commitment of the child is no longer critical (choice D) are incorrect as the interventions for communications are not a secondary consideration; they are not fast paced—rather they are individually paced, and commitment to the individual child is always critical. (Competency 5/Skill 4)

97. C

Personal amplification device is correct as this choice is assistive technology for individuals with hearing impairments, not visual impairments. Screen magnification software, digital book readers, and screen readers (choices A, B, and D) are computer programs for visually impaired individuals. (Competency 5/Skill 3)

98. A

Pre-reading, learning to read, transitional reading, reading to learn is the correct answer. The other three responses are out of sequence for reading development. (Competency 5/Skill 5)

99. A

Read critically is the correct answer. Reading to learn represents a more advanced state of reading development. Develop fluency, develop alphabetic principles, and manipulate language sounds (choices B, C, and D) are found at the learning to read stage and are more basic skills in reading development. (Competency 5/Skill 5)

100. C

Choose a few key strategies to teach in-depth is the correct answer since thought toward in-depth teaching should be part of reading instruction. Plan to teach all nine comprehension strategies in the school year (choice A), teach exactly what your core reading program suggests (choice B), and start the year with teaching inferencing (choice D) are incorrect as these responses do not allow for more in-depth thought of content areas. (Competency 5/Skill 6)

101. B

A powerful motivating tool is the correct answer. Giving the students choices is very motivating. An option for enrichment for certain students, appropriate within basal programs only, and detrimental to classroom management are incorrect as choices should be included in all reading groups and is an important means of classroom management. (Competency 5/Skill 6)

102. B

Give them challenges appropriate for their skill is the correct answer. A student who presents with reading challenges will respond successfully if the teacher is aware of the students' skills and abilities. Not encourage them to take risks (choice A), give them extra literacy homework (choice C), and let them work on their own (choice D) are incorrect as these responses do not address the unique individual needs of the student. (Competency 3/Skill 8)

103. D

The student is less likely to feel isolated if all students in the class are working on one theme or content area. Make all instruction whole-class (choice A), have all students reading the same text (choice B), and ask stronger readers to read the texts to weaker readers (choice C) would highlight weaker readers' difficulties. (Competency 3/Skill 8)

104. A

Learned helplessness is the correct answer since these students see little relationship between their efforts and school or social success. Social skills problem (choice B) refers to students' inability to interact with peers and adults. Self-control training (choice C) is for students who know what to do in social situations, but lack the self-control to behave appropriately. A behavior contract (choice D) is for students who have significant conduct problems and thereby would benefit from a behavior management system. (Competency 5/Skill 7)

105. D

Conducting an environmental inventory will define what modification is needed to increase the participation of students in the classroom as well as in community environments. Enable a student to learn to solve problems and complete tasks independently (choice A), teach students to reinforce themselves (choice B), and give students a chance to show their strengths (choice C) are strategies that will enhance student self-image. (Competency 6/Skill 2)

106. D

Students learn pre-skills as basic skills necessary for performing more complex skills as pre-skills are part of instruction. Students learn their strengths and weaknesses (choice A), students learn the support they need to succeed (choice B), and learn the skills required to communicate their needs positively and assertively (choice C), which will enable them to become self-advocates. (Competency 6/Skill 3)

107. B

Involving the student in household chores and allowing the student to take responsibility in as many age-appropriate life activities as possible allows families to become directly involved in their students' progression to adaptive life skills. Developing high school skills for graduation (choice A) only addresses graduation requirements. Providing assistive technology devices (choice C) only addresses assistive technology. Completes all necessary paperwork for transition (choice D) only addresses paperwork for transition. (Competency 6/Skill 4)

108. A

Job coach or vocational educator is the correct answer as this observation must be conducted by a person who works or coaches in the environment in which the student is actually performing the task. Classroom teacher, principal, and physical education teacher (choices B, C, and D) are not the professionals who would necessarily work in the field. (Competency 6/Skill 4)

109. B

The sequence of the four stages of career development is awareness, exploration, preparation, and placement. The other responses (choices A, C, and D) do not correspond to the proper sequence for the four stages of career development. (Competency 6/Skill 1)

110. C

Students gain knowledge about various careers by studying community service workers. On-campus jobs, service learning projects, and community-based shadowing (choices A, B, and D) are activities relating to career exploration, not awareness. (Competency 6/Skill 1)

111. D

Employment activities assist students in choosing appropriate postsecondary training for entering the workforce immediately after graduation. Instruction (choice A) involves strategies designed to teach a skill or set of skills. Related services (choice B) include supportive and therapeutic services and activities that students may need to achieve their goal. Community experiences (choice C) provide students the opportunity to practice skills in actual settings in which they will be used. (Competency 6/Skill 1)

112. C

Transition plan is the correct answer. Behavior intervention plan (choice A) is a plan for students with significant behavior problems. Due process (choice B) is a strategy for monitoring students who receive special education services. Mediation (choice D) is a system put in place for parents as an initial means for resolving conflicts with schools. (Competency 6/Skill 4)

113. D

Develop a career portfolio in which students accumulate information related to career interests is the exception. Effective family involvement includes answer choices A, B, and C. (Competency 6/Skill 4)

114. B

Through job shadowing students can develop a better understanding of their personal interests and capabilities. Internships (choice A) allow students to spend an extended amount of time (several weeks or months) on a single job site. Apprenticeships (choice C) usually last three to four years. Volunteerism (choice D) provides students an opportunity to practice employability skills. (Competency 6/Skill 4)

115. B

Personal-social, general community functioning, employment, leisure-recreational are the essential domains of transition planning. Answer choices A, C, and D do not specifically address the domains of transition planning; these answer choices refer to aspects of transition, but do not focus on the domain of transition planning. (Competency 6/Skill 2)

116. A

Refer Debbie's grandmother and Debbie to a Social Security work incentive consultant for clarification of the Social Security benefits Debbie receives is the correct answer as it accurately identifies the concerns over Social Security benefits. Answer choices B, C, and D do not accurately address the grandmother's concerns for Social Security benefits. Promise the benefits will be available for Debbie regardless of her paid position (choice B) offers false promises to the family. Dismiss the concerns of Debbie's grandmother and avoid the situation entirely (choice C) does not provide support to the family. Talk about the transportation options for Debbie (choice D) is not a necessary discussion as transportation has already been resolved. (Competency 6/Skill 4)

117. D

Participate in guitar lessons at the YMCA is the correct answer as it involves leisure and recreation. Complete a career portfolio, receive tutoring in science, and participate in job shadowing experiences (choices A, B, and C) are activities associated with the other domain of transition planning. (Competency 6/Skill 2)

118. A

Set up a savings account for expenses related to purchasing a car is the correct answer as money and budgeting are part of the personal-leisure domain of transition planning. Obtain a part-time job at Lowe's (choice B), complete a career portfolio (choice C), and participate in scheduling dance classes after school (choice D) are activities that correspond to the remaining domains for transition planning. (Competency 6/Skill 2)

119. B

A young woman with disabilities is the correct answer as young women are less likely to enroll in work-study and vocational education. Young men with disabilities, all children with autism, and middle school boys with ADHD (choices A, C, and D) are incorrect as the age levels of the students do not apply or the gender is incorrect. (Competency 6/Skill 3)

120. D

Socioeconomic status is the correct answer as the financial aspect of buying a home has to do with Glen's income status. Gender, cultural and linguistic, and career planning (choices A, B, and C) correspond to other aspects of Glen's transition planning. (Competency 6/Skill 3)

Index

Graphophonemic knowledge, 136–137
Grouping strategies for classroom management, 85
Group work, for adaptive life skills, 161
Guided practice, in systematic instruction, 71–72

H

Hands-on instruction, of adaptive life skills, 161
Hardcopy reading passage booklet, as accommodation, 51
Hearing impairment, 13
  assistive technology and, 127
  description of, 14
Hearing technology, 125–126
Heterogeneous groups, 85
High-frequency words, practice with, 139
Homogeneous groups, 85

I

IEP team
  data collection by–for positive behavioral support, 108
  purpose of, 81
"I'm Going on a Trip," 133
Inclusion
  compared to mainstreaming, 16
  defined, 16
  least restrictive environment and, 16
Independent living centers, 156
Independent practice, in systematic instruction, 72
Individual Educational Evaluation (IEE), 24
Individualized Education Plans (IEPs)
  compared to IFSP, 11, 20–21
  composition of team, 18–19
  confidentiality, 17
  content required, 19–20
  defined, 10–11
  meetings, 19
  transition planning and, 21, 151–152

Individualized Family Service Plan (IFSP)
  age of majority, 21
  compared to IEP, 11, 20–21
  defined, 11
Individual Placement and Support (IPS), 156
Individual-referenced assessment
  defined, 49
  progress monitoring assessment as, 49
  running record as, 49
  uses of, 49
Individuals with Disabilities Education Act (IDEA)
  accommodation requirements, 44–46
  assessment requirements, 43
  inclusion and, 16
  manifestation determination review, 107
  overview of, 10–11
  positive behavioral support, 106
  transition planning, 151–152
Individuals with Disabilities Education Improvement Act (IDEIA), 9–10
Infants and toddlers with disabilities
  defined, 12
  developmental delay areas, 12
  early intervention services, 25–26
  support for, 25–26
Instructional activities and procedure modification, 80
Instructional material modification, 79
Instructional practices
  classroom management, 83–88
  content standards and, 90–91
  differentiated instruction, 77
  explicit and systematic instruction, 74–75
  goals for learning and, 69–70
  integrating communication-related skills, 76
  modeling, 76
  scaffolding, 75–76

  selecting and evaluating print and non-print media for, 89
  systematic instruction, 70–72
  team approach for, 81–82
  text features and, 87–88
  text structure, 88–89
Instructional task modification, 79–81
Intellectual disability, 13, 14–15
Intensive intervention programs, 135–136

K

Keyboard commands, as accommodation, 51

L

Language
  components of, 118–120
  grammar, 119
  orthography, 120
  phonology, 118
  pragmatics, 119–120
  receptive *vs.* expressive, 117–118
  semantics, 118
  sequence of development, 120–121
  types of communication deficits, 121–125
Language impairments, 124
  assistive technology and, 128
  defined, 124
  expressive language disorder, 124
  mixed receptive-expressive language disorder, 124
  phonological disorders, 124
  prevention and intervention, 125
  specific language impairment, 124
Learning-to-read stage, 129
Least restrictive environment (LRE)
  defined, 10
  inclusion and, 16
Line reader highlights, as accommodation, 51
Literacy development, 141
Local organizations, 32

NOTES

NOTES

NOTES

NOTES

NOTES

NOTES

NOTES

NOTES

NOTES

NOTES